Hugh Oram's **French** Blogs

Hugh Oram's French Blogs
NOVEMBER 2012-NOVEMBER 2013

HUGH ORAM

Order this book online at www.trafford.com
or email orders@trafford.com

Most Trafford titles are also available at major online book retailers.

Printed in the United States of America.

ISBN: 978-1-4907-2274-0 (sc)
ISBN: 978-1-4907-2275-7 (e)

Trafford rev. 01/02/2014

www.trafford.com

North America & international
toll-free: 1 888 232 4444 (USA & Canada)
fax: 812 355 4082

FOREWORD

For the past year, I've been writing a weekly blog almost entirely about France, travels in that wonderful country, French politics, economics, social trends, just about anything to do with life in France, with lots of little anecdotes and stories along the way. Into this heady mix, I've also added comments about politics here in Ireland, where we live, and about some of the odd things that go on not just in France, but right here in Ireland, in fact just about every country. Still, If life always went smoothly, it wouldn't so interesting! In France of course, everything is enmeshed in the web of bureaucracy, which can make life doubly difficult, but that doesn't detract from the storied history of the country, the beauty of many of its landscapes and above, the fascinating people of France and their unique way of life. I decided that we couldn't just let these weekly blogs disappear into the digital ether, so here they are in book form, covering the 12 months from November, 2012 to November, 2013. The book follows very closely the content of the blogs, although I've omitted the illustrations.

DEDICATION

'd first of all like to dedicate this book to my wife Bernadette, for all her help, support and encouragement, above all patience, then equally importantly, I'd like to offer a dedication to my sister Emma Louise Oram. She is the technical genius with the blogs, doing what I can't do, putting them into place each week and organising illustrations. Without her help, the task would have been impossible.

November 15, 2012

Murder and mayhem in Corsica

J ust a few hours ago I read in the online edition of Le Figaro, a leading Paris-based newspaper, of the assassination of a well-known business person in Ajaccio, Corsica.

I always enjoy reading Le Figaro online, it's very accessible and a quite comprehensive guide to the news of the day in France, which isn't always pleasant reading. The assassination in Ajaccio took place in the mens' outfitters shop owned by the victim, who was prominent in the local Chamber of Commerce and someone with good nationalist credentials, essential in Corsica. The dreadful news—the 17th assassination of the year in Corsica—brought back so many memories of the one and only time we went to Corsica—we've never been back.

The shop where the murder took place is in the Rue Fesch, which is right in the centre of Ajaccio, whose main claim to rather dubious fame is that it was the birthplace of Napoléon Bonaparte. When we were in Corsica, we stayed in the Rue Fesch, which was like something out of an Italian opera set. It's a narrow street, where the houses rise on both sides of the street to five or six stories. In the evenings, when all the windows are open and families are gathering, it's a noisy bustling place of much conviviality. The street was much more like something you'd find in Naples than in France, and that goes for much of Corsica, which is really France's Italianate protectorate in the Mediterranean.

I always remember, in the Rue Fesch, going into a small draper's shop to buy a scarf for my wife. The woman who ran the tiny shop was very elderly and wore the traditional Corsican style of dress, enveloped in black from head to toe. Yet she was very friendly, came from behind the counter and gave my wife a big hug. It was a touching moment, a friendly gesture of solidarity.

Yet the memory that sticks longest about Corsica was the most chilling and even to this day, when I think of it, the episode sends shivers coursing up and down my spine. One summer's afternoon, typically very sunny and very hot, we decided to go the other side of the bay from Ajaccio to a luxury hotel so that we could have a few drinks and chill out poolside. We got there easily enough on the bus—like most places in France, public transport, by bus or train, is quite good, efficient and affordable. French public transport isn't run down, an afterthought, the way it is in other countries, like the UK.

We strolled down the driveway to the hotel and had just got into the lobby when we saw something odd going on. A group of men, carrying guns, and rather large guns at that, were running out of the lobby. For a split second, I t seemed like some kind of pantomime charade and then we realised that we had run into the middle of an armed robbery, a very frequent occurence in Corsica. We were standing there looking like a couple of eejity tourists and dressed accordingly and I had my camera slung around my neck. The robbers had to run right past us to get out of the revolving doors. The thought immediately occurred to me that just a couple of days previously, on the French mainland in the south of France, something very similar had happened and that the robbers had casually killed several people as they made their exit.

The hotel staff were frozen in shock, but eventually, they told us, long before the gendarmes arrived, that this gang had burst into the hotel, demanded to be taken to the safe in the manager's office and then cleaned out the contents. As it happened, most of the contents were made up of credit card paperwork from guests who had paid by card. The safe actually had very little hard cash, which must have made the robbers very frustrated and doubly dangerous. That evening, there was a brief mention of the incident on the local television news and that was that; this type of robbery is so commonplace in Corsica that they come with the scenery.

The hotel staff offered us drinks as we sat by the pool, looking out on an incredible view across the bay to Ajaccio. It must have been a touch of the stiff upper lip syndrome, or something, but while my wife opted for something suitably alcoholic, I stuck to mineral water!

It was only later that evening, when we had got back to our hotel in Ajaccio that the real horror of that afternoon's events sunk in along with the realisation of what might have been.

That whole episode also points up another truth: so much of what you read about fabulous French holiday destinations is pure pr guff. They'll tell you about the absolutely incredible beaches in Corsica and the equally incredible inland scenery, with all its mountains and maquis, and you'll be told about these storied medieval towns like Bonifacio in the south of Corsica, and it's all quite true, but will you find a word about the true situation in Corsica? Of course not. In the official France, Corsica is just another department and it's often a case of "try to forget about the problem for long enough and it will go away".

Corsica has had a very convoluted history and strong nationalism and an equally rampant banditry play a large part in its affairs. It's an incredibly beautiful island and hospitality is usually warm and heartfelt. But Corsica comes with a health warning and that's something you won't find out about in all the reams of pr. I usually ignore all the pr stuff I read about France and much prefer to find out the real situation, on the ground, for myself, meeting the people of whatever locality I'm in, much more fun and much more rewarding.

Having said all that about Corsica, another much more pleasant memory still sticks in our memory. One afternoon, we had taken the famous narrow gauge train that runs across the central and northern part of Corsica, only to find that night that for some mysterious reason, the train that was scheduled to make the return trip to Ajaccio never turned up. Ten o'clock that night in a small mountainous village in the centre of Corsica—how in the name of bejasus were we going to get back to Ajaccio? We went into the one and only bar and explained our predicament. The local taxi driver was sitting there having a drink and he said, no problem, I'll take you back to Ajaccio. That late night drive at high speed zipping along mountain roads was really something but what made it really special was the music that the taxi driver put on at high volume—the songs of Jacques Brel. Utter bliss, utter magic—that's what a true French holiday is all about!

November 21, 2012

Drinking the profits away!

S omehow, book launches and lashings of drink go together, but these days of course when everything is so politically correct, it isn't always possible to marry the two to create an evening of splendid verbal pyrotechnics and maybe even a little general mayhem!

I launched my latest book, Ballsbridge Then & Now, about the district of Dublin where we live, in that very grand and worthy institution, the Royal Dublin Society. It all went very well and everyone said that they really enjoyed the evening. The only trouble is that the refreshments had to be limited to tea and coffee, since many of the people there had to drive home afterwards. In one way, this was perfectly right and proper, since even here in Ireland, driving under the influence has become totally unfashionable, a good way of becoming a social pariah.

That's an excellent advance and one that I wholeheartedly recommend but it still takes a little fun out of the proceedings. However we hope to put all that right this Thursday evening when we do a book signing in Baggot Street Wines, in Upper Baggot Street, Dublin 4. For the people coming to the do, they'll all be within walking distance of home, so hopefully, modest refreshments of an alcoholic variety will be the order of the evening!

Which brings me to similar events in Paris. On various occasions, we've been to launches of exhibitions in the Musée de la Publicité, which has an extraordinary collection of publicity material. Some of those earlier French advertising designs, especially from the 1920s and 1930s are quite extraordinary, for perfectly ordinary consumer items. Just think of the Vache qui rit! It's amazing to think that in those far—off days, design for packaging for the most humble kitchen products could be so entrancing!

The museum itself was founded in February, 1978, by Geneviève Gaeton Picon and for the best part of 20 years, it had a rather splendid address, in the rue de Paradis in the grimy 10th arrondissement of north-east Paris. This is part of working class Paris, the eastern portion of the city, which is so much more interesting than the haunts of the high bourgeoisie and the super rich, the 16th and 17th.

That's by the way. The museum moved in 1997 to a wing of the Louvre museum, where it remains to this day along with a textile museum and the Musée des Arts Decoratifs. The rue de Rivoli is a rather grotty street, dull, boring and lacking in any redeemable architectural qualities. But once you're in the Musée de La Publicité, all changes, and especially when they're having a launch.

Mind you, they rather make a habit of these in Paris, where the traditional vernissage or previews of art shows are still legion and you can feast yourself on canapés and wine. They're usually all very civilised and while Paris has always had a certain reputation for snooty formality, I've always found people in Paris, who live and work there, very approachable and friendly. The traditional image of Parisians doesn't do for me at all! I know it helps if you have a little French but even if one's vocabulary is limited, making the effort is all important.

One of our favourite galleries in Paris is the Galerie Maeght in the rue de Bac in the 7th, which specialises in contemporary art. It's small, but perfectly formed and has lots of interesting artwork. It's an offshoot of the Maeght Foundation at St Paul de

Vence down in the south. For anyone who hasn't been to St Paul de Vence on the Côte d'Azur, it's a marvellous medieval town, full of artistic traditions and wealthy socialites. Funnily enough, the Maeght Foundation, despite its modernity, fits in well.

So that's the Galerie Maeght in the 7th—if you ever get a chance to drop in on any of the innumerable vernissages in Paris, do go along. You'll have as much fun there as at big venue art centres, like the Grand Palais.

And as for the Musée de la Publicité, once it moved out of the rue de Paradis in the 10th., into the same building moved the Baccarat crystal museum. Baccarat is one of the best-known and revered crystalware brands in France. Eventually, it too moved on, to really plush premises in the 16th., where it can display all its wares to stupendous effect. If you want to see the best style and elegance anywhere in the world, you go to Paris and they've really pulled out all the stops in this museum in the 16th., where you can also dine to your heart's content, in the first floor restaurant, after you've been bedazzled by all the crystalware displays.

The address of the Baccarat museum and company headquarters is 11, place des États-Unis. Behind that address lies an intriguing story. The building was once a hotel particulier, in other words, a very splendid townhouse, that had been built by the grandfather of Marie-Laure de Noailles, the Vicomtesse de Noailles (1902-1970). She was one of the 20th century's most daring and influential patron of the arts, a friend and supporter of such creative spirits as Salvador Dali, Jean Cocteau, Man Ray and Luis Bunuel. In true French aristocratic tradition, the happily married Maire-Laure was also very prone to horizontal liaisons, a great French pastime, with many of the artists she admired. So the Baccarat museum comes trailing glories of French aristocratic history!

Of course, the publicity museum and the Baccarat museum are just two museums in Paris. There are several hundred more to choose from and fortunately, the French aren't so keen as other nationalities, like the British, in discarding their heritage and concentrating solely on the here and now. I always applaud the French for preserving their patrimony.

Just to end on a completely different note, French politics, these too are endlessly fascinating and they are usually as much written up in English as they are in French. Never mind the big split in the QMP party, once the preserve of Nicolas Sarkozy. What is really interesting is that the French went to such trouble to boot Sarkozy out of office earlier this year. Everyone thought that while François Hollande might be dull, at least, he'd have plenty of good ideas about getting France out of the economic doldrums. I loved the recent cover of The Economist, showing the disappearing president, a tiny figure beneath a Napoleonic tricorn hat. Like so many new governments everywhere, the new one in France promised so much and has delivered so little. he sense of disenchantment over Hollande and his non-performance that has set in within just a few short months is incredible. Perhaps Sarkozy is set for a return, in a puff of smoke and a flash of lightning. Who knows?

At least, it's a great talking point in France, a country where there's never any shortage of things events and personalities to talk about, especially at all those art gallery openings!

November 28, 2012

What I hate about the Côte d'Azur

Mention the Côte d'Azur and all kinds of dreamy summer images come up, endless blue skies, blazing sunshine, pastis in a seaside bar, I n other words, the perfect place for a holiday.

But as with all idealised pr images, the truth is somewhat more prosaic. For starters, you need to pick your time carefully to go to the Côte d'Azur. Whatever you do, avoid the peak months of July and August. For some strange reason, people in France simply refuse to change their age-old tradition of everyone taking their holidays in July and August. If you're in Paris, it's great, because the city is much quieter than usual yet you will still find plenty of places open. But if you're on holiday elsewhere in France in the middle of summer, it can be a nightmare, with endless traffic jams on the autoroutes, including the A6 from Paris to the south of France.

It's all part of the French holiday tradition, the bison futé, which lists all the really bad spots for traffic jams. In many respects, life in France is ordered logically, yet when it comes to summer holidays, the French just refuse to alter the way they do holidays, totally illogical. They all want to go on holiday at the same time. Not alone will getting to the Côte d'Azur mean crowded motorways, planes and TGV trains, but once you get there, all the seafront walkways, of which the Promenade des

9

Anglais in Nice is the most spectacular, will be absolutely packed with holidaymakers, sightseers and backpackers from all over the world.

So if you want to holiday in comfort on the Côte d'Azur, far better to go out of season. Even in November or December, the weather is usually quite mild and often sunny, so very pleasant weather for walking or just wandering. Mind you they do have the odd earthquake. They had an enormous one in Nice and Menton stretching right into Italy, but that was way back in 1887 and everyone has long since forgotten about it. Funnily enough, there are quite often minor earthquakes in the south of France, up to about two on the Richter scale, but they never do any damage and no-one bothers talking about them.

Once you've settled into the Côte d'Azur for a nice quiet winter vacation, away from the maddening crowds of summer, the next thing you need to consider is where to go. Everyone has their own personal preferences, so yours may well not agree with mine. First of all, the places to avoid. Three spots along the south-east coast of France drive me nuts—I can't stand them!

The first is Nice. Everyone raves about Nice as the perfect holiday resort, but I don't agree. The best thing about Nice is when you're leaving it. The airport is built out into the sea at the western end of Nice and it's the second most important airport in the whole of France. If you happen to leave on a clear day, with the skies bright blue, which will be the case much more often than not, the views from your window seat are just incredible. You'll see not only Nice but virtually the whole of the Côte d'Azur, stretching right back to the mountains of the Alps.

Nice itself was once Italian—it's only been French for about 150 years, and much of the late 19th century architecture in the city centre is heavy and dull looking, in other words, totally uninspiring! These days, every effort is made to promote the city with its countless museums, parks and gardens, but I'm still not turned on! True, the old town quarter in Nice is delightful and many's the salade niçoise we've had there. The old port quarter too is rather appealing, but as for the city centre, no!

The Promenade des Anglais is the great walkway that fronts the beach in Nice. It's been around since earlier in the 19th century, a time when so many English people made the Riviera their home, and the present version was opened nearly 80 years ago by the Duke of Connaught, one of Queen Victoria's sons. These days, many of the uber rich who live in these parts are Russian.

These days, the English connection with the Riviera is well and truly past history, although the place is still a favourite holidaying place for English holidaymakers. The Promenade des Anglais in its present guise looks a bit like any motorway anywhere, but at least it's a terrific spot for walking. At the western end of the walkway is the Hotel Negresco, one of the famed historic hotels in Nice, with a strange looking cupola on its roof, the design of which was allegedly inspired by the breasts of La Belle Otéro, a great society figure in France in the late 19th/ early 20th century. There's another popularly peddled story about the Hotel Negresco that definitely isn't true; the huge window in the Royal Lounge wasn't the work of Gustav Eiffel, better known for a certain tower in Paris.

Nice also has a big problem with crime—where doesn't?—and that doesn't help either.

The other French city on the Côte d'Azur that I find equally repellent is Cannes. True, it's the home of big film and other festivals, but that doesn't make the place any more acceptable. Neither is the seafront part of Cannes any great shakes. If you go inland in Cannes from the seafront, it's even less pleasant, with plenty of boy racers, especially in the evening.

You're probably wondering why I don't include St Tropez on this list of not-so-nice places. I actually like St Tropez, which is nearly 100km west of Nice. I like the harbourfront walks, I ined with many restaurants and bars; even the monster sized yachts can have a certain appeal. But there's a proviso in all this; don't attempt to go anywhere near the resort in the middle of summer, it's jam-packed and not very pleasant. But if you go just before Christmas, as we've done, all the innate charm of the place is easily seen and appreciated.

Finally, in this list of places in the South of France that I can't stand is the principality of Monaco, which is almost entirely covered by Monte Carlo. The perfume here is particularly obnoxious, that of the super rich who live and holiday here. I can't say that I find anything of any great interest in Monaco and I'm not particularly turned on by all the Prince Rainier/ Grace Kelly love story stuff. I've been to Monaco just once and that was quite enough, thank you very much.

Despite these negatives, there are loads more places all along the Côte d'Azur that are much more interesting and attractive, ike Antibes with its newly refurbished Picasso museum and Menton, which gives a better insight into what the old style Riviera was like than anywhere else. And before I forget, Nice has one big plus when it comes to seeing all these other Provençal hotspots. The main SNCF railway station in Nice can be the starting point for trips all along the coast, in both directions. Trains along the coastal route are pretty frequent and there are various saver fares if you're on holiday.

Don't let me put you off the Côte d'Azur, anything but. However, the three biggest cities along the coast are the least attractive places in Provence. And above all, don't even think of going to the Côte d'Azur in the middle of summer!

December 5, 2012

The president who poops

T alk about irreverence and really crappy irreverence at that! And it's all proving a big hit in France this Christmas, small porcelain figures that show well-known personalities and politicians with bare backsides, having a dump.

Don't blame the French for this, although the French can be extremely bloody minded about their politicians. This time, it's the Spanish, in a country that seems not only to be on the verge of breaking up but having a little revolution at the same time, all over the appalling austerity its people are suffering. These caganer santon figures have been a tradition in Catalonia, the region that desperately wants to break away from the rest of Spain, since the 18th century, and they've lost none of their popularity.

These little figures of the bare backsided cagener has long been a great Christmas seller in Catalonia, where they've made them in recent years of such figures as Carla Bruni, Barack Obama and the Pope. See what I mean, seriously irreverent. The figures shows noted figures relieving themselves and in Catalonia, the tradition was to put them in the crib so that the deposits will make the soil in the crib rich for the coming year. Sticking one of these figurines in the crib was supposed to mean that you'll get luck and happiness in the new year.

There's a similar tradition in Provence but what has given these little figures a big sales uplift this year, especially in France, I s the new one that has been done of French President François Hollande. The disillusionment with the new French president is astonishing and even though it's only six months since he came to power, the way in which public confidence in him has waned is quite incredible. So many people in France were keen to dump Sarkozy and now they've got an even worse presidential figure, who seems totally incapable of leading France out of the recessionary mire.

This could well be a Mediterranean tradition that catches on in this part of the world, Britain and Ireland. We can all name politicians who came to power promising miracles and who, in the event, have delivered bugger all squared. If you're short of a party game at Christmas, here's an idea. Get everyone to name their favourite political pooper as an ideal candidate for a caganer figure!

If you want to buy one, all you have to do is go to the website, www. caganer. com and you'll be doing the business!

Talking about such matters, French actor Gérard Depardieu is in the news again for all the wrong reasons. Very recently, he fell off his scooter in the 17th arrondissement in Paris and it turned out he was well over the alcohol limit for driving. So it looks like he's going to be in big trouble. Earlier this year, he got into an altercation with a fellow motorist and ended up beating up the poor man. Then in August last year, when he was in an Air France plane preparing to take off from Paris for Dublin, he wasn't allowed to go to the loo, tried to urinate into a bottle while he was in the first class section, failed and did it all over the carpet, giving new expression to the phrase "pissed off".

While we're on such matters, I must tell you about one of the most intriguing museums in Paris. It's not quite as popular as the Louvre, but it still gets about 90, 000 visitors a year. It's the sewers museum, near the Pont d'Alma. You pay a small entrance fee, then climb down into the sewers and go for a little promenade, all rather different from your usual bucket and spade seaside excursion.

Paris has a great underground tradition; as well as the sewers, it has nearly 300 km of catacombs, caves and galleries. In the late 18th century, to relieve overcrowding in the city's cemeteries, the mortal remains of six million Parisians were put into the catacombs. A small section of them can be inspected.

Then eight years ago, in 2004, an amazing underground site came to light, literally. Some 20 metres beneath the Palais de Chaillot, which is in the 16th arrondissement, directly across the River Seine from the Eiffel tower, the sewer police discovered this huge cave that had been turned into a fully equipped cinema. It even had three working phones! This was literally just the tip of the iceberg—Paris has a maze of these underground caves that have been put to all kinds of uses. You can well say that what lies beneath the surface of Paris is just as interesting as what you see everyday above ground!

On a similarly byzantine tangent, I'd like to mention a very unusual plaque at the top of the rue de Bellechasse in the 7th— it's at the top of the same street as the Musée D'Orsay. In 1910, Paris had the worst floods for 300 years and much of the low-lying parts of central Paris were flooded. The mark in the rue de Bellechasse shows just how far up the water came. There's a great book on the subject, with some magnificent photos. It's called: Paris Under Water—how the city of light survived the great flood of 1910. It's by Jeffrey H. Jackson and was published in New York in 2010 by Palgrave Macmillan. If you can get hold of a copy, I t's well worth having, for the photos alone.

Meanwhile, all France is preparing for another apocalypse, which to my mind sounds pure rubbish to say the least! The ancient Mayan culture in Mexico devised a calendar that ran in cycles each of which lasted for over 300 years. The calendar began 5, 000 years ago and the Mayans sculpted it so that it runs right up to December 21, 2012. After that, the calendar is a blank. Many cults have intrepreted this as meaning that the world's going to come to an end on December 21. Down in the south-west of France, beyond Carcassone, there's a very odd looking mountain, called the Pic de Bugarach.

Locals say that the rocks at the top of the mountain are younger than the ones further down. Many cults believe that on the big day, December 21, this mountain will be all that will be saved on earth and all kinds of strange rumours are going round, like the one that says the mountain will burst open, revealing an alien spaceship. So strong have become the rumours in recent weeks that even the Pope has come out against them. I'm perfectly sure we will all be here on December 22, attending to all the preparations for Christmas.

Which reminds me of the time we decided to spend Christmas in Paris. It was tricky, because the weather was so lousy and so many places were closed. French people aren't really keen on Christmas-wise people!—and prefer instead to put all their energies into New Year's Eve, looking forward instead to the new year. One New Year's Eve in France we were amazed to see that one of the attractions on one of the main TV channels was an admittedly mild enough striptease!

But anyway, back to this particular Christmas visit to Paris. We arrived at Roissy late on Christmas Eve, having booked into one of the gigantic hotels at the airport. It turned out we were the only guests in a place that had nearly 600 rooms, but the staff were great fun and very decent. They opened up the disco just for the two of us! We also saw snatches of a great French tradition at Christmas, a screening on television of one of the most tremendous French films ever made, Les Enfants du Paradis. It was made while France was still under German occupation and released in 1945. After all these years, the film is incredibly fresh and appealing.

Still, during that trip, the taxi ride from the airport into central Paris on Christmas morning was something rather special.

Just shows, no matter how adverse the circumstances or the weather in Paris, you'll always find something to fascinate you. And while I'm on the subject of fascinating things for Christmas, don't forget your caganer santon!

December 12, 2012

Yipee, free from television!

N oel Coward, that great maestro of the quick witticism, had it exactly right over 50 years ago when he said about television that it was for appearing on, not watching.

In those days, television was in its infancy and no-one had thought of reality TV; the height of banality was Crossroads, the motel serial with the wobbly sets produced by ATV in Birmingham and networked across ITV, yet oddly compulsive viewing as was Emergency Ward 10 from the same station. Even the Eurovision song contest was quite watchable in those long ago days, while big technical advances, like the first trans-Atlantic live TV transmission by satellite, were really exciting. I vividly remember being in the ATV studios in Birmingham to see their first ever test television of colour telly, years before it became everyday practice. My uncle had a great time before World War II appearing as a jazz singer in the early days of BBC television.

Like so many ventures, television was wildly exciting when it was starting up. Now that it's a mature medium, it has lost much of its fun and excitement, relegated to near junk status like so many national economies in Europe.

Politicians are getting on their high horses about regulating junk food, because of its perceived dangers to adults and children alike, but they seem little concerned about the vast quantities of audio-visual rubbish on television. That too has a bad effect, mentally and physically, on young and old alike, but the politicians don't care. Perhaps that's because it suits them to have voters subdued by what is in effect a kind of valium designed to dampen creativity and original political thought. The politicans know damn well that important issues of the day, like the probable exit of the UK from the EU, the possible collapse of the EU itself and the more than likely demise of the euro, aren't going to be properly covered on TV. Viewers are much more concerned about the latest episodes of the truly imbecilic reality TV offerings.

I'm thinking now of Noel Coward, gone 40 years from us in 2013, and his highly apposite remark about television, because recently, the television networks in Ireland switched from analogue to digital, among the last in Europe to do so. The changeover was made successfully. Even though the Irish government made nearly €1 billion from selling the analogue frequencies so that people can enjoy 4G mobile phone services from mid-2013 (quelle joie!), they didn't give a cent to help older and other disadvantaged viewers make the switchover. In the North of Ireland for instance, as part of its UK package, the BBC was offering such viewers a £40 package deal to help them make all the necessary arrangements. Similar arrangements were put in place in France long ago for its digital changeover.

Despite this stinginess in Ireland, the switchover went very smoothly and complaints were few and far between. But we decided, n a moment of standing aside from the rest of the population, not to bother getting a digital set. We still haven't got one and over the past two months, we can't say we've missed anything about not having a television. True, I do miss things I really enjoy, like horse racing, but other things, like news, we don't miss at all. We don't miss seeing all the tedious and banal politicians trying to put a spin on things and making promises they can't keep, or all the vulgar consumerist commercials. As for all the reality shows, we can't say we feel deprived because we never watched them in the first place.

When it comes to television, few people realise that the French got there before the British, starting their first television service in Paris in 1931, a full five years before the BBC did the same at Alexandra Palace in London. Today, the television market in France is highly developed. There are 36 national channels, which include high definition versions of four of the most popular channels. There's also a whole host of regional and local TV services, where again, France out-performs the UK in developing local television. Some of the names are fascinating, like Voo TV in Dijon.

On our many trips around France, we've often seen regional news coverage on the France 3 network, sober and unsensational. Breakfast TV too has always been good in France and I remember one trip, when we were staying in Vichy (where France's World War II pro-Nazi government was based) and doing our own catering, it was great fun to watch breakfast TV as we were having our first meal of the day. It was all very entertaining and informative.

But having said that, much of the programming at peak times is simply boring and especially in Paris, it's a sin to think of staying in for the evening to regarder la télé when you could have so much more fun being out for the evening, especially enjoying a good meal in a restaurant. I still remember vividly the time we were in our favourite restaurant in Paris, which just happens to be Chinese, and seeing two other patrons, a very elegantly dressed and elderly couple, who had obviously once been big names in the arts, quietly singing lullabies to one another. How many memories from the television will stick in your mind like that?

Having said all that, sometimes TV in France can be quite innovative, like the Euronews channel, which was set up in 1993 by 10 European public service broadcasters. It's based in Lyon and aims to tell world news from a European perspective, now broadcasting in 11 languages.

If we lived in France permanently, which in many ways I regret we don't, although French bureaucracy is a fetish best avoided, we probably would have television, but here in dear old Ireland, we can well do without and we don't feel we are missing anything. Instead, we are reading more books and newspapers, listening to more music and generally having a more satisfactory and sociable time. Since our main purpose in watching television was news, we find that we can actually get more from online sources, complete with their own videos, like the ones that many leading newspapers now do.

We certainly won't miss the telly over Christmas but then we have a very unorthodox approach to Christmas anyway and don't for instance go for stuffed turkey on Christmas Day. Being vegetarian makes cooking over the Christmas holiday much more straightforward, but funnily enough, while vegetarianism is widely accepted in this part of the world, especially in the UK, it's enough to make many French chefs throw up their hands in horror and go and seek out some disgustingly once alive piece of meat! But thinking of France, it was saddening to see the latest statistics on the number of poor people in France, 8. 6 million at the latest count, all living on less than €964 a month.

So count your blessings and enjoy Christmas and even more, new year, with or without telly. We'll be managing perfectly well without that screen in the corner, audio-visual opium for the masses. That great master of the ad lib, Noel Coward, certainly had his finger on the button, the off button.

December 19, 2012

Drink up for Christmas!

W here would we be without lashings of drink at Christmas? 'Tis the season to be merry and to hell with all the health advice!

In Dublin, they have a great institution called the 12 Pubs of Christmas. The idea is that a group of friends visits 12 pubs along a carefully designated route and everyone has at least one drink in each pub. The sessions start at lunchtime and by the time they finish, it's around midnight. It's all in complete disregard of the official advice on how much you should drink, but so what, as long as you don't try driving home afterwards.

All of which reminds me of the most spectacular drinking session we've ever had. I was on a press trip to the Champagne district in France, together with my wife and a fellow writer from Glasgow. The night we arrived, we were taken to a superb restaurant just outside Épernay. The restaurant had its own accommodation, which turned out to be a very sensible idea! We were invited to have dinner, order what we liked and enjoy ourselves.

The drink tally was astonishing, nine bottles of Champagne between the three of us followed by a double cognac chaser apiece. We finished up about midnight, too drunk to be drunk, staggered into our rooms next door yet we were in the fields around Épernay inspecting the grapes the morning after at

9am and remarkably sober! We were actually so sober that the famous windmill near the town wasn't doing anything utterly bizarre, like going round and round and up and down.

Épernay and its big brother, Reims, have plenty to offer tourists who want to examine this wine region in detail. The region is only a short distance from Paris and easy to get to by train or road. But if you're stuck in Paris, still the world's number one tourist spot, according to a very recent survey, there are plenty of places in which to while away the time over a drink or two.

Very often, we've been to restaurants along the boulevard St-Germain, where most of the lunchtime clientele is made up of civil servants, all knocking back their wine with the best of them, until 3pm or even 3. 30pm in the afternoon. Then it's back to the office—there are lots of government ministries in this district—for a little very light work before going home for the day.

Two of the best-known bars along this boulevard are the Deux Magots and the Café Flore, but these can be quite busy and hectic. Some of the lesser known bars along here have just as much atmosphere and I must admit my favourite bar in the district is such because it has such fantastic oeufs durs (hard boiled eggs)!

Perhaps the best-known bar in Paris is Harry's Bar in the rue Daunou in the 2nd (sank roo daunoo). It's been going for just over a century now and has long been celebrated as the home of American expats in Paris, the likes of Ernest Hemingway, Rita Hayworth and Humphrey Bogart. It was at the piano here where George Gershwin composed An American in Paris. It's still got loads of atmosphere, a great place for a straight drink or a cocktail.

Another bar that's equally venerated, but in much more down-to-earth style, is the Mélac bistro, in a street in the 11th with an unfortunate name, the rue Léon Frot. his street is between the Bastille and the place de la République and the pub is run by a man called Jacques Mélac, who looks like an old-fashioned troubadour with his enormous moustache. He grows vines in the cellar, enough to produce about 35 bottles of wine a year. Come

September and he has a fantastic harvest festival to celebrate the new vintage. All great fun!

The Ritz Hotel is another celebrated place for drinking; it has some superb bars, but the whole place is closed for renovations for two more years. It was in the Ritz that Lady Di had her last fateful meal at the end of August, 1997, before being killed in a traffic accident in a nearby road tunnel. The Ritz was founded in 1898 and Sophie Loren described it as the most romantic hotel in the world. Hopefully, when it eventually reopens, it will be even more memorable and its bars even more extravagant.

There's also a vineyard in Montmartre, running to all over 1,546 square metres. Out of its grapes are squeezed 1, 700 bottles of wine a year; the Clos Montmartre vintage sells for about €45 a bottle. The annual grape harvest is the excuse for a fantastic festival that runs for five days at the end of September and the beginning of October. There's so much carousing and merrymaking that it draws half a million tourists to Montmartre in the early autumn.

Slightly more formally, you could go to the Paris wine museum, which is in the square Charles Dickens in the posh 16th. The old limestone quarries here were used by the Friars of the Passy monastery in the 16th and 17th century to store their ample supplies of wine. Today, he old wine vaults have been turned into three vaulted cellars for the museum's restaurant. You can also do guided and unguided tours of the museum and a glass or more of wine is included in the admission price, depending what price level you go for. The museum even offers an assorted plate of cheese for a mere €7.

Sometimes, going for a drink in Paris can produce results far beyond a feeling of relaxation and comfort. One of the most intriguing places in Paris, for a meal or for a drink, is Le Train Bleu restaurant in the Gare de Lyon. It was founded in 1901, complete with amazing murals on the ceilings and walls. The red banquette style seating isn't the most comfortable, but the atmosphere is such that you forget about things like that. Around 40 years, the railway company, SNCF, wanted to do what authorities everywhere love doing, demolish this much loved building. Parisians are great at creating an almighty hullabaloo when something or someone threatens the landscape of their beloved city. When word got out about the planned demolition of the Train Bleu, SNCF, had to back off in a hurry and the subject was never mentioned again!

The restaurant has been properly idolised over the years and has made various film appearances, including Mr Bean's Holiday, released in 2007. It has especially memories for us, as once when we were there some years ago, we struck up a casual conversation with the couple at the next table. The gentleman turned out to be a distinguished member of the medical profession and artist in Paris and his wife was a renowned scientist in her own right. We began an immediate friendship with this couple and eventually they told their life history. They were Polish and had fled from Poland to Paris just before World War II nd managed to survive through the war. He eventually gave all his papers to an American university where they make a unique archive about life in Paris over the years. It was a remarkable and enduring friendship for us, that all began over a drink in the Train Bleu, and we still cherish the drawings he gave us.

There's just so much to see in Paris and one of the best ways of getting started is by going for a drink in the right places, although Paris still has to get in on the 12 Pubs of Christmas theme that's so popular in Dublin right now.

January 3, 2013

A very strange Christmas

Christmas just gone in Ireland has been very strange indeed, marked by the passing of several notable people. So it's hardly any wonder that the 40th anniversary of Ireland's accession to what was then the EEC was marked with total indifference by the general public, who are adapting the same "couldn't care less" attitude towards Ireland's current six monthly presidency of the EU. The same indifference can be seen in France.

A poll over the holiday in France found out who were the top 50 personalities in France. The new French president, the invisible man, M. Hollande, didn't even appear! To make matters worse, 62 per cent of French people feel decidedly nostalgic for the franc, which disappeared in favour of the euro 11 years ago.

As for Ireland and the "disparitions" of Christmas and the New Year. The passing of a bard in Ireland is always the occasion of the greatest grief and quite rightly so. Denis O'Driscoll was a noted poet, a gentle and unassuming person with the highest literary attributes, who died on Christmas Eve, aged 58.

For all his working life, since he was 16, he had been employed in the offices of the Revenue Commissioners, the Irish tax office, and only retired from there recently. He found nothing incongruous in having a day job like this (shades of T. S. Eliot) but it didn't stop him writing some amazingly down-to-earth, uncompromising, honest, almost brutal, poetry. Last summer, he brought out his latest book of poetry and strangely a reviewer found that it contained much about dying young. The reviewer hoped fervently that what O'Driscoll wrote wouldn't come true for the poet himself, but sadly it did.

If you have a look at his website, www. denisodriscoll. com, you'll see what I mean about his poetry. He also wrote extensively about the art of poetry, ncluding many collaborations with Seamus Heaney. His passing has left a huge void, the death of one of the best contemporary poets anywhere in Europe.

His death came shortly after a government minister took his own life by hanging, just a few days before Christmas. The budget that was brought in in early December had many measures that heaped misery on people with few resources, including families with sick children, and pensioners, yet was an almost total breeze for anyone fortunate to be well-off. The rich scarcely noticed the December budget; the sick and the poor certainly did. As a result, government ministers endured an unprecedented outpouring of truly vile comments from the public, using social media websites. The ferocity of attack on politicians by the public was unprecedented. No-one had ever done this to long-suffering politicians before, using Twitter and Facebook. The sheer torrent of abuse from the public aimed at politicians was said to have been the main reason for the minister's suicide.

Then on the Thursday after Christmas, the 16 year old son of two of the best-known people in Ireland's restaurant industry, was working on a car at home when it collapsed on top of him. The Clarkes, husband and wife, run L'Ecrivain restaurant in Dublin, often feted by Michelin for its culinary excellence. The death of their teenage son, a motor enthusiast, in an accident at home, which turned out to have been suicide, has been the occasion of much outpouring of grief.

This theme has continued into the New Year. One of Ireland's best known mountaineers, Ian McKeever, was leading an expedition up Mount Kilimanjaro in Kenya when the day after

New Year's Day, an electric storm burst around them and the leader was killed by lightning.

With all these awful events, it's hard for anyone to feel inspired about the New Year, but at least, in France, there are some pieces of good news.

One of the few good things that Sarkozy decided to do when he was president was sanction a new, ultra contemporary concert hall for the Philharmonie of Paris. he futuristic design was to go ahead in the Parc de Villette in north-east Paris. The hall was designed by Jean Nouvel, who also designed the Institut de Monde Arabe in Paris and the Quai Branly ethnographic museum, also in Paris. The new concert hall is a really daring design, but it's running two years late and probably won't open until 2015. It's also costing twice as much as originally planned, now €400 million, but the current government has decided that as so much has already been built, they may as well continue on to completion. It's a great French tradition—French presidents always want to leave outstanding works behind them. Mitterand was the greatest in this respect, including the new national library in Paris, all glass, even if they forget to include proper shades on the windows to protect the books!

The French love grands projets. Another that's coming to fruition is the Berges de Seine project to liven up the long neglected banks for the River Seine in Paris. The idea is to create parkways, walkways and cycle paths beside the river as well as five floating gardens with restaurants and cafés. With all this new flora and fauna, the first results should become evident in 2013, including the stretch from the Orsay museum to the Pont d'Alma.

At least we have one thing to look forward to, spring in Paris. Just ignore all the junk that floats down the Seine, I ncluding shoals of dead fish, and look out for the new riverside attractions!

January 13, 2013

Vive La Marseillaise!

I f you ever want a dynamic and highly energised city to visit in France, I strongly recommend Marseilles, with its strong North African ethos and a history stretching back 2, 600 years, putting Paris in its place! It's the second biggest city in France, yet too often, people overlook it, perhaps because of its fearsome reputation for gangland crime.

Yet it's well worth making the effort, especially this year, when Marseilles shares its 2013 European city of culture status with Kosice in Slovakia. Marseilles has long played a crucial role in French history. In 1792, during the French revolution, the people of the city were so supportive of what was happening in Paris that 500 people walked from Marseilles to Paris to lend a hand. While they were on their way, they sang a revolutionary song called La Marseillaise which of course is now the French national anthem.

Marseilles has traditionally been the entry point into France for migrants from North Africa and after Algeria gained independence 51 years ago, many French settlers from Algeria returned to this part of France, followed in due course by many others of North African origin. When we visited Marseilles, we made a point of walking through the Arab quarter near the city centre, even though we stuck out like a couple of proverbial thumbs, dressed like a couple of all too obvious tourists. It was an absolutely fascinating and it seemed as if we had been transported from Europe to somewhere in the Middle East, a place that absolutely no connection to France.

When we came to Marseilles by train, we arrived at St-Charles station, which is built on a hilltop overlooking the city. When you emerge from the front of the station, you go down the grand escalier into the city proper. But the view from the top of the staircase, right across the city on all its hills, the old port and the surrounding bay is so astonishing it's just unbelievable. Before we went there, an old maritime friend who had travelled the world had said that this view from the top of the staircase at the station was one of the most remarkable in Europe and so it turned out to be. Amazingly, thanks to the TGV, Marseilles railway station is only around four hours journey time from Paris!

One of our next stops was at the five star Sofitel Marseille, the hotel at the entrance to the old port. You can sip cocktails, as we did, gazing out on the old port, which can trace its history right back to ancient Greek times, and also see the great bay, complete with its four islands. One of those islands has the Château d'If from the Dumas novel, The Count of Monte Cristo. At the western end of the bay is the delightful small fishing village of L'Estaque, a favourite haunt for artists over the years, including Braque, Cézanne, Dufy and Renoir. The Fondation Monticelli was set up here in 2010 and features many paintings of the area. The location of the Foundation provides one of the most eye catching vistas of the Bay of Marseilles—you just can't get away from those views!

Soon, we found another high point to climb, up to the19[th] century cathedral, Nôtre-Dame-de-la-Garde, which perches on a hilltop overlooking the whole city. When you're standing outside the cathedral, you are presented with yet another absolutely wonderful view. You can't go anywhere in Marseilles without being confronted with extraordinary views, even though the main drag, La Canebière, which begins at the back of the Vieux Port, s rather heavy and dull.

Needless to remark, having done all this climbing, we found ourselves in need of a relaxing lunch and without any problem discovered a very agreeable small restaurant a little out of the city centre. We didn't try any of the specialities of the region, such as pastis, the drink made with aniseed; aioli, the sauce created from garlic and of course, bouillabaisse, he rich fish soup of Marseilles. But we had an excellent lunch and observed a small group of civil servants taking a respite from their chores and having a seriously vinous lunch. This is the only way to run a civil service and since we've often seen civil servants taking great pleasure in their lunches and their wines in other parts of France, can only conclude that this practice is quite usual. And yet I've never heard of any malfunctions due to the practice. Maybe civil servants elsewhere in Europe should make more of a habit of getting tanked up at lunch!No doubt, too, that their decisions made with the help of a little wine, are sensible and down-to-earth!

Close by our lunch rendezvous, we found the most startling architectural gem in Marseilles, the Unité d'Habitation, the apartments designed by Le Corbusier and built between 1947 and 1952. They are absolutely stunning; it's almost like coming to the original source of so much modern architectural design. These apartments were damaged by fire during 2012 and are still awaiting designation as a UNESCO World Heritage site.

Marseilles is a very gritty city, yet in recent years, has seen much modernisation including a new tramway system. Yet from the 1950s to the 1990s, the city was the fiefdom of the Socialists and the Communists and it's only in recent years that much of this political allegiance has switched from left to the far right, the Front National. It's also a city noted for its hip-hop music, I ts opera house and much else besides on the cultural front, with a raw energy that could almost be bottled. This year, as part of the city of culture celebrations, many intoxicating cultural events will be staged in Marseilles and elsewhere in Provence.

Towards the end of our time in Marseilles, we strolled along the corniche to the immediate east of the city—the corniche is named after the late President John F. Kennedy—and found a cosy hotel where we could sit for the afternoon, enjoying poolside drinks as we gazed over the absolutely incredible views of the coastline. From here for about 20 km, a series of limestone cliffs called the Massif de Calanques run all the way to Cassis, a stunning small seaside town.

Normally, in summer, when we were there, Marseilles is very hot and very sunny, while it's appropriately mild in winter. But just a few months ago, the weather got very capricious, producing one of the strangest sights seen in Marseilles for a long time. The storms were so severe that they blew a large ferry that normally plies between Marseilles and Corsica, right up on to the quayside. There it sat, totally marooned until it could be returned to the sea.

But as always Marseilles come up with surprises. One rarely thinks of airports as places of gastronomic excellence, quick, expensive food more like. But before departing Marseille's airport, at Marignane, north-west of the city and beside a great inland lake, the Étang de Berre, we had an absolutely splendid lunch in the cosy surroundings of the airport restaurant. Yet another plus point for Marseilles and believe me, this is a city absolutely bursting with five star plus points!

January 16, 2013

Mont Saint Michel

T he death yesterday, January 15, of an old priest friend set me thinking on that spiritual haven in France, Mont Saint Michel, that welcomes over three million visitors a year, if that's not a contradiction in terms. When the hordes arrive, reflecting in silence is an absolute impossibility.

The priest friend who died was Fr Tom Cahill SVD of the Divine Word Missionaries. He had an extraordinary life, having worked in Asia for many years before returning home to Ireland. That was how I got to know him; he became editor of a monthly magazine called The Word published by his order—no connection at all with another well-known magazine of the same name. Fr Tom was the perfect editor, liberal, open to all kinds of ideas, secular ones as well as religious, for his magazine. Working for the magazine was a perfect commission, since Fr Tom and myself were very much on the same wavelength. Everything was perfectly organised and even better, the magazine paid well and on time.

This magazine flourished for years, but in the end, succumbed to the fate of so many printed magazines. The Word may have be no more, but Fr Tom was eventually sent to Rome by his order, where he worked for a number of years, labouring heroically with the challenges of communicating digitally in Italian. Eventually, he returned home to Ireland and at the time of his death, was the

Biblical Apostolate for his order. In between all his editorial and religious work, Fr Tom had a great penchant for keeping fit and one of his favourite pastimes was climbing Ireland's holy mountain, Croagh Patrick, which he did countless times.

Certainly, Fr Tom was a great character and tomorrow, January 17, sees him laid to rest in the order's cemetery at its headquarters in Ireland, Donamon Castle in Co Roscommon.

Reflecting on all the years my wife and I knew Fr Tom and appreciated his zestful take on life reminded me of the time we went to Mont Saint Michel in Normandy. There's been a monastery on top of this islet ever since the 8th century and the day and night we spent there was quite mesmerising. The night we arrived, we dined splendidly in the restaurant of the hotel where we were to spend the night. Awakening the next morning, it was amazing to look out and see that the sea around the island had totally retreated.

Early the next morning, long before tourists were about, we climbed up to the monastery on top of the islet and savoured its remarkable Gothic architecture. At that hour of the morning, it was a place of great spirituality, long before the hordes of tourists overran the place. We also much enjoyed exploring the little town on the two sides of the steep narrow street that leads up to the monastery. Amazingly, about 50 people live here all year round. Mont Saint Michel has over 20 restaurants, the most famous of which is La Mère Poulard, famed for its suitably expensive soufflé like omelette and its autograph wall. This has been signed over the years by numerous famous people who've come here, from Ernest Hemingway to Yves Saint Laurent.

The islet used to be approached from the mainland by a causeway, but in recent years, a huge engineering project has been carried out here, to build a dam that is designed to remove the silt that has accumulated around the islet. The dam is now completed and the next stage is to build a bridge from the mainland to the islet, so that once again, Mont Saint Michel will be surrounded by sea.

I'd definitely recommend a visit to Mont Saint Michel, but would strongly advise going offpeak. If you go in summer, its sense of religious spirituality is seriously diminished, due to the sheer volume of camera toting tourists.

Near Mont Saint Michel, on the Normandy mainland, is a delightful port town, Granville, that is well worth exploring in its own right. When we were in Granville, It was a little offputting to find out that the municipality had rigged up loudspeakers in all its main streets in preparation for a big local fair. I don't know how many decibels were being belted out music wise but it must have been at the top end of the scale!

We took a boat trip for the 17 km from Granville to the Chausey Islands. Hardly anyone in France has heard of them; they are to the south-east of the English-speaking Channel Islands. At low tide, 365 Chausey islands are visible, but at high tide, that number shrinks to 52. Only the biggest island, Grand Ile, is inhabited, by about 30 people. There's little to do except walk and admire nature and from a distance, see the Château that once belonged to Louis Renault of motor car fame. When we were there for the day, we enjoyed a wonderful and truly authentic farmhouse lunch, well washed down with copious wine. The lady who cooked the lunch talked about her occasional trips for shopping to the mainland; to her, mainland France seemed a world away.

It's well worth looking at the website for the islands, www. ileschausey. com with its array of mostly ancient photographs.

I'll end this blog, thinking of the Chausey Islands and Mont Michel, in Normandy, a wonderful region of France, and in doing so, drink a virtual toast to the memory of Fr Tom Cahill, a truly enlightened magazine editor.

January 23, 2013

Whatever's happened to the fighting Irish?

T he reputation of the Irish of fighting for their rights has taken a battering, as apathy and passivity sweep the country during this interminable recession, but the French have kept the reputation of the Fighting French alive and well.

If there's any perceived injustice in France, or any social group feels that their rights are being undermined, then out come the protest groups. Recently, huge protests took place in Paris, saying that true marriage can only be between a man and a woman; it's a view that many regard as antiquated and outdated, that lots of other people have just as much right to get married. The organisers of this particular protest said that around 800, 000 people came out on the streets, while the police say the number was half that. Whether all this protestation will have any effect on the current French government's policies in this area is very doubtful, but the whole episode proved once again, there's nothing large numbers of French people like more than a really good street protest. Out with the banners and the placards and the recent bad weather was no deterrent!

Another very recent protest was by a large vested interest group, the taxi drivers. Altogether, France has 55, 000 taxi drivers, of whom 17, 000 are in Paris. They are up in arms over government plans to liberalise the taxi licensing regime and open it up to competition. The taxi drivers organised a campaign called Opération Escargot, which involved large convoys of taxi drivers driving at a snail's pace and holding up all the traffic, an objective which succeeded all too well. I must admit, any time we've taken a taxi in Paris, we've always been well looked after and the drivers quite happy to chat away while driving at what seemed to us very high speeds!

French protests can involve every imaginable grievance or put-down; no cause is too insignificant not to demand a street protest. Sometimes, the protests can be for very high-minded campaigns. One such outpouring took place in Paris just over 40 years ago. The Gare de Lyon has a marvellous historic restaurant called the Train Bleu, that's just over 100 years old, with many fine artistic decorations. In the early 1970s, the French State-owned railway company, SNCF, wanted to demolish the whole caboodle, in a stupid decision worthy of any large state -owned bureaucratic monopoly. However, the citizens of Paris weren't having any of this and so successful was their campaign at blocking the moves to demolish the restaurant that SNCF promptly backed off and never tried to repeat the exercise. Today, Le Train Bleu still stands in all its restored glory, even if the banquettes are more than a little uncomfortable to sit on.

And as any traveller through France knows all too well, the employees of said SNCF are the best at upholding the ancient French tradition of walkouts and strikes at any perceived lessening of their rights. Deduct their weekly wages by a euro and the entire network will go on strike! All too often, disruptions by irate workers mean suspensions of SNCF service and the French public just accepts these perturbations as part of the every day scenery.

This spirit of marching out to protest against any loss of rights is one that seems to have disappeared in Ireland: the spirit of the fighting Irish has really gone for a burton. Just think, 1916 and the Easter Rising, when a small minority was willing to give its lives in exchange for nationhood, or the vast farmers' protests during the 1960s when farmers demanded and eventually got the right to a decent standard of living. There were also some great street demonstrations years ago about the high levels of personal taxation and all these protests had their desired effect; the governments of the day had to listen to the people.

Nowadays, in the middle of a recession, it seems that everyone in Ireland is too busy busy watching soaps like Coronation Street or Eastenders (practically all the soaps on Irish television are of British origin, although few notice the irony) to care a whit about the troubles of society or bother doing anything about them.

The Irish just don't seem to bother when the sick, the disabled, the unemployed, the poor pensioners, take yet another hit as the most marginalised in society, while the rich get away scot free. Exactly the same thing is happening in the UK, where the rich get richer and the not so rich and the poor just get done down day-by-day. In Ireland, the politicians, aided and abetted by the troika of the European Commisision, the European Central Bank and the International Monetary Fund, keep throwing buckets of the proverbial horseshit over the Irish public and they just keep coming back for more. Talk about lying down and being walked all over!

Some recent government decisions in Ireland are going to cause a lot of hardship and deepen the recession, not help end it. One is the forthcoming property tax. Every home owner will have to pay a tax depending on the valuation of his or her house. It never occured to the wise people who drafted this legislation that the value of property in Dublin and other cities is far higher than in rural areas. So a family living in a four bedroomed house in Dublin could end up paying around €1, 500 a year for their property tax and the forthcoming water charges, while someone who lives in a rural house of exactly the same dimensions as one in Dublin will only pay about a quarter of what the property tax in Dublin will be, although their water charges will be about the same.

No wonder that Vincent Browne, one of the leading political commentators in Ireland, said last weekend that the present Irish government is talking baloney on every subject it addresses. But what government minister, of whatever hue in any country you care to name, isn't doing exactly the same?

Despite this, is there any sign of protest? Not at all, the great Irish public seems quite happy to let it all wash over them, the horse shit that is, without the merest murmur. The notion of people in Ireland being the fighting Irish should be quietly retired— there's no point in maintaining this myth in the face of such passivism. The troika can keep on telling public sector workers that in future, they will have to work longer hours for less money, and no-one seems too bothered at all. In the UK, the coalition government, Conservatives and Lib Dems, is getting away with exactly the same kind of nonsense, so it's not purely an Irish phenomenon.

Next time you're waiting for take-off while French air traffic controllers or Air France employees do their thing, just think of how the French react against the smallest perceived injustice and how in Ireland and Britain, it's all swept away by a tsunami of apathy.

However, I have a funny feeling—and I hope to goodness I'm proved wrong—but I think that the way 2013 is starting to shape up, we're going to have a worldwide wave of blips this year. Not just acute weather events, but terrorism and political and economic blips galore. Just think of the Senkaku Islands in the East China Sea, a tiny spot that hardly merits a mention in the western media.

The islands are owned by Japan and claimed by China and some well-informed Asia experts predict that these tiny islands could become a real hot spot this year. With so many hot spots of so many kinds bubbling away all over the world, 2013 could be a lot more dynamic than we want, for all the wrong reasons.

Perhaps after all, keeping the finger on the snooze button and allowing apathy to reign relentlessly, may be the best way of doing things!

January 30, 2013

Marching in Co Cork and celebrating the TGV

I n north-west Co Cork, a small village called Ballyhea (population 1, 000) has been garnering the headlines, not only in Ireland, but internationally.

It all started in February, 2011, when a sports journalist with the Irish Examiner in Cork called Diarmuid O'Flynn decided that enough was enough. He was angered by the ongoing taxpayers' bailout of the banks in Ireland, saying that it has been the biggest bank robbery in history, but that the difference is that this time, the banks are robbing the people. O'Flynn says he was inspired to start the protests by the Arab Spring. He sees the protests as part of a movement for organising change in society from the bottom up.

Ever since then, people have been marching through Ballyhea in protest, sometimes once a week, sometimes more often, and just recently, they passed the 100 march mark. People come from all over Ireland to take part, so it's no longer a local curiosity, and people carry placards with slogans like "stop punishing the poor for the sins of the rich". When the protests started, they were little more than the smallest pebble in the boot of the European Central Bank, but now they have become something much more significant, aided by the amount of national media interest they have created in Ireland. More and more international media sources too are finding the protests interesting, including most recently, the English language service of Al Jazeera.

Gene Kerrigan, a journalist with the Sunday Independent newspaper in Dublin, says that when the history of this ignoble little era comes to be written, Ballyhea will be a byword for honour. Amazingly, the Irish Republic, with a population of 4. 2 million, is carrying 42 per cent of Europe's bank debt.

An excellent example of how Ireland is so out of kilter came the other day when the latest Scottish unemployment figures were published. In the latest period under review, the figures fell by 14, 000, giving Scotland just over 200, 000 people out of work. Scotland has one million more people than the Irish Republic, but the unemployment rate in Ireland is close to half a million. Given the similarities between the two economies, no-one has come out and explained the obvious: why the huge disparity?

Actually, you'd wonder what the hell is going on. The French employment minister, Michel Sapin, caused something akin to panic earlier this week, when he said that the French state is "totally bankrupt". That may have been an exaggeration, but there's probably a grain of truth in what he blurted out. A further problem in France comes from the fact that so many people have fallen out of love with buying new cars. Sales of new cars in France are back to what they were 15 and 20 years ago, which is creating huge problems for the French economy. And in Italy, scandalised chatter surrounds the country's third largest bank, the Banca dei Paschi di Siena. People want to know: is it going bust? But finding the straight answers is the hard bit. Meanwhile, the Republic of Cyprus, the Greek part of the island, is going through its own financial traumas: where is it all going to end?

Trying to find answers anywhere is difficult. Gerry Adams, the president of Sinn Fein, who's also a member of the Irish parliament, said on RTÉ Radio this week that he wouldn't send the present Irish government out for a bottle of milk. Exactly the same could be said for many governments across Europe, including the UK coalition, where the austerity programme seems to have done nothing except create more austerity. This UK coalition government is due to run its term until 2015, but I wonder will it make it that far?

At least, we have something to celebrate this week. At the Gare de Lyon in Paris the other day, there was a ceremony to mark the two billionth passenger on the TGV network of super fast trains in France. Originally, the trains were designed to be powered by gas turbines, but the oil crisis of 1973 put an end to that and the engines were modified to be electrically powered. It's very unfashionable to admit it, but most of France's electricity is nuclear generated, which is a far safer source of energy than oil. The first TGV came into service in 1981 on the Paris-Lyon route. Eventually, the line was extended to Marseille.

Over the years, the network has been rolled out across France. When the second phase of the eastern section of the TGV is completed, journey time from Paris to Strasbourg will be cut to a mere one hour, 50 minutes. The TGV is due to reach Bordeaux in four years' time. The highest speed ever reached with a TGV was 574. 8km/ h, on April 3, 2007. The network of high speed lines in France has now reached just over 2, 000 km.

The TGV has prompted other countries in Europe, such as Belgium, Germany, Italy and Spain to follow suit with their own high speed trains and of course, Eurostar between London and Paris and Brussels, has proved equally successful.

When you're on the TGV, as we've been on several occasions, the sheer speed is impressive. But the train is going so fast that you the countryside flashes past in an instant blur, too quick to see much detail. The trains travel so fast that the signalling is automatic; the traditional lineside signals would be useless for the drivers because of the speed of the train. What is equally astonishing is how the French railways system, SNCF, has rolled out the TGV system across France with so little disruption or protest and so efficiently, too.

I've a funny feeling that the planned high speed rail links between London, Birmingham and Manchester and the north of England, will never come to pass. There'll be so much disputation over the routes, and acquisition and a host of other issues, that by the time everyone has stopped arguing the toss, the system will remain unbuilt.

All of which brings me to a wonderful project I heard about on Radio 4 the other day. The Black Isle is a wonderful part of Scotland, right up in the far north-east, not far from the city of Inverness. A memory project is under way to preserve the memories of older folk in this very distinctive area: who lived where and in what buildings, the kind of local history that's swept away as the generations pass. Inverness is also a fast-growing city and a lot of people who are working there now live in the Black Isle, which is increasing development pressure and hastening the oblivion of old memories. So this very worthwhile project is well under way and yielding a lot of information that will be vital for future generations.

I've recently been involved in a local history project, or a book called Old Achill Island. It's the largest island off the Irish coast and naturally, being Ireland, it's had a very turbulent but fascinating history. The book I did that was launched recently has lots of old photographs, all taken around a century ago. What's been really interesting about the launch is that it has had zero coverage in the traditional media, yet the book has really taken off, thanks to word of mouth and such social media as Twitter. That's all an interesting conundrum to ponder, just as much as the real state of the French state finances.

But at least we have St Brigid's Day here in Ireland on this Friday, the first of February. It's the first day of Celtic spring and by February, you can see a big improvement, with the mornings getting much brighter and the evenings doing the same. It's a real marker that the horrible days of this past winter are now behind us.

February 6, 2013

The bells of Nôtre Dame

P aris never fails to surprise; there's always something new and inventive happening to lift the spirits and this week, the good news comes from the cathedral of Nôtre Dame.

The cathedral is currently celebrating its 850th anniversary (construction started in 1163 and was completed in the mid-1240s) and to mark that momentous occasion, its nine new bells will be rung for the first time on Saturday, March 23, just in time for Easter.

It had been obvious for a long time that the old bells were out of tune, not only with each other, but with the great Emmanuel bell, which was cast in 1681. So at a cost of €2 million, raised from private donations, eight new bells to replace the five old ones were made at a foundry in Villedieu-les-Poeles in Normandy, and a ninth bell, called the Marie bell, was cast in the Netherlands. Recently, all the new bells were brought to the cathedral and put on display. Each bell is named after a saint or a prominent Catholic figure and when they ring out for the first time towards the end of March, it will surely be a joyous occasion not only for the faithful of Paris but for the innumerable visitors to the city.

And if you're fortunate enough to be in Paris to hear the new bells, it's well worthwhile making the short journey from the island that Nôtre Dame is located on, across the small bridge to the neighbouring Ile St Louis. The latter is an absolute gem, with its few well-preserved streets and quayside walks that will remind you of a long vanished upper class Paris. If you cross from Nôtre Dame to the "mainland", don't miss the fabled bookshop of Shakespeare and Company.

Meanwhile, the Académie Française pursues its endless quest to keep French pure. The academy, with its curious customs and outfits, has been the guardian of French cultural purity for the past 378 years and over the past three decades, has been fighting a not always successful battle to translate the legion of words about Information Technology into French equivalents. However, while the academy may have moral authority behind it, the institution doesn't have any legal powers to enforce its rulings on the French language.

Some of its translations have become more or less accepted as standard in France, like courriel for email and logiciel for software. Its latest attempt is to persuade people in France to use the word mot-dièse for hashtag. Dièse means "sharp", so "sharp word" in translation!

Despite all these sometimes unsuccessful attempts to keep French in its pristine form, the uphill struggle continues. Just the other day, I got an email flyer from France which urged me to believe that "Happy Hours, c'est maintenant". Enough to make the elders of the academy splutter!

But the French have an addiction to bureaucratic rules and edicts. One of the most ridiculous ones, as applied to Paris, was only officially abolished the other day, despite having been ignored for decades. On November 7, 1800, I t was declared that women in Paris couldn't wear trousers without a permit. There were certain exceptions, such as for horse riding or riding a bicycle. Now the edict has been declared unconstitutional, but of course, it's been simply ignored for six decades and more. No sooner had this archaic edict been done away than two more came along.

The French government has decreed that as from July of this year, all shops and offices in France will have to turn off their lights at night, in order to save creating some 760 tonnes of carbon dioxide a year. It seems fair enough to keep offices in the dark at night, if no-one is present, but what about shops, especially all the shops in fashionable parts of cities like Paris, where tourists love to window shop as they browse? Another new edict that's due to be introduced will see children be confined to school when they do their homework. The reasoning behind this is that children from better off homes, where the parents are well educated, get all kinds of benefits from doing their homework at home compared to children from poor backgrounds. It all reminds me of what a one time Taoiseach (prime minister) of Ireland, the late Dr Garret FitzGerald, said once about a proposed new law: "In theory, it works fine, but the question is, will it work in practice?"

No wonder the French continue to be so dismissive about their president, François Hollande. One of his nicknames in France is Monsieur Flanby. In case you're wondering, Flanby is a packaged dessert produced by Nestlé; it's a brand of big wobbly caramel cream. Recently, Frederick Forsyth was even more damning of the French president, whom he described in the Daily Express as having less talent than his Jack Russell terrier. He explained that he meant the dimmer of his two dogs.

I wonder what the French will make of the Irish president when he visits France later this month. Michael D. Higgins may be small in stature, but he has a big humanitarian heart. During the past 30 years, he has been very outspoken on many issues, but the protocol surrounding the Irish presidency means that his scope for making comments on controversial issues is now very limited. A friend of mine who once studied at the university in Galway well remembers Michael D as a lecturer in political science and sociology there. His lectures were so electrifying that the students all made sure to be present for his lectures at 9am on Mondays, they were so unmissable, quite an achievement and not done for too many uni lecturers!

Still, it's not much better here in Ireland, where daft decisions continue to be made. One recent decision concerns the building of 2, 300 wind turbines in the midlands of Ireland, which have the least amount of wind of any part of the country. In Britain, many people are turning against the monstrosities of wind turbines that now blight many landscapes there. But Britain still needs all the green energy it can get, so it has signed a deal so that all these extra wind turbines can pepper the landscapes across the midlands of Ireland, with the power generated, on the days that the wind blows, flowing into the UK grid.

Ireland is so depressing these days; all the talk is of cutting costs and of bringing in ever more ludicrous red tape to tie up even more aspects of people's lives. No-one seems to have anything creative or original to say!

Once, many people in Ireland had a rather loose relationship with the law; if they didn't like a particular law, they simply ignored it, an attitude that was a hangover from colonial days. In certain cases, the introduction and application of new laws has been long overdue and very welcome, as with the much tighter controls on driving, ncluding drink driving, but these days, the Irish penchant for petty bureaucracy is getting every bit as bad as France.

Just this week, I heard from a friend of mine who moved to Melbourne, Australia, about three years ago. He had a good job in the media industry here in Ireland but when he and his wife had their first child, a daughter, they decided that Ireland was no fit place in which to bring up a young child, so they packed up everything and moved to Melbourne. Despite the fact that it's one of the most expensive cities in the world in which to live, they've been doing well, like the countless other Irish people who've emigrated since the great economic crash began nearly six years ago. Every week, some 2, 000 Irish people, mostly younger people that the country can least afford to lose, are quitting Ireland in favour of places like Australia and Canada, where the wave of negativity that washing over Ireland simply doesn't exist.

That 2, 000 figure, incidentally, doesn't include all the people from other countries who came to work in Ireland during the boom, some of whom are now returning home. The days when

Irish newspapers ran regular supplements in Polish are long gone, as Poland continues an economic miracle that's long vanished from this part of the world.

In contrast, it was so moving to hear the Desert Island Discs programme on Radio with Aung San Suu Kyi, the Burmese opposition leader. She was incredibly moving, uplifting and inspirational. We need someone of her moral authority and positive determination here in Ireland and many other European countries are the same. In Britain, for instance, all that the Tories seem able to do apart from inflicting yet more harsh measures on the poorest and most deserving in society, is faction fight among themselves on such issues as continued EU membership and gay weddings.

So here's to one rare and truly inspiring international figure and to the new bells of Nôtre Dame!

February 13, 2013

Lightning strikes St Peter's

J ust when I was wondering what on earth I was going to write about this week, along comes Pope Benedict XVI who threw a real ecclesiastical spanner in the works. Did you see that incredible photograph, taken a few hours after his resignation speech? An electrical storm was raging across Rome and this amazing bolt of lightning is seen striking the very top of the cupola on top of St Peter's. It looked so eerie, almost literally heaven sent.

But in the absolute torrent of words that's been pouring forth since the news came about the Pope on February 11, that he intends to resign from the Papacy as of Friday evening, February 28, a really good story about the Pope and the Vatican seems to have been missed by the media. Has no-one ever heard of the prophecies of St Malachy, the cleric who was an archbishop of Armagh in Ireland in the 12ᵗʰ century?

He wrote a whole series of prophecies about future Popes and in the centuries since, they've often been proven perfectly accurate. But it's his prophecy about the pope who comes after Benedict XVI that's really striking. By Easter, we should know who the new Pope is, but if St Malachy is right, then the new Pope is in for a hard time. Malachy says that the next Pope will be the last and that the seven hills of Rome will be destroyed, marking the end of both the Papacy and the Catholic church.

Meanwhile, on matters artistic, there's also been plenty happening in recent days. In 1866, a French painter called Gustave Courbet painted something that caused great outrage at the time. The painting is called L'Origine du Monde and shows the lower half of a naked woman. The painting looks rather revolting for the simple reason the model has an absolute mass of genital hair, which is a general turn-off these days. There was much speculation at the time that the model was an Irishwoman called Joanna (Jo) Hiffernan, known in Paris as La Belle Irlandaise. But people who know about these things now say that it couldn't possibly be her, since she was a natural red head.

The other intriguing part of the story is that for years, the top half of the painting was missing. However, someone says he picked it up a couple of years ago in a bric-a-brac shop in Paris for €1, 400. This piece of the painting has been verified by the world's leading expert on Courbet and if he's right, this portion of the painting could now be worth €40 million. The painting has only been on permanent display within the last 20 years; it's in the Musée d'Orsay in Paris, which is planning a major exhibition centred around the painting, next year.

As for Courbet, he was quite the little revolutionary and during the Paris Commune of 1871, he was put in charge of the museums in Paris. He wanted to pull down the great Napoleonic column in the Place Vendome, which was done, but in 1877, long after the commune had been banished into history, the city council decided to restore the column and send the bill, in 33 instalments, to Courbet. The painter, who was addicted to heavy drinking, conveniently died the day before the first instalment was due; there must be a moral in that!

What was interesting was how the media covered this particular story. In France, newspapers and websites like Le Figaro thought nothing of showing all of the painting. For Paris Match, it was a world exclusive, so naturally, they put the painting in all its genital glory on its front cover. People on the Continent are often much more relaxed about the workings of the body, a much more sensible attitude, and I always remember the time we were staying in the delightful Normandy town of Valognes, near Cherbourg. One day, we were walking down the road from the railway station to the centre ville, when an elderly man, who looked like a farm worker, came along. He was in urgent need of relieving himself and promptly pissed against a wall in full view of all the passersby, ncluding ourselves, without the slightest hestitation or shame, and no-one thought any the worse of him.

Yet in the media in the UK and Ireland, prurience reigns and everyone went out of the way to be so coy about Courbet. The Irish Independent newspaper and website for instance, showed a photo of the world expert on Courbet, but little detail of the famous painting. Such faux coyness often verges on the ridiculous.

The other recent French story about art came from Lens, the former coal mining city in north-eastern France, where the new branch of the Louvre was only opened in December. One of its works is the famous Delacroix 1830 painting, Liberty leads the People, which shows a bare breasted woman carrying the tricolour and leading the mob. The painting represented the July, 1830 revolution in Paris. A woman in the art gallery put a graffiti sticker on the painting, which fortunately didn't do any lasting damage. It turns out the sticker represents a group called AE911, which through its website, ae911truth. org, wants the US Congress to have an enquiry into what really happened on 9/ 11. They say that the attacks that day were the result of a conspiracy and had nothing to do with Islamists.

My final painterly note this week is about the Picasso Museum, which was founded in 1985 in the Hotel Salé in the third arrondissement of Paris. It's undergoing a major revamp and the latest news is that it is due to reopen to the public this summer, with over 500 works by Picasso on four levels. But don't bank on this opening date actually happening; dates for such construction projects have a nasty habit of going south! But we were very amused when we visited the museum in its original form some years ago; one of the exhibits was made up of some of Picasso's laundry lists Any takers for my shopping lists?

Something else we had a look at in France many years ago was the Bayeux tapestry in Normandy. This shows 1066 and all that, but the tapestry was never finished. What is on display is most interesting, in a fasacinating Normandy town, where it's been since 1945. Now 400 of the good burghers of Alderney in the Channel Islands have stitched together the missing section, showing the coronation of William the Conqueror after the Norman invasion of England, and it's been put in the Alderney museum.

Alderney itself is a strange island. When we went there, we were mystified because there was such a palpable eerie feeling around the harbour area; we didn't find out until later that during the World War II occupation of the Channel Islands by the Nazis, many frightful atrocities had taken place in this part of Alderney.

Just to end on a funny peculiar note. The other day, I was reading the website of the French language Tribune de Geneve, a very respectable newspaper. I spotted a headline to the effect that a top Swiss chef had allegedly been making a cake from shit. For one split second, I thought, dear me, the standards of haute cuisine in Switzerland are really dropping. But of course shit is a slang word for heroin and what this chef was supposed to have done was bake a cake laced with heroin, which of course made the two women who ate it very ill and needing hospitalisation.

These days you just don't know what story is going to come up in a very uncertain world, which of course makes life much easier for bloggers!

February 20, 2013

The delights of Strasbourg

One of the most interesting cities in France is Strasbourg, even if it is one not much visited by English tourists. The best time to go is August, even though it's usually very hot, for the simple reason that the European Parliament isn't in session and the Eurocrats have all gone off on their holidays, so that Strasbourg puts in a rare appearance as a reasonably normal city, with not too many crowds.

We benefitted from this August calm, one year, by checking into Le Hotel Grand, which is just across the street from the railway station. The train journey from Paris to Strasbourg used to be awfully tedious, although the TGV, with some upgrades still to come, is a big improvement. You can also fly from Paris to Strasbourg, with flying time an hour. When we flew to Strasbourg, the runway at the airport was being repaired, so our flight was diverted to a small airport in the region and with typical French efficiency, when we touched down, no-one had thought about how all the passengers were going to be transported from there to Strasbourg. Anyway, after a lot of pushing and shoving and a bravado Jean d'Arc performance by my wife Bernadette, in her best French, it wasn't too long before Air France got coaches organised.

Anyway, we found the wholly delightful Le Grand Hotel really comfortable with an excellent breakfast area. Yet if we had tried to book in at any other time of the year, it would have been close to impossible because of the Eurocrats in residence. The whole European Union as it is presently constituted, fills me with horror because of all its bureacracy and as for the European Parliament, it strikes me as one of the most useless and irrelevant institutions ever devised, although great for MEPs and their expenses! As you can guess, I'm a fan of neither!

But as for Strasbourg itself, we went as high as we could up the cathedral, fuelled by a rather boozy lunch, which speeded our climbing abilities, and saw the marvellous spread of the city, the River Rhine and then just across the river, Germany. We also marvelled at the great horological clock.

In the vast square close to the cathedral is a fantastic restaurant, the Kammerzell, where we had had a spectacular vinous lunch. The building was constructed in 1427 and today, you can both dine and stay there. The area around the cathedral is most interesting, with so many of the medieval buildings preserved, but other parts of the city are much less interesting and look very hick, like a dull provincial city, Kilkenny, Ireland, in the 1950s. However, it is easy enough to get round Strasbourg using the new tramway system.

In terms of eating out, we also had a very pleasant meal at the station restaurant and had a great chat with one of the waitresses, who was full of bonhomie and fun, great for practising our French. And it's funny how a little wine loosens the tongue! How often could you say those kind of things about a railway restaurant in Ireland or Britain? Also in Strasbourg, we went on a boat trip exploring the Petite France district of city, with its medieval waterways—but watch out for mosquitoes!

Alsace is such an interesting part of France but we only had time to see a few other places. We went to the wine town of Riquewhir, one of the Plus Beaux Villages de France, only to find it absolutely jam packed with tourists. The main street looked like Oxford Street, London, on a Saturday afternoon. But it's a very attractive medieval town, including its ancient Main Street, if you can see the buildings for the people. I've always had a soft spot for Alsatian wine, not so much the reisling, but most certainly the gewurztraminer. Gewurz comes from the German for spices and in a good quality wine, you can taste both the spicey flavours and a certain sweetness. Delicious!

Our best trip outside Strasbourg was to Mulhouse, a dull industrial city with two incredible museums. The national automobile museum, founded by the Schlumpf textile industry family, has literally hundreds of vintage and veteran cars in pristine condition. I've no great interest in old cars, but this museum was really wow! I was totally hooked! Then we discovered an even more astonishing museum that was much more to my taste, the Cité du Train railway museum, the largest such museum in the world.

The old locos and the old carriages were so thrilling to see and the museum really brought back the best days of the old Wagon-Lits service, when you could travel by across Europe and beyond in wonderful style and enjoy the most magnificent meals and scenery.

As we travelled around Alsace, storks, one of the region's symbols, were very much in evidence, perched on the chimney tops. We also enjoyed getting to know the work of Hansi (1873-1951) one of Alsace's great artists who loved to draw and paint many traditional scenes in Alsace, including the ubiquitous storks.

Alsace has very much a German as well as a French heritage and over the years, the region has changed hands on various occasions between the two countries. We travelled across the Rhine by rail into the German spa resort of Baden-Baden, on the edge of the Black Forest. It's a delightful town, very clean and well presented, with the Kurhaus at the centre of its spa business and a host of other delights such as the Fabergé Museum.

This is very much a part of Europe where countries and cultures merge. We also visited Basle, the Swiss city on the Rhine where Switzerland, France and Germany meet.

I can't recommend Alsace highly enough, one of the most distinctive parts of France, with strong traditions of its own in food and wine, but with its own very vibrant cultural tradition.

Back to more usual quarrels. I was rather astonished by the outburst of the novelist Hilary Mantel about the poor, put—upon Duchess of Cambridge. While Mantel's speech might have been plain speaking at its plainest, she treated the Duchess almost as an automaton, rather than as a real, living person with feelings and thoughts of her own. No doubt the row will rumble on in the red tops for days if not weeks to come, with both sides of the argument making the most ridiculous statements.

I was also interested to hear the other day of ongoing progress in Birmingham, with the new Library of Birmingham and the new theatre for the 100 year old Repertory Theatre both nearing completion. Add to these Symphony Hall, opened in 1991, and Birmingham is soon going to get an amazing variety of cultural institutions in the heart of its city centre. Incidentally, it was in Birmingham where as a young teenager I got my introduction to Irish culture and customs, I n the Irish Centre, and I've never lost my fascination with Ireland in the decades since. It was wonderful that I got to know some of the people in the Irish Centre and it opened up a whole new world for me. If I had depended solely on the curricula reading at school, I would hardly have known that Ireland even existed, it was like a country that just didn't figure in the English imagination, perhaps because the English legacy there had often been so bad. It still doesn't figure; to a large extent, Irish people love to know everything that's going on cross-channel, but an awful lot of English people live in blissful ignorance of what's happening in Ireland.

As for Ireland, in three years time, the country is due to commemorate the centenary of the 1916 Easter Rising, which led to two-thirds of the island of Ireland being granted partial independence, all of which has now been handed to the EU. The leaders of the Easter Rising had some very noble ideals and aspirations for the Irish people; it's a shame that they have been so totally betrayed by successive Irish governments, driven more by a spirit of gombeenism, place seeking, cronyism and a pathetic desire for lower middle class respectability rather than by high moral principles that would have benefitted all the people of the nation.

February 27, 2013

More taxes and the Italian election

T his week, much of the news is dominated by the Italian general election and generally bad economic news everywhere, as the UK lost its triple A credit rating from Moody's.

It's hardly surprising that the UK has lost this valuable trophy rating, since the policy of the UK coalition government has produced little except more austerity and depressed consumer demand, which in turn, accelerates the pace of austerity. Now the Italians have thrown their general election result into the European melting pot. It seems that forming a government in Italy will be well nigh impossible, given the political statement and somehow, it seems highly appropriate that a stand-up comedian, Beppe Grillo, should have been this catalyst for change.

Where is Italy in particular and the eurozone in general going after this fiasco? Looks like nowhere fast.

Another Italian conundrum is also coming up fast. With the resignation of Pope Benedict XVI happening later this week, a conclave to elect a new Pope is likely to be speeded up. Given the church scandals that have emerged so far, who knows what else is in the woodwork and about to emerge? The sensational news of the resignation of Cardinal O'Brien of Scotland is hardly likely to be the last scandal of its kind in the race to find the new Pope. Watch this space!

Amid all the general economic gloom comes more from France. Since François Hollande became the French president last May, the French economy has been going steadily downhill. Now, it seems, it isn't in much better shape that those on the periphery of the Eurozone. The first nine months of his presidency have been an economic disaster for France.

The latest forecast shows that French unemployment rates are about to return to the worst levels seen since 1997. There's also bad news for French businesses and households with the news that electriciy prices are set to soar by 30 per cent between now and 2016, a mere three years away.

While France depends for much of its electricity on nuclear generation, the country now has to invest heavily in renewables, so that close to a quarter of electricity will be generated from renewable resources. This is going to cost French consumers dear, as most of the increase in energy prices will be due to investment in these new resources.

At least, one cheap new offer has come along, the TGV at bargain prices. SNCF, the French State-owned and run railway company, is introducing a new low cost Ryanair style TGV service, which will operate from Marne la Vallée, near Paris, to Lyon airport and Marseilles. Some of the initial tickets on the route were priced at €10, but the rest of the tickets will be low cost, too, with those for under 12s priced at a mere €5 each. The only snag is that to make room for more passengers on the new Ouigo service, the bars on the trains have been removed.

Another interesting piece of news from France is the election to the Académie Française of an Englishman, 74 year old Michael Edwards, an academic and poet. His wife is French and they live in Paris. His two previous attempts to get elected failed, so it's third time lucky in this unusual precedent.

Meanwhile back at the ranch here in Ireland, things just go from bad to worse. The upcoming property tax may well be the cause of the next uprising in Ireland. The tax authorities are collecting the new tax. Draconian powers are being used to make sure that every house in the country is registered and then in order to ensure that the tax is paid, the tax authorities are being given the power to dip into people's personal bank accounts and to deduct it from social welfare payments and other sources of income. But it looks like the government is going to count on the incredible docility of the Irish people, who just seem to lie down and take whatever bad fortune comes their way.

Since 40 per cent of the population of Ireland is now estimated to be living on the breadline and another recent survey shows that three-quarters of Irish families can't even pay their energy bills, it's not hard to imagine the consequences of this new tax. Countless thousands of families will find themselves compliant with the new tax, yet will become destitute of funds to keep themselves going. This new tax is going to turn into the latest bureaucratic nightmare in Ireland. As for the government in Dublin, it seems blissfully divorced from the reality of everyday living for so many people and more than happy to dream up a brand new tax just about every week.

Just this week has come news of yet another household charge, or tax. At present, people with television sets have to pay an annual TV licence fee. But since so many people now don 't watch television on traditional TV sets but on tablets and the like, the government plans to bring in a broadcasting charge payable by every household. Even if a family doesn't have anything beyond a portable radio, they will still have to cough up.

In the general election two years ago, the two parties that now form the coalition government promised a clean break from the corrupt and incompetent practices of the previous government, which had ruined the country. Now it's been revealed that the present government has been stuffing boards and agencies with its political supporters—nothing has changed. No-one in Ireland now believes anything the government says it is going to do, except impose further taxes and charges.

In the meantime, what's next week's tax in Ireland going to be? We'll have to just wait and see. In the meantime, we are surviving perfectly well with no television. It's four months since the switchover from analogue to digital, a change we didn't bother making, and I must admit that in the intervening weeks and months, we haven't missed the telly one little bit. It's the source of just so much audio-visual junk and the news on telly isn't exactly an enlightened source to tell you what's really going on in the world. Television is also becoming totally infested with utterly irrelevant entertainment news in line with much of the media industry. More prozac for the masses!

Just this week, I was reading about a young Irish nurse, well qualified and skilled, in a good hospital job here, who has decided to emigrate. As the latest news came through about the current proposed round of pay cuts for Irish public service workers, she said she couldn't care less. She has got herself a good nursing job in Australia, where her takehome pay is going to be double what she gets in Ireland. Her only thought was that she was just to so glad to be getting out of Ireland. The country seems permanently mired in recession and the absence of original political thinking on how to cure the country's ills is quite astonishing. Many people will admire this nurse for what she is doing and many of Ireland's best and brightest young people are going to continue following suit.

That's it for this week, another dull and dreary week in the Eurozone, to match the weather. The Italians have now got a standup comedian calling the shots and saying that the traditional political systems have failed completely. Maybe every European country needs its own Beppe Grillo to engineer an escape into a more promising future!

March 6, 2013

The down-to-earth delights of Trouville

Northern France has an abundance of delights, easily and cheaply reached from England as well as Ireland and every bit as interesting as the south of France.

We found this for ourselves the time that we stayed in Trouville, which we reached via a retch inducing sea voyage from Rosslare in Ireland to Le Havre. Once we were on dry land, however, we were fine. Our first find in Trouville was an inexpensive place to stay, the Hotel St James.

The hotel was modest but comfortable, but it did have one disconcerting trait. The woman who owned and ran the hotel was an undoubted cat lover and the breakfast room was full of cats. It was the kind of place where if you don't mind the moggies bedding down on the breakfast table, everything was fine. People who aren't cat lovers mightn't take to this feline takeover quite so kindly. Anyway, during our time in Trouville, the Hotel St James was an acceptable home from home, with plenty of cats to watch us as we ate our modest breakfasts.

What we quickly discovered about Trouville is how down to earth it is. The Fish Market was well worth seeing, an historic monument since 1922. We also discovered a wonderful restaurant close to the sea front called Les Vapeurs, which has been going strong since 1927. We found it full of atmosphere and its menu boards resplendent with all kinds of catches from the sea. Close by is another historic restaurant called Le Central Brasserie, but somehow, Les Vapeurs is a far catchier name.

Trouville is considered to be the oldest seaside resort in France, enjoying this status since the early 19th century. The beach is still superb and the planches, the wooden walkways along the top of the beach, are splendid if you feel like stepping it out. This we often did around midnight, with not a soul in sight, perhaps not the most sensible thing to do, but a wonderful way of getting fresh sea air before bed. The town has all sorts of other old world delights, like the Dickens Pub, even the casino, if you're into that sort of attraction. Overall, we found Trouville modest, unpretentious and thoroughly enjoyable, much more so than Deauville, which is the far side of the Touques river.

Unsurprisingly, uber chic Deauville is often known as the 21st arrondissement of Paris because it is so glam. Paris is a mere two hours distant by train.

The walkway at the top of the beach in Deauville is the last word in glamour, complete with its complement of poodles (the four legged kind). If you're into fashion, smart horse racing, casino going or watching the stars arrive for the American Film Festival every September, then this is the place for you. Speaking personally, we found the much more workaday Trouville far more modest and pleasing.

It's also a great place from which to see other delights of this part of the Normandy coast. I'm thinking in particular of the wonderful old maritime town of Honfleur, on the southern side of the Seine estuary. With its old fashioned houses, either half timbered or covered in slates, and its streets dutifully cobbled, the harbour area in particular is an absolute delight. But of course since it is such a stunning old fishing town, it is always jam packed with tourists.

We also enjoyed Cabourg, another seaside resort along the coast here, despite its avaricious mosquitoes, which do have a very nasty bite to them, as we discovered for ourselves. The promenade is very pleasant, complete with its Grand Hotel, even if the town behind the seafront isn't particularly interesting. It's a comparatively recent seaside town, since development only began in 1853. Cabourg of course is best known for its connections with Proust and his Remembrance of Things Past. The fictional seaside town of Balbec that he created was based on Cabourg.

This particular trip to northern France was most enjoyable, fortified with some of the local spirit, Calvados, distilled from apples. Tasting sessions made the experience very enjoyable and I always think that it's a great pity that in Ireland and elsewhere outside France, Calvados is seen as a speciality drink. That means you are very unlikely to find it in the local supermarket, so you'll have to go to a specialised off licence to stock up.

We ended this particular trip by nearly missing the ferry home from Le Havre. For some reason or other, we were running very late and looked like missing the sailing. As we moved along the quays in Le Havre, towards the ship, along came a local sailor driving a battered old estate wagon. We were slightly amazed, because he stopped to see if he could help, which he most certainly was able to do. We explained our dilemma and within five minutes had us at the gangplank for the ferry.

We were very amused, because he initially thought we were a couple of very polite English tourists. He in turn was perfectly polite, explaining how he always enjoyed playing rugby against the English, such excellent and civilised foes on the field. Then we told him, but no, we live in Dublin in Ireland. His reaction: "The English, that crowd of bastards!"

Meanwhile back at the ranch here in Ireland, I t looks very much as if the revolution is about to get under way. Preparations are in full swing for the swingeing impositions of the new property tax in Ireland. It's likely to cause widespread social disruption and protest and its imposition will make Ireland as a place to live even more like the old East Germany, with the Stasi keeping its eye on everything its citizens are doing. Up to now, people in Ireland have been remarkably quiescent about all the austerity imposed by the troika.

We don't have a Beppe Grillo in Ireland, but perhaps all the groups so opposed to all the new taxes will manage to come together and form a credible and workable opposition to the new taxes coming down the line, not just property tax, but water charges too. A forlorn hope, but you never know!

March 13, 2013

All the seaside delights of Youghal

Nearly every week, I write about what's happening in Paris and France generally, a subject close to my heart, but this week, I want to write about a lovely seaside town in south-east Ireland, Youghal.

It's on the western shores of the very wide Blackwater estuary and it has a fantastic maritime tradition. In the 19th century, some 150 sail schooners were based in Youghal and it's said that wherever Youghal sailors went in the world, they instantly recognised fellow townsmen because of their unique whistle.

Youghal continued its unique maritime tradition in 1954, when a film was made of the great Herman Melville novel about whaling, Moby Dick. The Irish-American film director, John Huston, who a couple of years before had made another epic, The Quiet Man, came to Youghal and converted its waterfront into a replica of New Bedford, Massachusetts, America's premier fishing port and in the 19th century, a great whaling centre.

A fantastic cast was assembled and came to Youghal, I ncluding Gregory Peck as Captain Ahab, who in the novel, sought revenge on the whale that had wrecked his previous boat and cost him a leg. Others in the cast included Richard Baseheart, Bernard Miles and James Robertson Justice; even Orson Welles had a cameo part. The filming in Youghal went on for the best part of six months and bystanders came from all over Ireland and beyond to see the action.

The studio scenes were shot at Elstree Studios in London and when the film was released, the nitpickers had a field day. The joins in the painted backdrops could be clearly seen and equally vivid were the aircraft contrails in the sky. (The novel was set long before planes had been invented). One of the ships moored in Youghal had a Plimsoll line; this hadn't been devised until the 1870s, although the novel was set in 1841. Despite the blips, the film went on to become an epic in the annals of the cinema and it grossed $10 million at the box office, having cost just under half that to make.

When the film was being made in Youghal, its production centre was Paddy Linehan's pub in the Market Square, close to the harbour. After the day's filming was done, cast and crew repaired to Linehan's pub for some fantastic storytelling and reminiscences over copious refreshments. The pub had just one phone and everyone queued to phone home, even Gregory Peck.

Paddy Linehan was assidious about collecting memorabilia relating to the film. He died in 2004 and the pub was taken over by his son Kevin, who has kept all this material. Visitors to the pub can have a great time looking through all the press cuttings and photographs, as well as the visitors' book.

Linehan's pub has helped keep alive the spirit of the Moby Dick filmmaking in Youghal and now there's an annual event which has exactly the same purpose. The Moby Dick Festival runs from Mary 31 until June 2, the June bank holiday weekend, and will examine all aspects of Moby Dick and its filming in Youghal. There'll be lots of Moby Dick memorabilia, as well as prose and poetry readings. Guests have been invited from the Melville Society in New York. But the festival is not just for Moby Dick aficionadoes; it's for all the family and has lots of activities to appeal to all family members, regardless of age, even a teddy bears' picnic. By the time this festival is on, the latest Irish rebellion, against the hated new property tax, will probably be well under way (that never happened, of course) but the festival will provide a lovely haven of normality and family-filled fun.

You'll find all the details on the website: www. youghal4all.com

As for Youghal itself, it's a gem. Sir Walter Raleigh, who was mayor here in the late 16ᵗʰ century, I s reputed to have brought both the potato and tobacco to Ireland, introducing them when he was living at Myrtle Grove, a magnificent 16ᵗʰ century mansion that still stands today. The house is close to the Church of Ireland Collegiate church of St Mary, which probably dates back to around AD450. Its interior is well worth exploring for all its decorative treasures.

Also in Youghal, you can see the 1777 Clock Gate, spanning the Main Street. During the 1798 rebellion, many rebels were hung from it, but these days, Youghal is far more ecumenical and peaceful. Many interesting pieces of architecture include the Red House, designed in the 18ᵗʰ century in the Dutch style. Just behind the town are the magnificent walls, which are far superior to those in Derry, although they've managed to remain much more of a secret. Add to all this a wonderful harbour area and plentiful beaches and you'll agree with me that Youghal is a totally delightful seaside town.

Sadly, one thing Youghal no longer has is a railway station. The line from here to Cork city, just over 30 km away, was closed down in 1963. Although some of the line, close to Cork city, has been restored to use, it's highly unlikely the rest of it will be brought back to life. In the old days, the line brought many packed excursion trains from Cork to Youghal.

Close by Youghal are more delights.|On the far side of the Blackwater estuary is the wholly delightful seaside town of Ardmore, once home to the late Molly Keane, one of Ireland's greatest 20ᵗʰ century writers. Also close to Youghal is Ballymaloe House hotel and restaurant, run by the Allen family, renowned for their culinary excellence. The cookery school here is regarded as the best in Ireland and the whole complex has lots of other delights, including a Ballymaloe shop and a grainstore where many musical gigs and exhibitions are staged. You can stay at Ballymaloe house itself as well as in self -catering cottages.

So all in all, this is a great part of Ireland to explore. I know the whole district well and can thoroughly recommend it for an excellent visitor experience, topped off of course by the forthcoming Moby Dick festival.

Now it's back to France, where President François Hollande is the most unpopular French leader in recent memory. A recent political poll showed that only 30 per cent of the population trust him to find cures to France's problems. Unemployment is close to 3. 2 million, which nearly equals the record jobless levels of 1997. The government is planning to cut a further €5 billion from government spending, yet it says it's not going to bring in an austerity programme, so there are many very unhappy campers around. This sense of disillusion is spreading across the Atlantic, with the news that President Obama's ratings are sliding down the poll rating, less than two months since he was inaugurated for his second term, because people in the US don't believe he can fix the economy, despite all his fine words.

Add to this the comments from Jean-Claude Juncker, the prime minister of Luxembourg, who has drawn many comparisons between Europe in 2013 and Europe 100 years ago, in 1913, the year before the start of the First World War. He says that there's so much enmity between countries in Europe now, especially anti-German feeling, that it's not impossible for conflict to break out again. In 1913, European countries were so intermeshed industrially and commercially that everyone thought another war would be impossible. It wasn't and Juncker has a strong feeling that we could be in for a repeat performance.

Not that you would know this from much of the mainstream media, in Ireland, the UK and the rest of Europe. There's so much emphasis on frivolous entertainment and celebrity news that big issues like this simply aren't examined. But if you want to get away from all this doom and gloom in mainland Europe, all you have to do is head for Youghal at the beginning of June, the perfect antidote to the woes of a troubled continent.

And before you go, spare a thought for the 500 passengers on the Irish Ferries ship, the Oscar Wilde. Normally, the crossing from Rosslare in Ireland to Cherbourg in Normandy takes 12 hours. This week however, the journey took nearly two days, because conditions at sea were so stormy and the vessel only docked in a snow-paralysed Cherbourg on Tuesday afternoon after being at sea since Sunday. Much of northern France, indeed Paris itself, has been inundated with snow this week, up to 40 cm in parts of northern France. The Channel Islands, normally so mild, have been blanketed with snow. The snow has made for spectacular photos and video footage, but for people on the ground, it's been a white hell. Maybe one of these days, we may get a proper spring, even though against this snowy backdrop, the daffodils are already coming out.

March 20, 2013

Damp and drizzly Paris

O ne of the seminal events in Parisian history during the 20th century was the great flood of January, 1910, now largely forgotten. But a repeat performance is expected and the authorities in the Paris region are well prepared.

The prelude to the 1910 flood was a long spell of prolonged, heavy rain, just as we've been experiencing in this part of the world during the first three months of 2013. When the floods hit Paris, about 300 streets were flooded and much of central Paris was under water; people had to go along the boulevards by rowing boat. Parts of the Champs-Elysées were under water up to treetop level. A total of 12 out of the 20 arrondissements of Paris were flooded, with 20, 000 buildings flooded and 200, 000 people made homeless. Amazingly, official figures show that only one person died as a result of the floods, although unofficially, the toll was said to have been higher.

However, the flood did have one beneficial effect; it created a unity among Parisians that proved vital during the First World War, which started four years later. A fascinating book on the subject of the 1910 floods was published three years ago; it was written by an American history professor called Jeffrey H. Jackson and published by Palgrave Macmillan in the US. The photographs in Paris Under Water: How the City of Light survived the Great Flood of 1910 are absolutely extraordinary.

You can see one of the high water marks of the flood in the 7th arrondissement. It's at the top of the Rue Bellechasse, the same street that houses the Musée d'Orsay. The mark shows how during the flood, the water level of the nearby River Seine crept about 30 metres above its normal levels.

A similar flood is expected in the reasonably near future, but of course, no-one can forecast exactly when. Recently, the bateaux mouches were banned from going under the bridges around the Ile de la Cité, because the Seine had reached a height of 3. 6 metres, compared with over 8. 6 metres during the 1910 flood. Next time round, the damage would be much more significant, with estimates of up to five million people affected; a million people would be deprived of electricity and 1. 5 million of drinking water. Virtually the whole of the Métro would be flooded as would much of the RER network and the Péripherique motorway would be impassable. It wouldn't affect just Paris but much of the Ile de France. The next big flood could last for about two months and cause €40 billions' worth of damage, compared to the €1 billion in today's money caused by the 1910 flood.

Already, many preventative steps have been taken, including the construction of four new reservoirs to control the flow of the Seine and Marne rivers. Precast sections of wall are being made that will be used to heighten the levels of the riverside walls. The rivers have been dredged and emergency evacuation plans are being developed.

It all sounds very commendable and hopefully practical in the event of the next big flood. Before the 1910 flood, no-one knew it was going to happen and so no preventative measures were put in place. In 2005, Hurricane Katrina hit New Orleans, similarly unprepared, but the French are determined not to be caught out next time.

And talking about infrastructural projects, there's a very agreeable one under way in Nice, where a city centre greenway for walkers is being built. It stretches from the National Theatre of Nice to the Albert 1er gardens, In other words, a good stretch through the city centre. The Coulée Verte should be ready for people to stroll along at their leisure, by September. Elsewhere in France, the news isn't so good. The auto industry, for long a mainstay of French industry, is having a torrid time; people just aren't buying new cars and many speculate that the love affair between younger people and cars is coming to an end. One of the three big French auto brands, Peugeot, is planning to lay off 10, 000 people and close its huge factory at Aulnay near Paris.

Now comes news that the French budget minister Jérome Cahuzac has resigned, the first minister to quit the Hollande regime. Cahuzac was in charge of managing the the programme to cut the French public deficit, but he had been accused of salting away money first in Switzerland and then in Singapore, to avoid tax.

This time last year, most people in France were clamouring for the replacement of Nicolas Sarkozy as French president; what they got was François Hollande, which just shows you shouldn't wish too hard for what you want! Now, many people would welcome back the dynamic Sarkozy, a fine turn of events!

Meanwhile, the Cyprus bailout, considered a small issue irrelevant to the rest of the eurozone just a few days ago, is now a potential Eurozone-wide crisis that's growing by the hour. And don't believe a word of what the politicians are saying. The Irish government has been making much of the fact that the Cyprus situation is unique to that small economy and the measures proposed for Cyprus will have no bearing on Ireland.

I always think it's a good idea to stand politicians' promises on their head to find out what really likely to happen. If they think it's a good idea to slap a levy on people's savings across the Eurozone, especially in the more fragile economies, then that's exactly what they are going to do. Don't say you haven't been warned! After the two parties that now form the coalition government in Dublin came to power two years ago, they made a whole rash of promises, few of which have been kept. And

71

how many of the promises made when the Tories and the Lib Dems formed a coalition government in London in 2010 have been honoured?

France has also had to put up with some very bad weather, just as has happened in the UK and Ireland. Last week, lots of snow engulfed much of northern France, including Paris. It gave rise to some spectacular photos of Paris in the snow, as opposed to Paris in the spring. The past few days have also seen some really wet and chilly weather in the south east of France, including the Côte d'Azur. This coming Saturday in Paris, it looks like the city will be getting cloudy but dry weather, but with a maximum daytime temperature of only around 9 degrees Centigrade, a far cry from the lovely spring weather we can normally expect in Paris at this time of year, as the greenery bursts forth in the city.

At 17h00 French time on Saturday (6pm in UK and the Ireland), the new bells of Nôtre Dame will ring forth for the first time. The inauguration of the new bells promises to be a monumental occasion and a promise of hope in a sorely troubled world. Who knows, one of these fine days, we may even have the arrival of a normal spring!

March 27, 2013

Effete troika and the delights of Biarritz

I'm indebted to Fintan O'Toole of The Irish Times in Dublin for coining a marvellously apposite phrase to describe the troika, that unholy and wholly unaccountable triumvirate of the European Union, the European Central Bank and the International Monetary Fund. He borrowed an expression from that gritty 1996 film about Scotland, Trainspotters, in which one of the characters says that Scotland is ruled by effete arseholes.

Fintan O'Toole applies exactly the same expression to the troika, with deadly effect, to described their totally cack handed approach to the Cypriot financial meltdown. The featherbrains of these three institutions made a total and absolute cockup of their handling of the situation in Cyprus. These days, it's Germany that sets the pace and makes the decisions in the EU, which it now seems to regard as the old German empire made new. Funnily enough, in the time of President Sarkozy of France, both France and Germany maintained an illusion that they formed a duopoly to mastermind the EU, but since Sarkozy was ousted, this illusion has been totally shattered. Present day France under President Hollande seems to have no part to play in keeping the Germans in check and this is the way Germany likes it. As a result,

Germany has been treating Cyprus like some Second World War vassal state, humiliated in defeat.

The whole deal with Cyprus seems brainless in another respect, too, since it's clear that Russian investors in Cypriot banks are going to be the ones who lose out big time, with the haircuts on their deposits. Since when was it a good idea to offend the Russians in this manner? Western Europe is lucky that Russian President Putin doesn't retaliate by turning off the gas taps.

There are plenty of other effete arseholes around elsewhere, especially in governments across Europe. Look at the coalition government in London and the way in which it has been able to impose cruel and callous cuts that affect people least able to survive them, like the people who worked in the Remploy factories or people who are going to start suffering from the so-called bedroom tax from the start of April. These are just two of the cuts that remind so many people of the uncaring Tories at their historical and hysterical worst. In Ireland, too, many thoughtless cuts have been imposed on people least able to cope with them and it's typical that here in Ireland, despite the unseasonably cold weather for the past few weeks, not a thought has been given to how to protect vulnerable people, like the elderly, by those in government. It's as if all they want to do is cut, cut, cut, without a notion of what the consequences will be. But at least, even if people in Ireland and the UK seem quite ready to take all this lying down, the people of Cyprus have shown a really determined attitude towards what's being done to their country.

After the unwise precedents set in Cyprus, imposing levies on bank deposits, and the chaos left by the troika in the wake of their decisions imposed on Cyprus, it's a relief to contemplate another trip we did in France, this time to Biarritz in the south-west. It's very easy to get to Biarritz by air from Ireland, the UK and elsewhere in Europe, direct to Biarritz airport, or if you're in France, to take the train. It's a five hour journey from Paris. We took the train from Bordeaux, travelling across the dreary sandy terrain of Les Landes, to the south of Bordeaux.

As for Biarritz, we found the town itself no great shakes; the town centre isn't particularly interesting. There's a limit to how many 19th century villas or examples of Art Deco architecture that you can look at. The place is best known for its beaches, especially the spectacular Grande Plage. Just south of this beach, there are many rocky outcrops, most notably the Rocher de la Vierge (The Virgin's Rock), and lots of walkways that make for interesting strolls.

The town is of comparatively recent construction. In 1854, the Empress Eugenie, wife of the then French head of state, Napoléon 111, had a palace built by the beach; this vast building is now the Hotel du Palais. Other royals took up the idea of recuperative trips to Biarritz, Including Queen Victoria and King Edward V11, as well as royalty from other parts of Europe, such as King Alfonso 111 of Spain. This royal patronage quickly made Biarritz fashionable. Many English people with money took to travelling to Biarritz and so too did many wealthy Russians; one of the results of that Russian interest was the construction of the 19th century Russian Orthodox church in the town, which is still one of the most spectacular buildings in Biarritz. Another outstanding landmark on the town is the lighthouse, the subject of a famous Picasso painting; it shows the lighthouse on its headland, in the background, while the middle ground is occupied by a sailing boat and the foreground by three women in bathing costumes.

It also has other places of interest for tourists, including Le Musée de la Mer (museum of the sea) with no less than 25 aquaria, a Caribbean lagoon, seal feeding and lots of sharks. Biarritz also has a museum of chocolate. The first casino in Biarritz opened in 1901 and now the town has two. Even if the beaches are spectacular and the town itself very missable, we did bring home a unique souvenir. Someone we met there presented us with a model of Bibendum, the Michelin man. It's a fine looking model, standing close to 30 cm tall. It's a reminder of one of the legends of tourism in France, the Michelin guides. It's amazing how Michelin was entirely dependent for the best part of 100 years on printed products, maps and guide books; it then switched effortlessly to its digital offerings and the Via. Michelin. com website is an invaluable way of finding your way around France, indeed the world.

When we stayed in Biarritz, it was in a small hotel close to the main beach, where guests had to share space with the various dogs owned by the lady who owned and ran the hotel, but it was comfortable and reasonable enough in price. Today, there's a great variety of hotels in the town, about 50 in all, such as the well-equipped Le Windsor, which charges around €130 a night for a room in low season, rising to about €230 in high season. You'l l also find thalassotherapy facilities in abundance in Biarritz.

My suggestion for Biarritz is not to make the town your sole destination in the region. It is however a great place for exploring other nearby seaside towns, like Bayonne, and the French Basque country. The inland areas of the Pays Basque have much riveting scenery, such as mountains, forests and quiet rural villages, a delightful terrain indeed. The Basque country includes of course much of northern Spain and between the Basque lands in France and Spain, some 2. 5 million people live there. You'll find many examples of the extraordinary cultural and historical heritage of the Basque region, not least the Basque language, the oldest in Europe. It also pre-dates the Indo-European languages that make up all the other languages in Europe, making it the only language in Europe not of Indo-European origin, so the Basque language is a very unique heritage indeed.

When we left Biarritz, by train, we travelled through two particularly interesting towns. The inland town of Pau, about 100km from the coast, is much more interesting than Biarritz. Wellington left a garrison there after his battles in the Napoleonic era and English tourists began arriving in Pau long before the railway arrived. There are many reminders in Pau of this 19th century English influence, similar in many ways to what was happening on the French Riviera. Another very interesting place, especiallyif you are a believer, is the town of Lourdes, visited by an estimated 200 million tourists and pilgrims since 1860, shortly after the appearance of the visions of the Blessed

Virgin Mary. Today, many pilgrims still consider that the spring water in Lourdes has many exceptional healing properties, so these days, the drawing power of Lourdes as a place of pilgrimage for the faithful, including the disabled, is as strong as ever.

Such belief in faith and the power of prayer is a welcome relief to the sheer scale of incompetence in modern secular life; here, deep in south-west France, you can safely get away from the ubiqitous clots who run life in modern day secular Europe.

April 3, 2013

The Louvre is still tops

The Louvre in Paris is still the world's most visited art museum, according to the latest figures from the Art newspaper. Last year, it had 9. 7 million visitors, a million more than in 2011. In 2012, the Metropolitan Museum of Art in New York was the second most visited art museum, while museums in London took third, fourth and fifth place.

Since this poll began in 2007, the Louvre has always topped the list. People go to the Louvre not just to see the Mona Lisa, but a vast array of other works of art. The Louvre also has a habit of coming up with new delights, such as I. M. Pei's glass pyramid, inauguarated in 1989 amid protestations of shock and horror. It has since become an accepted part of the landscape in the Louvre.

The new wing of Islamic art has also created something very new and worthwhile for visitors, it has a dramatic roof that looks like a flying carpet. It's considered the biggest collection of Islamic art in Europe. It has about 3,000 objects on show in its gallery, such as mosaics from the Damascus mosque and a delicately carved ivory box dating from AD 928. Altogether, the Louvre has 18, 000 pieces of Islamic art in its collection. One of the key backers for the project was former French president Jacques Chirac, a constant advocate of cultural dialogue between the West and the Muslim world. The biggest single donor to the new wing was a Saudi Arabian prince, Alwaleel bin Talal bin Abdulaziz al-Saud, who gave €17million.

In terms of new architecture, you don't just have to go to the Louvre in Paris. The city has many other fine examples of modern design. The oldest is the Maison de Verre in the 7th., built between 1928 and 1931, an outstanding example of modern design using glass. There's one very odd facet to this building. When an old building on the site was purchased, to make way for the new block, an elderly tenant on the top floor refused to budge, so the Maison de Verre had to be built below the level of the old top floor. Very odd, but typical French obstinacy!

Then at the end of the 1950s, the renowned architect Le Corbusier designed the Maison de Brésil in the 14th; it's now a World Heritage site. In recent decades, astonishing new buildings have come along at a great pace. The Institut du Monde Arabe in the 5th is a landmark building that promotes the cultural and spiritual values of the Arab world and it incorporates many features of Islamic design into its structure. A then young and up and coming architect called Jean Nouvel was very involved in its design. In much more recent times, the mature Jean Nouvel has created the Musée de la Quai Branly, very close to the Eiffel tower.

The very concept of the museum has created much controversy, since it contains nearly 300, 000 objects representing indigenous art and culture from Africa, the Americas, Asia and Oceania. But Jean Nouvel's design for the museum is indeed striking and it's worth going to have a look just at the exterior, before you step inside.

French presidents have long had the idea of getting ambitious building projects up and running in Paris, to leave monumental works behind them, long after they have departed from office. François Mitterand had an especial eye on his legacy and one of his creations was the new national library in the 13th. The new blocks of this library, with their vast expanses of glass, had huge cost overruns during construction, so much so that the place became known as the very big library, a play on the very fast train, the TGV. Its design also showed a certain lack of practicality. No-one thought of including blinds for the windows, to stop the sun beating in on the books inside.

The Grande Arche at La Défense, to the immediate west of the city, is also a striking edifice and from it you can see straight down the Champs-Elysées to the Tuileries gardens. An earlier presidential creation was the Pompidou Centre in the 4th., with its inside on the outside design and much refurbished since it first opened in 1977. It also has a new "wing", at Metz. Finally, among this plethora of new buildings in Paris, don't miss the Cité de Science in the 19th., the biggest science museum in Europe.

Paris presents a great contradiction; on one hand, many citizens are aghast at anything being done to tamper with the great historical buildings and landscapes in the city. Yet on the other hand, Paris is a great place to see some really exciting new architectural work, that is visually stimulating, rather than merely banal, which seems the curse of much modern architecture.

The latest spot in Paris to undergo regeneration, according to the BBC Travel website, is the Pigalle district of northern Paris, for so long renowned for its sleazy sex clubs and even a museum on the subject. Now it seems that south Pigalle is becoming one of the hottest places in Paris for an entirely different reason. In the past two or three years, some really hip bars and entertainment places have opened, starting at the end of 2010, when Le Carmen opened in what had once been the home of the composer Bizet. One of the latest openings is the Dirty Dick bar, a tongue in cheek reference to the sordid goings on elsewhere in Pigalle.

But one thing never changes in Paris as in the rest of France, this incredible obsession with bureaucratic meddling. Lara Marlowe is the American journalist who has recently returned to Paris to become for the second time, the Paris correspondent of The Irish Times. She had spent from 2009 to 2012 in Washington as that paper's correspondent there and was clearly delighted to get back to Paris. But she has described the mind-numbing ordeal of having to go through so many bureaucratic hoops in

Paris as she set up her new home there. But as the headline on the piece said, so pithily: " The magic of living in Paris punctures the endless pain of French bureaucracy". Why the French have this incredible and perverse love of bureaucracy, I'm not quite sure, but only a Frenchman could have invented the concept of VAT and did. And incidentally, Lara Marlowe was once married to Robert Fisk, the veteran Lebanon-based correspondent of the London Independent.

At the moment of course, Paris should be utterly delightful in the spring, but it isn't. Like most of the rest of Europe, northern France and Paris has endured some of the worst weather of all time during the month of March and it continues in April. In fact, it's been the coldest March in France since 1987 and you'd have to go back to the weather records of 1970, 1962 and 1955 to find equally low temperatures. The forecast for the coming week is that the north is going to continue cold, with some snow, spreading down into middle France, while the south is going to have a lot more rain. This is exactly what has been happening in Spain, absolute deluges of rain. On Monday, in the region of Castille-la-Manche, in the south of Spain, the rains caused a bridge over a local river to collapse, throwing a car and a truck into the water and killing the two drivers. We can only hope that this awful weather simply can't last for ever; I've a funny feeling that in recompense, we're probably going to get a scorching hot summer. And hot summers in Paris are really something!

April 10, 2013

Remembering Maréchal Pétain

A small event in a very small village in the Lorraine region of north-eastern France triggers off a whole host of memories this week. The tiny village of Belrain, which has just 50 inhabitants, has had a Rue du Maréchal Pétain since 1930, but no more. It has decided to scrap the name of the street and has invited local people to come up with an alternative. What makes it so unusual is that this was the last street in France named after Pétain.

Belrain is only 40 km from the site of the devastating battle of Verdun, fought during the First World War and it was at Verdun that Pétain made his name, becoming a national hero in the process. Mind you, Pétain nearly didn't make it. As the battle was about to commence at Verdun, Pétain, a notorious womaniser, was nowhere to be found, but one of his staff officers had a very good idea where Pétain was, in other words, which of his mistresses he had taken to which hotel in Paris. So it turned out and Pétain was able to make it to the front in time to command the French troops.

For 20 years after the end of the First World War, Pétain managed to retain the affections of the French people and after France was defeated by the Germans in 1940, he came the head of state, in charge of a collaborationist government in Vichy, in central France. Until 1942, the central and southern part of France was controlled by the Vichy government and remained free of German troops. But after 1942, those troops occupied the whole of metropolitan France, yet the Vichy government managed to survive, until the liberation of France in 1944.

Pétain was a remarkable man and it's astonishing to think that he had a great-uncle who had served in Napoléon's Grande Armée. After the end of the Second World War, Pétain was lucky, because although he was put on trial and sentenced to death, he managed to escape with his life. During the First World War, a junior officer under his command happened to one Charles de Gaulle. By the time that Pétain was sentenced after the Second World War, de Gaulle was the president of the provisional government of France and it was he who spared Pétain's life and sentenced him to life imprisonment on account of his great age. Pétain died in prison on the Ile d'Yeu, off the west coast of France, in July, 1951, aged 95.

Nearly a century ago, Pétain was the great French hero; today, no-one in France even wants to have a street in their neighbourhood named after him, he is considered such a villain of the Second World War period.

All this brought back memories of our time in Vichy; we knew someone in the Irish diplomatic service who had represented Ireland in Vichy during that war and her memories were very vivid. So when we got a chance, we decided we'd go and see for ourselves. Vichy is quite easy to get to; from the Gare de Lyon in Paris, the quickest train will take three hours. The town became renowned during the 19th century for its thermal baths and in the years immediately before the First World War, close on 100,000 people a year were going to Vichy to take the waters. Of course today, the name lives on in the Vichy range of beauty products owned by L'Oréal because you're worth it.

In addition to the thermal baths, the town saw a great building boom, when many Belle Époque mansions were built and we were able to see the facades of those that housed the various government departments in Vichy during the Second World War. In the past 20 years or so, much restoration work has been done in Vichy, including revitalisation of the thermal baths and the rejuvenation of the great opera house. These days, Vichy is still quite a small town, with close on 30, 000 inhabitants, but it has a great array of facilities for tourists, ncluding a fine selection of restaurants.

We were rather amazed to find that the railway station, itself much improved in recent years, had a very pleasant restaurant, where we could enjoy a very vinous dinner at night in very congenial surroundings. Imagine being able to enjoy such fine dining with excellent wines at a regional railway station in either Ireland or Britain! Once we'd had our meal in the railway station restaurant, what we used to do was cross the tracks by the footbridge; we'd discovered that if you went to the eastern side of the station, within about 1, 000 metres, you were in almost open country, which made for a very pleasant late evening walk.

We were lucky as well because the hotel we chose was close to the station. Another big advantage was that our room was so big and had such good facilities that we were able to treat it as a self-catering apartment. We used to have great fun making our own breakfast and then sitting down to enjoy it while watching breakfast television.

Something else I discovered in Vichy was the local library; it was here that I found masses of material about François Mitterand, later destined to become a President of France. As a young man, he had joined the Vichy government, working as a mid-level funtionary, looking after the interests of prisoners of war. As I discovered in the library, later in the war, he was active in the resistance and I discovered that he had many code names; later, he became best known for being "Morland". Mitterand was a fascinating and complex character, a president who left behind a great legacy.

Yet another extraordinary story about him—and there are many—concerned the coronation of Queen Elizabeth II in London in 1953. Mitterand attended, as a representative of the French state. He sat beside Princess Marie Bonaparte and Mitterand passed the time during the coronation being pyschoanalysed by the princess, who was the great-grand niece of Emperor Napoléon I. The princess had had a marvellously interesting career; in the 1920s, one of her main subjects of interest was research into improving female orgasms. No wonder that in 1953, herself and Mitterand talked so much they managed to miss virtually all the coronation ceremony!

But going from Mitterand to the present day, I notice a sense that rebellion is brewing on a wide scale in France, on both sides of the political divide. Nothing new about la Belle France being so rebellious, except that this time, the revolutionary surges are coming from both left and right. On the left is Jean-Luc Meléchon, who leads the Front de Gauche. During last year's presidential campaign, he made some of the most dramatic and rabble rousing speeches, although many people were secretly delighted he didn't get anywhere at the ballot box.

Instead, the French people have got the biggest presidential turkey of all time, François Hollande. The latest story about him concerns the camel he was given as a present in Mali, as a "thank you" to France and French troops for saving the day in that war-torn African country. He tried to get it repatriated to France, but this didn't work out, so he arranged for it to be looked after by a local family in Timbuktu. It turns out that they have now used the camel as the main ingredient in a Saharan tangine stew. I'm sure that Hollande has really got the hump on this one, or did the family concerned, as a gesture to the person who had been given the camel, serve it with hollandaise sauce?

Back to the feelings of revolt. In addition to the always restive left wing in France, t now seems that sections of the middle class are fermenting a right wing revolution, as evidenced by such manifestations as the recent massive protests against gay marriage. If right and left manage to agite separately and create trouble on a big scale, will we see a double reinactment of 1968?

One right wing revolutionary is being commemorated but not celebrated in France, Margaret Thatcher, who died last Monday. Le Figaro, the newspaper and website, came up with a very good description of her, the iron lady with a heart of stone. What a legacy she left behind! Sinn Féin wouldn't be the party it is today in both parts of Ireland if it hadn't been for Mrs Thatcher. Neither would the process of Scottish devolution got such a following with the result of wiping out the Tories in Scotland, if it hadn't been for the effects of Thatcherite policies in the 1980s, which destroyed much of Scottish industry, and the legacy of the poll tax, first introduced in Scotland. What a legacy she left behind her-many people in England think she was an even greater prime minister than Churchill, while in Scotland and Ireland many think the exact opposite.

But enough of politics! There's a fascinating outdoor event going on in the 7th arrondissement in Paris from April 11 to 18. It's called the La Nuit aux Invalides and it uses the latest audio and 3D video technology to project a Son et Lumière style interpretation of French history on the façade of the Hotel des Invalides. All it needs is night time weather that's an improvement on what Paris has been enjoying lately!

And don't forget the sheep! Four black sheep, who had been made redundant by more intense and competitive farming, have been put to work keeping the grass well trimmed in public places in the 19th arrondissement in Paris. The eco pasture movement has been well established in France for the past decade but in the past two or three years, It had really taken off.

So the sheep are now at work grazing the equivalent of eight tennis courts in the 19th., which is a working class suburb in north -eastern Paris. It's also home to the Cité de Sciences et de l'Industrie, the largest science museum in Europe. In between their work sessions, the sheep are housed at the Ferme de Paris, the farm owned by the city of Paris in the Bois de Vincennes. No doubt in due course, we'll see sheep hard at work in many other places in Paris over the next year or two, as this ecologically friendly movement replaces lawn mowers! What a lovely tag for Paris, the city where sheep may safely graze.

April 17, 2013

French bureacracy confirmed—in triplicate

Now we know, officially, that France is overwhelmed by petty bureaucracy. Alain Lambert, who is head of the government's consultative commission on the evaluation of norms, has said that France is so tied up in red tape that the country is in danger of being paralysed. At least, we've now got an official analysis of the situation, but whether it will ever be translated into reform is another matter entirely.

It's now been revealed that France has 400,000 petty rules and regulations covering almost every aspect of life. If your child goes to kindergarten and has an egg for lunch, then there's a strict rule for that—they can only have half an egg. If you have a box for the post at the front of your house, there are precise rules for how it can be placed—it can't stick out too much. And so it goes on and on, very wearying and often utterly ridiculous. Much as I love France and everything French, I wouldn't dream of actually living there and having to put up with this totaly overwhelming and often pointless bureaucracy. Not only is France infected with this modern disease of having rules for everything in life, but the rot is insidious throughout the EU; it couldn't run without vast amounts of red tape and the people in charge of the EU have learned their lesson well from the French. You can't of course go to the other extreme and have a free for all; there has to be a reasonable amount of regulation—and redress—for the ordinary citizen, but not on the scale it's practised in France, where red tape threatens to tangle up the country entirely.

Which brings me to the free flowing documentary on Radio 4 the other day about Juliette Gréco, the singer and performer who for so long has epitomised the bohemian way of life in the Saint-Germain-des-Prés district of Paris. She was born in 1927, which makes her 86; she was born in Montpellier in the south-west of France but quickly made her mark in Paris after the Second World War. From 1950 almost up to the present, she created an extraordinary amount of albums and sung so many songs. One of her most famous songs came out in 1967, called Déshabillez-moi (undress me), which she sang in her characteristically sultry style and which featured in the Radio 4 programme. Amazingly, her most recent album came out just two years ago. If anyone sums up the lifestyle of the famous residents of the Left Bank, she does and what a tradition it is, the essence of café life in the artistic quarter of Paris.

But if you want a counterpoint to all this, an intriguing new book called Quiet Paris by Siobhan Wall has just been published by Frances Lincoln (£12. 99), which details all kinds of quiet places to enjoy in Paris, from hotels and restaurants and cafés, art galleries to libraries. One of the intriguing places she mentions is the Musée de la Vie Romantique in the rue Chaptal in the 9th., close to Pigalle, which gives great insights into the lives of 19th century Parisian literary figures.

Back here at home in Ireland, it's the usual story of cock-ups and near misses. A typical story comes from the Central Bank of Ireland, which has just issued a €10 coin commemorating James Joyce. The coin has a brief quotation from Ulysses, but whoever created the coin managed to include a word that wasn't in the original text. The pedants have had a field day! The coins were selling for €46 each and all the publicity for the mistake helped ensure the whole lot sold out in double quick time. No doubt in time they will become collectors' items. Stephen Joyce, the grandson of the great writer, has described the creation of this coin as a great insult to the memory of his grandfather. But sadly, this slovenliness is all too typical of so many areas of present day life in Ireland, when persuading people to do what they say they are going to do can quite often prove problematic.

It's no wonder that a recent opinion poll in the Sunday Independent newspaper in Dublin found that 75 per cent of the people questioned thought the present coalition government in Ireland was doing a bad job and only 17 per cent were prepared to commend it. These are the kind of ratings that the government and president in France are getting, where the Hollande regime seems to be in freefall. Just when you think things can't get worse, along comes yet another blunder. It's got to the stage where every week, there's news of yet another calamity, despite all those rules and regulations that are supposed to make life in France totally antiseptic and hazard-free.

Still, I suppose that if you wanted to get away from all this present day madness, one good place to go would be the islands of Saint Pierre and Miquelon, just off the coast of Newfoundland in eastern Canada. They've long fascinated me; they are all that's left of the once mighty French empire in North America.

There are eight islands in all, but only two are inhabited. The present population is just under 6, 000, but even though it's such a small outpost of France, the islanders are proud of their French heritage and speak French much more in the metropolitan style rather than in a Canadian idiom. The rain-swept islands have long been dependent on fishing; other attempts at diversification haven't been very successful.

During the prohibition era in the US, the islands became the "warehouse" for whisky brought in from Canada and then smuggled into the US. When prohibition ended in the US in 1933, it brought economic ruin to the islands as they lost so much of their daily revenue. But somehow, the islanders have managed to keep going, with the help of generous subsidies from Paris. n 1999, the islands got a brand new airport, which is big enough to allow planes flying directly from France to land there. For tourists, the islands are a marvellous example of unspoiled wildlife, a virgin landscape and environment, so remote from what passes for civilisation they are an utter revelation. Yet the population is so small that on the two inhabited islands, street names are rarely used; people's real names and their nicknames are all you need to find whoever you are looking for.

Yes, these wonderful islands are a terrific retreat from the modern world, yet have all the facilities people need, including an impressive array of restaurants—nearly all authentically French, a sufficient recommendation for me!

Retreating from the modern world is a great idea and another slant on this theme came in an intriguing piece recently in The Guardian by Swiss writer Rolf Dobelli. He argued that people shouldn't become news junkies. In a typical year, a person would read something like 12, 000 news items from a whole variety of online sources, yet questioned Dobelli, how many would actually be relevant to the everyday life of the person reading them?

He also condemned present day news coverage for its superficiality, since it gives readers no insights into the wider movements of social, economic and other trends. In other words, since readers are encouraged to concentrate on the smaller picture, they miss out entirely on the big picture of what's really happening in the world. He makes more significant accusations, too, that this fixation with instant news soundbites does to the brain what junk food laden with sugar, fat and salt does to the body. Dobelli, who practices what he preaches and astains from this daily fix of instant news, says the deluge of news leads to fear and aggression and what is even worse, kills off creativity. Now you know what the world is in such a bad state—it's run by news junkies!

April 24, 2013

Springtime in Villeneuve-lès-Avignon

W e've been enjoying the past few days of real spring weather, after weeks and weeks of bitter cold (lets hope this spell of spring sunshine doesn't constitute the summer!) and when we get weather like this, it always reminds me of the time we spent in Villeneuve-lès-Avignons in the south of France.

Villeneuve has a population of about 10, 000 and lots of medieval streets, as well as a castle to match, and it's just across the River Rhone from Avignon itself. To my mind, Villeneuve is a far better place to be based in than Avignon itself, even though the distance between the two places is a mere five km; Villeneuve is far less touristy, much more authentic.

We visited Villeneuve as part of a grand tour of France by train; we did a complete circuit of France by train in a fortnight (God bless the energy we had then!). We had started by flying from Gatwick to Montpellier and as the plane came in to land at Montpellier, we had a great sight of the masses of red flamingoes that inhabit the lagoons close to the city. After an overnight in a very comfortable Sofitel in the centre of Montpellier, we headed to Avignon and thence to Villeveuve, where we stayed in the five star Le Prieuré, an hotel based in a converted 14th century monastery. It offered the last word in comfort and dinner in the gastronomic restaurant was just as enticing. In Avignon itself, we did all the sights, including a walk on the famous half bridge that partially spans one section of the river. In the old days, most people seemed to know the song about being "sur le pont d'Avignon", but I'm not so sure the song is so well known these days.

I should mention also, talking about Villeneuve-lès-Avigon, that the town is having a fantastic music festival on June 21, with a great array of artistes. And it's all free!

Avignon, incidentally, has just set an unwelcome record. Very recently, a man who was on leave from his work in the oil fields of Angola, was beaten up and left for dead outside a bar in the town. When he was rescued, it turned out he had 11 g of alcohol in his blood, equivalent to having drunk four bottles of whisky in as many hours. This unfortunate man eclipsed the previous record for alcohol consumption, set in Ain in February, 2005, when a man at the wheel of a car (just imagine!) was found to have had 10 g of alcohol in his blood.

From Avignon, we headed to Paris and then to Épernay, in the heart of the Champagne district, where we met up with our old friend François Bonal, of the Champagne producers' association. Plenty of refreshments were the order of the day!

From here, it was back to Paris, to travel on a slow diesel train to St Lô in Normandy, where we took in such sights as Granville, the Chausey islands and Mont Saint Michel (currently in the throes of a massive restoration project, not entirely visitor friendly). Then we took a leisurely and restful train back to Paris on a sunny Sunday afternoon.

We had intended to overnight in Paris, but every hotel in the 7th arrondissement, where we usually stay, was booked out. So we took the next train down to Orleans, where we stayed in a rather grubby and downbeat Sofitel, quite a contrast to other Sofitels we've stayed in. Next stop was the much more interesting town of Poitiers, replete with bookshops (always a good sign!)

From Poitiers, we took the train, through Bordeaux, to our second last destination, Biarritz, where there were some fine sights to be seen around the beach, including a splendid array of topless sunbathers. Our final destination was Toulouse, which didn't impress as a tourist destination. When I think of Toulouse, boring is the word that comes to mind.

One group of people whom France is failing to impress are the British. Figures from the Office for National Statistics in the UK show that last year, 8. 8 million Britons visited France, quite a fall from the 10. 9 million in 2008. The main reason for this is the continuing rise in prices in France, which has now become quite expensive for tourists. In the present economic crisis, other European countries, like Italy and Spain, have become cheaper and more competitive.

However, despite all that and the continuing right-wing violent street protests in Paris against the new gay marriage legislation, there are some really interesting things happening in the city of light right now.

One notable event has been the reopening of the Louxur cinema in the boulevard de Magenta in the 10th, close to the borders of the 9th., 10th and 18th arrondissements in north-east Paris. The cinema had been opened in 1921, designed in a neo -Egyptian style, hence it being named after the city of Luxor. It was then the flagship of the Pathé chain of cinemas and it managed to keep going until the 1980s. Then it became a nightclub, before being abandoned to dereliction in 1988. Now city hall in Paris has restored the building, including its amazing and capacious interior. The project took 10 years and cost €25 million. Once again, the Luoxor is showing films, mainly films from outside France in their original languages, as well as hosting cinema festivals and other movie-related events.

Then another Parisian institution is being feted, the green newspaper kiosks, which were set up 150 years ago. These days, there are fewer than 340 of these kiosks left; they were going the way of another Parisian institution, the pissoirs, which have just about vanished. But city hall has stepped into the breach and has given €200, 000 in financial aid to the owners of the surviving kiosks to tide them over during the present crisis in the newspaper and magazine industry. City hall has also extended the list of products that the kiosks can sell, which now include publications from the Ville de Paris, souvenirs, soft drinks and sweets. Mediakiosk, part of the giant J C Decaux outdoor advertising firm, looks after the maintenance of the kiosks and has promised to bring their numbers up to 370. It's great to see these two examples of really progressive support from city hall in Paris, outside which an exhibition on the green kiosks is currently being staged. It's not often that local councils do things this imaginative, especially in this part of the world, Ireland and Britain.

Coming up in Paris from June 10 to 21 is another unique event. The Grand Palais is being turned into a drive-in cinema. At any one screening of films, on the largest screen in Europe, measuring 30 metres across, 1, 000 spectactors will be accommodated in a fleet of Fiat 500 convertibles. People will also be able to enjoy dishes prepared under the supervision of Canadian star chef, Gita Seaton; she's promising such delights as cheesburgers, bacon and eggs, fried chicken and tempting chocolate dishes. It's the sort of mad idea that can only happen in France and, I guess, will probably work to perfection! After the summer, the Grand Palais is going to be turned into a giant ice skating rink.

However, not everything is done with aplomb in Paris. Anything connected with the Elysée Palace these days seems to be disaster-prone and I'm not just talking about M. Hollande. The palace decided to place a tribute to the late Baroness Thatcher on its website. While the English language script was word perfect, the reading of it was anything but. The English pronunciation was so mangled that it turned out to be high comedy. It can be heard in its original form on the Rue 89 website.

Talking of websites, I should mention an intriguing website in the US called beforeitsnews.com

For anyone who enjoys conspiracy theories, this is the place to go. Some of the stuff here is seriously wacky, but other pieces will give you reason to think. One of its current predictions is that this Sunday is going to be disaster day in Los Angeles, and it backs this up by running a story that an enormous list of movie industry celebrities are desperately trying to sell their properties in LA, a move that's been going on for some time. Obviously, they must know something that the rest of us don't!And just for the record, that disaster never materialised! Mind you, this particular website last week promised that a swarm of earthquakes was going to hit around the globe; there were a few bad ones, especially in China, but as for a swarm, there was none to be felt!

Here in Ireland, nothing much happens, except continuing tales of financial cutbacks, which gets very boring after a while, especially if you 're on the receiving end. It'd be great if lots of positive things were happening, but the negativity in Irish life is pervasive.

It's nearly six months since television transmissions changed to all digital and we didn't make the switch. We have a TV set sitting here totally redundant, apart from its DVD player, and I can't say we miss it at all. The schedules on RTÉ television are often awful and if there is an interesting sounding programme, it often turns out to be a repeat of a repeat of a repeat. Mind you, reading about a few of the programmes on the BBC Four television channel, one does sometimes miss having a set.

I don't often look at the RTÉ website for news—after all there are so many news sources on the Internet that you can find all kinds of interesting and revelant international stories that just don't get a mention in Ireland.

But I've a nasty feeling that if you were dependent on many of the 50 or so television channels in France, and the plethora of radio channels there, you'd have exactly the same feelings about them. Now that the brighter evenings and hopefully better weather are here, there are many more rewarding things to be doing than sitting at home watching an evening of tripe on television.

But at least, there's one interesting thing happening TV-wise in Ireland. The government is planning to bring in a broadcasting tax, which every household will have to pay, as a replacement for the traditional TV licence. This is because so many people now watch TV on their tablets or their Smart phones. The government, in true Orwellian style, now has details of every household in the country on its database, thanks to the new property tax, so everyone can be rounded up. Evasion of the traditional TV licence is still a serious problem in Ireland, so maybe this new system will make it harder for people to dodge this particular charge!

May 1, 2013

Summer's here?

<hr/>

May 1, when summer is supposed to start and all that; the big question is whether we will have a decent summer this year, having endured four horrendous months of bad weather from January to April. An image that always comes into mind at this time of year is the time we spent in Bayreuth, Germany, where the great composer Richard Wagner lived for many years.

His enormous house, now a museum, was called Wahnfried and I remember so vividly us going to see it one afternoon in early summer. The sun was blazing down outside and there was a veritable 'snowfall' of jinny joes (the Irish name for airborne dandelion and other plant seeds) into the garden outside. We sat in the cool of one of the downstairs rooms at the house, listening to recordings of the great Norwegian singer, Kirsten Flagstad (1895-1962), arguably the greatest Wagnerian soprano of all time. It was an hour or so when one really caught one's breath, as we listened to her sublime voice, looking out on all the greenery of the garden and the jinny joes floating down.

I'm also thinking of the summer days spent at Cassis in the south of France, a mere 20km east of Marseilles, but an idyllic seaside town. It's on a great harbour, filled with boats; Cassis is renowned for its cliffs and for the Calanques, the sheltered inlets that now form a national park in their own right. Close to Cassis is Cap Canaille, with some of the highest sea cliffs in Europe.

From the 15th century right up to 1789, Cassis was the property of the Bishops of Marseilles, who ran the place as their own fiefdom. Up to the 1930s, Cassis had many industries, including stone quarrying and clothing. Stone quarried at Cassis was used to build the quays in many great Mediterranean ports, including Alexandria, Algiers, Marseilles, Piraeus and Port Said; Cassis stone also forms the base of the Statue of Liberty in New York. But when all the traditional industries in Cassis went into terminal decline in the 1930s, the town turned to wine making and tourism.

Cassis became one of the first three wine growing areas in France to benefit from the appellation d'origine controlée system introduced in 1936 and today, it's one of the main wine producing areas of the Côte d'Azur, renowned for its whites and rosés. It's not to be confused with creme de Cassis from Burgundy, made with blackcurrants.

As for the town itself, it's a lovely mixture of quaysides and squares with fountains, all drenched in sunshine. Often, people will play petanque, a version of boules, that in its present form originated in nearby La Ciotat in 1907. Cassis has also attracted many painters over the years, including Vlaminck and Dufy. It's no wonder that the Nobel prize winning author Frédéric Mistral (1830-1914) said that if you've seen Paris and you haven't seen Cassis, you've seen nothing.

As for the nearby town of La Ciotat, his is where the Lumière brothers made their famous 50 second film in 1895 showing a train steaming into the station. When the film was shown in Paris on December 28 that year, the world's first commercial film show, it's aid that many in the audience were terrified by the moving picture of the train coming towards them. The Lumière brothers had their summer residence in La Ciotat and it was here that they developed the world's first colour photographic system, in 1904.

Beyond La Ciotat is Bandol, also famous for its wines, especially rosé. The bay here is very peaceful; just a seven minute boat ride from Bandol is the island of Bendor, owned by the Ricard family, who built a strange looking village here in the 1950s. I remember that the trip to Bendor was fascinating, but it was a boiling hot summer's day and I'd neglected to put on any suncream, so that by the time we got back that night to our hotel in Cassis, I resembled nothing so much as a baked lobster! A very painful experience indeed.

At the other end of the Côte d'Azur, in Roquebrune Cap Martin to be precise, there's an intriguing tale unravelling about Eileen Gray, the Irish born designer and architect, who lived for many years in France. Gray, who had been born near Enniscorthy in south-east Ireland, trained at the Slade in London but after she made her first trip to Paris in 1900, with her mother, to see the Exposition Universelle, she was hooked on France. Gray designed lots of furniture and her Bibendum chair is one of the most distinctive pieces of 20th century furniture design. Four years ago, an armchair made by her just after World War I sold at auction in Paris for an astonishing €21. 9 million.

Gray also designed a unique modernist villa at Roquebrune-sur-Mer, called E1027. In recent times it has been badly neglected but for the past few years, restoration has been under way. A big fundraising effort is under way to complete the restoration and open the villa to the public before the end of this year. A film is to be made of the restoration project, with the title "Gray Matters".

Another film is under way, an Irish-Belgian co-production, about the life of Eileen Gray called The Price of Desire.

Winona Ryder is to play Eileen Gray and the details of the film, which is being directed by Mary McGuckian, are due to be released at the Cannes film festival later in May.

As for Gray herself, she spent the last years of her life in an apartment in the rue Bonaparte in the 6th arrondissement in Paris, where she died in 1976 at the grand old age of 98. For many years, this great modernist designer and architect was unjustly confined to the shadows, but hopefully now, with the new film, her outstanding genius will be fully recognised. Certainly in her personal life, she was a rather strange woman, avowedly bisexual, happy to have affairs with men, but more devoted to making love with other women.

And as for the Cannes film festival, that great annual extravaganza, it's almost a year since the new film about Renoir was released, directed by Gilles Bourdos. It had its first showing at Cannes 2012, but it isn't being released here in Ireland until the end of this June. The film depicts the final years of the great painter, when he was living at Cagnes-sur-Mer in the south of France, during the First World War. It was released some time ago in the US and most of the American reviews I've read of it have been unstinting in their praise, so let s hope that when it finally arrives in Ireland, it'll live up to the hype! In the event, it didn'! It was boring as hell and even Renoir's lovely naked model couldn't raise a flicker of interest.

But elsewhere in France, all kinds of interesting things are happening. Three beehives have been put on the roof of the national assembly in the 7th., painted in the colours of the French tricolore. They will contain 60, 000 bees, a welcome green environmental gesture at a time when the world's bee population is under such threat. he beehives on the roof of the national assembly are being managed by a firm called Le Rouge Apiculture, which dates back to 1878. For many years, it has managed a similar beehive on the roof of the French Senate, which is on the edge of the Luxembourg Gardens.

Talking about nature, Brigitte Bardot has been in the news again. At the end of March, her favourite cat, two year old Rontonton, went missing, frightened by the noise of pruning on the Bardot estate at St Tropez. Lots of people, more than 200, phoned in to offer help look for the cat and its disappearance made much national media coverage in France. Eventually and just recently, the cat was found, in good health, by the concierge of a nearby villa. he concierge received the finder's reward of €600.

But back in Paris, another piece of French heritage is being offloaded. The Elysée Palace has an incredible wine cellar of 12, 000 splendid wines, all French naturally, but in a gesture towards the austerity measures now being enforced in France,1, 200 of the bottles are being auctioned off at Drouot at the end of May. They are expected to raise about €250, 000. Mind you, even in the present French government, many dissenting voices are now being heard against the wisdom of the austerity drive and attacking the German demands for austerity which have had a dramatically adverse impact in many parts of Europe. In return for all the French remarks against German austerity, some German politicians are now saying that France could turn out to be the problem child of Europe.

When it comes to French history, an outstanding book has just been launched, Eleven Days in August, the Liberation of Paris in 1944 by Matthew Cobb, who teaches at the University of Manchester. It looks a fascinating read and many of the photographs are even more impressive, including the ones of the biggest demonstration ever held in Paris, when a million people turned out on the Champs-Elysées to celebrate the end of German occupation. There should be equally big demonstrations to celebrate when the German austerity regime ends.

Elsewhere in Europe, the news is equally interesting. In Italy, the new government is going to ditch the very unpopular property tax. Naturally, there's no sign of this happening in Ireland, where the political situation verges on the ridiculous. When the Indian woman Savita Halappanavar died in hospital in Galway at the end of last October, a very tragic and unnecessary death, it sparked off a whole chain of events. The recent inquest revealed all kinds of shortcomings at the hospital. Ireland became portrayed internationally as a country where a throwback to a medieval style barbarism could still exist in the early 21st century. The government is now to introduce limited abortion legislation, but this threatens to fracture the coalition government, perhaps even ensure its demise. The general discussion about abortion has overwhelmed public debate.

No matter that the economy is still in recession, that nearly half a million people are out of work and that countless thousands of young people and families are being forced to emigrate, none of this matters when it comes to all the energy and passion being put into the great abortion debate. If similar effort were put into solving all the other grave matters afflicting the country, Ireland would be a grand place altogether.

At least, the new king in the Netherlands, Willem-Alexander, was crowned peacefully, which was a little amazing, because when his mother, Beatrix, became queen in 1980, there was widescale rioting and disorder. It just shows—time moves on and times change, but not it seems in Ireland, where old antagonisms land entrenched attitudes live on as forceful today as they ever were.

May 8, 2013

A blast on the organ

This past Monday, there's one place in France where I'd have loved to have been, Nôtre Dame cathedral in Paris. Recently, the new bells were inaugurated at the cathedral, all totally in tune, which is more than could be said for the old bells they replaced. On Monday of this week came yet another stage of the grand restoration project to mark the 850th anniversary of the great cathedral: its magnificent organ has been wonderfully restored and it was unveiled publicly for the first time.

Apart from hearing the organ, it's also well worth seeing the temporary structure that's been put in place for a year on the forecourt of the cathedral. During the Haussmann renovations of central Paris in the 19th century, the medieval street that stood here was razed to make way for the forecourt. The 13 metre high temporary structure is a belfry and it has two splendid stained glass windows, made in 1937 by a renowned glassmaker, Jacques le Chevallier. One window shows Geneviève, the patron saint of Paris, while the other shows Saint Marcel, an early bishop in Paris. On the other side of the temporary belfry, there's a wide ramp that leads to a terrace that's five metres above ground level and from which excellent views can be had of the cathedral.

There's no music more majestic than that produced by a great church organ. One church that I know well in Paris is St Clotilde in the 7th. It's a truly magnificent church, with soaring steeples and interior and on various occasions when we've been there while organ recitals were being given, the acoustic occasion has been magnificent.

The church has had a long line of celebrated organists, none more so than César Franck (1822-1890), who was also a noted composer, ncluding for his only symphony. Someone else who established a long tradition playing one of the best church organs in Paris was Jean Langlais, who was blind. But from 1945 until 1987, he maintained the organ heritage in this wonderful 19th century church. It's surrounded by the 19th century high rise apartment blocks and government ministeries typical of this part of Paris but right in front of the church is a lovely little park, a real splash of green.

Other news, too, from Paris is optimistic this week. The new editor-in-chief of Le Monde was revealed publicly for the first time. Nathalie Nougayrede is not only the first female editorial chief of Le Monde but the first female national newspaper editor in France, a glass ceiling that was broken years ago in Ireland. She's 46 years old and began her journalistic career as recently as 1991, reporting from Prague for Liberation, Radio France International and the BBC. She succeeds Erick Izrealewicz, himself a highly talented editor-in-chief, who had a heart attack in the offices of Le Monde last November. He died there, despite the best efforts of colleagues who were skilled in resuscitation. He was just 58. His sudden passing was a huge loss for the paper, but the new editor-in-chief looks like an eminently suitable successor.

The national newspaper tradition in France is far less established than it is in other European countries, such as Ireland and the UK. It's only a couple of years since France Soir expired. In its broadsheet heyday in the 1950s, it was selling 1. 5 million copies a day, yet by the time it finally collapsed, it was down to daily sales of 20,000. Le Monde has long been seen as the pinnacle of French newspaper excellence, but it too was in dire danger of going under. It was rescued two years ago by a group of three well-known businessmen. Since then, all kinds of innovations have been added to the paper and its website and today, it's making money, which is great news in a beleaguered industry. French newspapers have always been remarkably cosy with the political establishment, so Le Monde set another precedent recently when it published many details of international tax avoidance and in the process, won many new readers to both the paper and its website.

Talking about newspapers, if you want a good belly laugh, Google the photos of the new headquarters in Beijing of the Chinese People's Daily. The building isn't finished yet, but the basic structure is in place and it resembles nothing so much as an erect male organ. I pity the bloggers in China; they can't poke fun at this new edifice. If they were in this part of the world, the bloggers would be having a field day taking the mickey!

Not all the news from France is good, however, especially in your name is François Hollande. It's just a year since he became president and the past year with him in charge of the country seems an eternity. No French president has fallen so far so quickly in the esteem of the public and his approval ratings are now down to 20 per cent. Le Figaro magazine published a cover to mark the occasion of his first year in office, with the caption reading "Four more years" as if this means four more years of grinding, groaning penance for the French people.

Not only is the French economy falling into a worse and worse state, with unemployment soaring to record levels, but what was once the mainstay of the European Union, the Franco-German alliance, has virtually collapsed. The ruling Socialist party in France is highly critical of the German approach to austerity, which it claims is only serving to make matters worse throughout Europe.

On the subject of the EU, I've just got my new EU driving licence and it's a fecky little thing that makes a Tesco Clubcard look quite superior. Typical EU! At least, within the past few days, two former leading politicians have spoken a lot of commonsense about the EU. Lord Lawson of Blaby, a former Chancellor of the Exchequer, who now lives in France, has declared that Britain's interests would be best served by quitting the EU. Oskar Lafontaine, who was the German finance minister so enthusiastic about the euro at its conception, has now changed his mind in dramatic fashion. He thinks that the euro should now be scrapped to help the countries of southern Europe (in this, he includes France) that are now struggling desperately under current EU austerity programmes.

Talking about international affairs, I've just been reading an absolutely magnificent book about what Vienna was like in 1913, the year before the outbreak of the First World War. The title of the book is Thunder at Twilight Vienna 1913/1914 by Frederic Morton, who himself is of Viennese origin, but long resident in New York. It's such a realistic account of what life was like in Vienna the year before war broke out that reading it is like being there on the spot, reading about contemporary life then. He explains in elaborate detail why it was inevitable that conflict between the Austro-Hungarian empire and Serbia would inevitably lead to world war.

On that fateful day, June 28, 1914, when the Austrian Archduke Ferdinand and his wife Sophie were assassinated in Sarajevo by a fanatical Bosnian teenager, Gavrilo Princip, it all happened almost by accident. The entourage with the Archduke and his wife took a wrong turn and while their enormous car was doing a U turn, this gave an unrivalled opportunity to Princip to fire the fatal shots at close quarters. If the driver of the car had kept on the right road, the assassinations probably wouldn't have happened and the lives of 10 million people killed during the war could have been saved.

I'd discovered the book when I was reading a story on the BBC website about how in 1913 and in a small area of Vienna, some of the most famous and notorious figures of the 20th century were in residence. They included Freud, Lenin, Trotsky, the man who became Yugoslavia's head of state, Tito, and another young, very demented man, a certain Adolf Hitler. The website recommended Morton's classic book and I was delighted to find that even though it was first published in 1989, a more recent paperback edition was readily available through our local and always immensely helpful independent bookstore, Hampton Books in Donnybrook, Dublin. What a joy to be able to get such a magnificent book so easily through the locally owned bookshop rather than having to use the likes of a tax avoiding online retailer!

The story of the book contains a real lesson for our present times. Could Syria be the new Sarajevo? Many analysts familiar with the Middle East go so far as to say that the next world war has already begun, in Syria. No wonder that years ago, the renowned physicist Albert Einstein said that the Fourth World War would be fought with sticks and stones.

On such topics, I read a fascinating piece posted by Mike Adams, the editor of naturalnews. com in the US. He listed a number of civilisation shaping trends in 2013 that are driving everyone into a social and spiritual crisis.

Number one was the rise of human engineered genetics, playing God with plants, animals and humans.

Number two is reality escapism, with growing numbers of people escaping life in the real world and preferring to live in the virtual world of social networking, Google Glass and virtual reality helmets.

Number three is the demonisation of normalcy. Adams says that normalcy is the new closet; if you are normal, you keep quiet about it these days. If you don't, you'll be berated by your peers for not giving in to their new wave of freakish ideas.

Number four is the rise of omission journalism. Adams says that journalism is becoming more and more a question of what is omitted from the news media rather than what is included. What's happening in Ireland is indicative of this trend; more and more news outlets are majoring on entertainment and celebrity news, rather than doing investigative journalism. Its much cheaper for the news outlets concerned and it's an escape from reality for readers.

Number five according to Mike Adams is that smart people are having fewer babies. He says that on the other hands, idiots are procreating in massive numbers, so that society is being filled by people with very low cognitive functions who represent the voting democracy—they carry the day at the ballot box.

Number six is censorship and the criminalisation of knowledge. Anyone who tells the truth is branded as a whacko, a conspiracy theorist or even worse, as a terrorist.

Number seven is selective dehumanisation, the abandonment of any value for the life of a newborn child or that of an adult who doesn't hold the same values as yourself.

Number eight is what Adams calls the theaterization of narrative for political gain-government is becoming a theatre production entity. This helps detach people from reality and makes them more malleable, more amenable to the whims of obedience to the government.

Number nine is the end of privacy, with governments having access to every uttered word, every email, every web page, in fact, all electronic communications.

Number ten is the rewriting of history; all the uncomfortable bits of history are being written out in favour of a bland conformity, so that the real truth and lessons of history are marginalised or obliterated.

This all sounds rather scary but Mike Adams is optimistic that a new wave of consciousness will sweep the world, placing the emphasis on personal responsibility and compassion.

So on that cheerful note, I'll I sign off for this week.

May 15, 2013

High summer in Collioure

With all the dismal weather continuing in this part of Europe, thanks to a low pressure system that seems permanently anchored in the Atlantic, we can't help but think back to a summer holiday we spent in the seaside town of Collioure, in south-west France, close to the Spanish frontier. At this stage, we've been to practically every seaside resort around the coast of France, as well as sampling some of those in Corsica, and I can quite honestly say that nowhere lives up to the expectations and the delivery of those expectations as Collioure. It's a small town, with a permanent population of around 3, 000. It's set on a spectacular bay, framed to the north by the church of Nôtre Dame des Anges, with its curious pepper pot tower, and to the south by the vast bulk of the Château Royal. On both sides of the church, Collioure has dazzling beaches, while in the town itself, along its quaysides, many restaurants recall the glory days of the town a century ago, when it attracted many famous painters, including the inevitable Picasso. Inevitably, too, the town has a little unspoiled Vieux Quartier. The whole area of the town centre is compact and undesecrated by developers, the mere thought of redevelopment an abomination not to be even considered. If this had been in Ireland, no doubt the place would be festooned with revolting modern concrete blocks without a semblance of design originality.

But with all kinds of hidden, traditional treaures, like weekly markets, Collioure maintains its status quo incessantly, despite the hordes of tourists from elsewhere in France during the summer. If the town changed its character dramatically, it would lose those tourists and the townspeople of Collioure are wise to retain as much of the old style as possible.

We had arrived in Collioure from Perpignan—it's just a short train journey down the coast. The railway station in Collioure is high up behind the town and it's a good walk from there down to the town centre. These days of course, the railway line passing through here has been much upgraded for high speed trains, now that you can do Paris to Barcelona by TGV in something over five hours.

When we arrived in Collioure, we had more or less decided to stay in one of the well-known historical hotels right in the middle of centre ville, but when we inspected the room they proposed to give us, we found that the walls outside the window were absolutely festooned in greenery, which in turn meant they were full of insects, a real turnoff. Whatever the view expressed in the past few days within the UN that we should really be eating insects as a daily part of our diet (ugh!), we had no wish to be in such close proximity, so we passed on the idea of staying at this particular hotel.

Instead, we opted for the Hotel Méditerranée, on the road up to the station. It's a modern style hotel with no great pretensions, not even a restaurant when we were there, but perfectly basic and adequate. In recent years, it has been much refurbished. When we wanted, we could create our own alfresco meals to enjoy on the balcony and it was all perfectly pleasant. We really enjoyed just wandering around Collioure and enjoying meals in restaurants in the small squares that dot the town centre and the quaysides.

The mere fact that we nearly came a cropper has never put us off Collioure. One sunny afternoon, we walked a considerable distance, just to the south of the town, along the road that skirts the Plage de Port d'Avall, until we came to a small jetty. A group of scuba divers were preparing to go out in a boat and we asked the skipper if anyone else was organising any boat trips that glorious sunny afternoon. No, he replied but if you want to tag along with us, you'd be more than welcome.

We sailed out into the bay, past the threatening cliffs to the south of Collioure, when all of a sudden the blazing hot sunny afternoon turned into a life threatening rainstorm. Not only did the temperature plunge, making it freezing cold, but suddenly, the sea became extremely rough, helped by a ferocious wind, and the rain poured down. Within a few minutes, the boat was going every which way, up and down, and we were soaked to the skin. We were wearing light summer clothes, but the scuba divers had the protection of their diving suits. The skipper shrugged his shoulders and said that this kind of sudden weather change was quite normal in this part of the Mediterranean. But even he began to get worried as he tried to turn the boat for home. Eventually, we made it back to the pier from where we had started; we were very wet and very seasick, but nothing that a few cognacs in the nearest bar couldn't put right. It was a truly frightening experience, and even to think of it now induces an awful feeling of seasickness, but it has never put us off Collioure.

These days, the town has yet another attraction; in recent years, wine growing close to the town has really blossomed and these days, it's much easier to find a really decent red, as well as whites and rosés that have been been produced in Collioure. Another place we travelled to, just down the coast from Collioure was Banyuls sur Mer, itself a very distinctive wine town, but with a completely different style of wine. Its vinuous product is akin to a really good quality tawny port or an excellent Madeira, a definite hint of sweetness to it. Also close to Collioure, and again just to the south of it, is the workaday port town of Port-Vendres, with a busy working harbour. The town is twice as big as Collioure, with a population of around 6, 000.

We also discovered a strange literary tale in Collioure. For years, an English writer whose nom de plume was Patrick O'Brian, lived in the town. He wrote the Aubrey-Maturin novels of seafaring life in Napoleonic times; shunning all modern means of putting words together, not even a typewriter. But he was such a brilliant novelist that he has often been compared with the likes of Jane Eyre. It was always assumed because of his name, that he was Irish and he did nothing to put people right.

Eventually, the Daily Telegraph and the BBC revealed that his Irish persona was entirely false. He had lived in Collioure for years with his second wife. Eventually, Trinity College in Dublin gave him an honorary degree and he quite often spent time in Dublin towards the end of his life, especially after his wife had died. Then at the start of 2000, just 13 years ago, he was found dead in his hotel room in central Dublin. He was buried with his second wife in Collioure. It was a very, very strange story, proof if any proof were needed, that behind the creation of the most brilliant of literature, there's often an equally fascinating human story.

Somewhere else we visited during that trip, even though it meant a rather long train journey, via Perpignan, was Carcassone. With its endless medieval town walls, turrets and castles, it's almost like a better class Disneyland, but much more authentic. The only trouble with Carcassone, especially in high summer, is that it's a tourist mecca, so it can be jam packed with visitors.

On the way back to Paris from Perpignan, we had an Airbus almost to ourselves and it was a very funny experience, because I ended up having a great chat with one of the stewardesses on the plane. She was French and lived in Paris, but in one of those curious twists, ended up discussing with her all kinds of festivities and other delights in Paris that she had never heard about! I suppose it's the same as everywhere else; if you're living in a particular place, you'll see it in an entirely different light to a tourist just passing through.

While Collioure has retained so much of its painterly atmosphere because no developer would dream of setting foot in the place, I read another delightful story with a similar theme this week. Apparently in Paris, in the 9th arrondissement, between the Opéra Garnier and Pigalle, an old fashioned apartment came to light. The owner of it, a Mme de Florian, had decided in 1939, just before the declaration of the Second World War, that it would be judicious to escape to the south of France. So she did just that and never set foot in the apartment in Paris again. It was only after she had died, three years ago, at the age of 91, that the apartment was discovered. It had been untouched for over 70 years, contained a vast array of art treasures, and resembled nothing so much as a scenario from the early years of the 20th century that had been set in aspic.

Talking about elderly ladies reminds me of another delightful contemporary story from France. SNCF doesn't usually get any bouquets, although I must admit I've never had serious disagreements over its services. But the other day, an elderly lady went to the wrong platform at the Gare de l'Est in Paris. She was returning home to Reims, but ended up on the TGV to Nancy, nearly 200km from Reims. It wasn't until she heard the on-board announcements that she realised she was on the wrong train. She told the man who was sitting next to her, who in turn alerted one of the staff on the train. The upshot was that SNCF arranged for the train to stop at a station it normally didn't stop at, just short of Reims. There, the old lady was able to disembark from the train to Nancy. The following train, which was going to Reims, also didn't stop at this station, but it made a special stop and a couple of SNCF workers were on hand to help her on board the train, which then brought her to her home station. What's more, one of the passengers on the original train, had told the old lady that they if they couldn't solve her dilemma, he would more than gladly put her up for the night at his house in Nancy.

Still, the other day, I found myself discussing with a friend from Brittany one of the more ridiculous fads that has gripped the Paris restaurant scene over the past five years or so, spreading to other cities, like London. It's the idea of eating in the dark; there is no light in the restaurant, so you have to concentrate on tasting the food. Neither can you see the other diners (which might be a plus point!).

Meanwhile, French politics gets murkier and murkier. The other day, former French President Nicolas Sarkozy said of his successor, François Hollande, that he is completely useless and has no authority. Sarkozy said that society in France was very fragile and that the snapping of one more straw could break it. He even went so far as to say that he could be obliged to make a comeback.

Sarkozy's words coincide with a major annual poll on what people in the eight largest countries in the EU, making up two-thirds of its population, think of the EU. The survey found growing disillusion with the EU right across Europe and found that nowhere was the decline in support faster than in France. This time last year, 60 per cent of people polled in France had faith in the EU, but now, that figure has fallen to 41 per cent. Not only have the French become totally disillusioned with President Hollande but with the EU itself.

No wonder that a three story museum has been created in Brussels, called The House of European History in Exile. It's in a disused boarding school just a 10 minute walk from EU headquarters. The man behind the venture, theatre director Thomas Bellinck, believes the EU will collapse in five years time, the result of the great depression in southern Europe (which now includes France), the growth of nationalism, separatism and neo-fascism. Perhaps it's time we all started thinking what lies beyond the EU!

May 22, 2013

Sizzling Sisley

One important group here in Ireland has much to thank the French for at the moment, no, not the rugby fans who saw some spectacular sport in Toulon's rugby victory over Clermont-Auvergne in the European Rugby Cup in Dublin last weekend, but Irish farmers.

The first four months of this year were absolutely lousy in terms of weather, with persistent wet and cold. This made the process of saving fodder for feeding cattle practically impossible. Many farmers are so cash strapped that they couldn't afford to buy in extra supplies and in a typically bureacratic response, many of the authorities involved could see what was coming down the line but did little to plan rescue measures in advance. In the end, consignments of French hay started arriving recently, much to the relief of many farmers in the southern part of the Republic. Never has French help to Ireland been so welcome!

This piece of good news was in contrast to the disturbing news that has come out of France in recent days. First of all, here were the economic reports that consumer spending and confidence in France is at its lowest level for 30 years. With France, a king pin of the EU, teetering on the brink of recession, it's hardly surprising that serious social problems are starting to emerge. Last week, a middle aged man committed suicide in front of a group of young school children in the 7th arrondissement in Paris. Then at the

115

weekend, two young children were found dead in an apartment on the outskirts of Lyon, having been apparently murdered by their estranged father.

Yesterday, Tuesday, saw an even more bizarre happening, when a 78 year old right wing historian, having ranted in his blog about the new law in France to legalise gay marriage, committed suicide by shooting himself in front of the altar in Nôtre Dame cathedral in Paris. At the time, 1, 500 tourists were inside the cathedral and they all fled, rapidly. The historian was apparently making a Japanese-style hara- kiri call to arms to the French people to oppose the now legal possibilities of gay marriage.

Just to round off this summary of strange news from France, at the weekend, it emerged that Marine Le Pen, leader of the far right Front National, had an accident while she was mowing the grass at one of her three residences. She managed to fall into the empty swimming pool and broke a bone in her back. Even more strangely, if there was by any chance of a French presidential election right now, it's quite on the cards that the Front National would produce the winner.

Marine Le Pen says that the onward development of the EU is destroying the identities of the countries that make up the European Union. Similarly, she is opposed to the euro, as part of this process of merging the various countries of the European Union into one single super state. Such is the state of disillusion with politicians in France, especially President Hollande, who promised so much last year and is delivering so little this year (rather similar to President Obama in the US), that the Front National seems the party set to benefit most. It's rather similar to the situation in England, where UKIP threatens to trounce the Tories. The Tories themselves seem set to dissolve into chaotic factions over the issues of gay marriage and Europe.

Among all these signs of debilitating, there is some more encouraging news. In Haut-Rhin this past weekend, a cyclist with a difference set a new kind of record. Riding what was really a jet-propelled bike, a vélo-fusée, at a disused military base, François

Gissy attained a speed of 263 kph. Just imagine if jet-propelled bicycles became the norm!

Then Disneyland Paris announced it was extending the celebrations of its arrival in France 20 years ago right through until September this year. Last year,16 million tourists enjoyed the festivities and it seems they will be equally popular this year. Brand new scenes are being added to the night time show, Disney Dreams. Another new feature of Disneyland Paris will be a new superior grade of accommodation, the Golden Forest Club, designed by French architect Antoine Grumbach. I remember well the consternation in many cultural quarters of France when it was announced that Disneyland intended to set up its stall in France. Many saw it as an unwelcome Americanised contrast to pure French culture, but these days, while so many tourists and their children continue to enjoy the Disney spectacle, the Disney presence to the east of Paris seems to be the subject of well, mere indifference.

Also to the east or more precisely, the south-east of Paris, we discovered a delightful small town that is full of resonances of Impressionism, Moret-sur-Loing. It's 74 km from Paris and easily reached by train from the Gare de Lyon. Moret is of course indelibly linked with one of the great Impressionist painters, Alfred Sisley. His work, especially his later paintings, are now considered among the finest in the Impressionist portfolio but that wasn't the case in his lifetime.

Sisley had been born in Paris in 1839. His parents were both British; his father was a wealthy silk merchant, while his mother was immersed in the traditions of classical music. Sisley himself wanted to take out French citizenship later in life, but it never happened, and he retained his British citizenship all his life. While in the first 30 years of his life, he had family wealth behind him, his father's business was ruined in the aftermath of the 1870 Franco-Prussian war and thereafter, Sisley had a poverty stricken existence. He eventually married his partner, Eugénie, who was Breton. Up until 1880, they lived in the country to the west of Paris. Then they made the big move, to a small village near

Moret-sur-Loing. This was close to the forest of Fontainebleau and the town of Barbizon, which had long been a painters' paradise—Millet was just one of a number of leading painters working there in the 19th century.

Today, Sisley and Moret-sur-Loing are inextricably linked. We had gone there to pay homage to Sisley and his work and see for ourselves this most delightful town of 5, 000 souls, set on the River Loing. The town has 1, 400 metres of walls dating from the 12th century, as well as two fortified gateways and 20 towers, besides the Prieuré de Pont Loup and the church of Nôtre Dame. We walked across the bridge that had so inspired Sisley and saw for ourselves the narrow streets that had also so inspired him. There's a statue to Sisley at the place de Samois, at the entrance to the town. Moret has another strange attraction, too, the Musée du Sucre d'Orge, the barley sugar museum. The nuns started making barley sugar in Moret in 1638 and their work is commemorated in this small but fascinating museum.

As for Sisley himself, who had spent almost the last 20 years of his life in and around Moret, he was a productive painter, who produced some 900 oil paintings, about 100 pastels and countless drawings. Yet in his lifetime, he and his work were scarcely recognised. When he died on January 29, 1899, a few months after his beloved wife, he was penniless. Yet today, if one of his paintings comes on the market, it will sell for millions. His work can be seen to good effect in the splendid Musée d'Orsay in the 7th arrondissement in Paris, the old railway station turned into a museum of Impressionism, yet to get the full measure of Sisley and what he was about, you need to make the trip to Moret-sur-Loing—well worth the journey!

I was reminded in another way of all the cultural and social differences that make France such a dazzling country, when I read of the efforts going on in the regional assembly in Corsica to make sure that the Corsican language is given equal status with French. France once had a multitude of regional languages and French didn't become the official language of the country until 1539. In 2001, Jack Lang, then a government minister, admitted that for more than two centuries previously, regional languages had been suppressed. They were seen as taboo, a threat to the unity of France. One of President Hollande' more interesting commitments, mmediately after his election last year, was to ensure the granting of legal status to minority languages in France.

These days, 24 indigenous languages are recognised in France. Some, like Provençal, have practically disappeared, in its case because of its similarity to French. Others continue to thrive, like Breton; around 200, 000 people speak Breton fluently, while around 400, 000 more have some knowledge of it. So Breton is alive and thriving, as is the unique Basque language in south-west France, which of course extends well into northern Spain. Another of the cross-border languages is Catalan, the traditional language in the region around Perpignan in south-west France and again, the local language of Catalunya in north-east Spain.

Non-indigenous languages are also doing well. It's estimated that around a million people in France have Maghrebi Arabic as their mother tongue. Many other languages have taken root in France; just think of the Russian influence. Then English has made quite an impact, not just in regions like Paris, the Côte d'Azur and the Dordogne. These days, English is much more commonplace in the Nord Pas de Calais region of north-eastern France, because English people have come to settle there whilst working in the UK. These days, it's almost as easy to commute by train to work in London as to be a commuter in the traditional commuter belt of south-east England.

All this linguistic diversity helps make France such a fascinating country, despite the best efforts of the Acadèmie Française and its striving to keep French a pure, undefiled language. France may be going through a very turbulent and unsettling time at the moment, but it will never lose its linguist fascination!

May 29, 2013

2013—the year without summer

The Tribune de Genève has confirmed today what many people have long suspected, that 2013 is going to be the year without a summer. This weather prediction, from a group of meteorologists, is specially directed at the French speaking part of Switzerland, but it is much more widely applicable across Europe. France has seen some appalling weather throughout May, with widespread rain and winds and temperatures far below the seasonal norms. In Normandy and Brittany towards the end of May, temperatures were plunging below zero, with 50 per cent of normal sunshine. At Sainte-Maxime in the Var, down in the south of France, a waterspout was spotted on the beach. Looking at photographs taken in the past few days of villages in the Vosges mountains in eastern France, on the borders with Switzerland, the impression is of snow-aden places in shots that could easily have been taken in the middle of winter. There's no doubt that this abysmal weather is due to climate change. Ice melts in the Arctic are having their effect and so too is the mass of Polar air pushing down over Europe for many weeks now. Climate change measures that should have been put in place years ago could have helped; it's probably too late now to stop the rot.

Over the years, we've experienced traditional summer weather in different parts of France. Naturally, the Côte d'Azur in summer has always been very hot and one of the most uncomfortable places we were in during a summer heatwave was Strasbourg. On the other hand, Paris in the middle of winter can be cold, wet and miserable. Perhaps the most equitable weather we've experienced in France came in Menton, in the far south-east, one December, when the temperature during the day was hovering around 14 degrees Centigrade, making it ideal for strolling round the town. But in the past year or two, the Côte d'Azur has had some very unseasonal weather, with large amounts of rain and very windy conditions, so even this notion of mild mid-winter on the Côte d'Azur can no longer be guaranteed.

All this rain, cold and lack of light is having a detrimental effect on crops, which are now weeks behind their normal growing patterns. In Alsace, so many fields are flooded from the non-stop rain that farmers despair of having anything like a normal harvest this "summer". At least there's one bright spot amid all this gloom.

The French agriculture minister, Stéphane Le Foll, said that the Government isn't going to impose any new taxes on wine, which is after all, a €7 billion industry in France, even if the idea of drinking wine has become less cool, especially among many young people.

In another respect, too, the government is refusing to budge. Labour minister Michel Sapin says that they are not going to change the laws on Sunday opening. Sunday opening of stores is very limited; furniture stores and garden centres can open for limited periods on Sunday, although DIY shops can't. Recent surveys show that the majority of French people want the restrictions on Sunday opening removed, yet paradoxically, a majority of people in France don't want to work on a Sunday. It's all a big contrast with Ireland, where almost round the clock opening has been the norm for years. On a Sunday in Dublin, you can go shopping in department stores and supermarkets without any restrictions. Smaller shops usually remain closed on a Sunday but if you can't resist shopping in Tesco on a Sunday, there's nothing to stop you doing just that.

From our own experiences in the 7th arrondissement in Paris, it's hard to find a shop open after 6pm in the evening, let alone on a Sunday, although at the Eiffel Tower end of the 7th., many smaller shops do open for much longer. And if you go to less middle class, more working class districts of Paris, you'll find a profusion of smaller shops and supermarkets open even on Sundays.

It may even become a debating topic in the next elections for mayor of Paris, due next March. One of the candidates, Nathalie Kosciusko-Morizet, usually known by her initials, NKM, Is running on behalf of the right-wing UMP party and early predictions say she could be the winner. One of her avowed aims, If she becomes mayor, is to tackle the restrictions on shop opening hours, so that tourists in Paris can get the same shopping experience as they do in London. This of course arouses the ire of traditionalists, who see such a move as yet another nod in the direction of Anglo-Saxon cultural and social values, which of course are rather contrary to those of French tradition. NKM also has another aim if she becomes mayor, a big cleanup on the pickpocketing and other crime that's endemic around major tourist sites in Paris.

She'll be battling it out with the left-wing Anne Hidalgo, who is the heir apparent to the present socialist mayor of Paris, Bernard Delanoë, who has been in office since 2001.T he choice of two female candidates from opposing sides of the political spectrum in next year's mayoral race in Paris means that for the first time in the 2, 000 year history of the city, it will have a woman mayor. Yet such is the male-oriented conservatism of the French political system that in 40 of France's largest cities, those with a population of over 100, 000, only five have women mayors. Conservatism in France is also seen in the continuing large scale protests over the new law to allow same sex marriage; in many ways, France is so deeply conservative that many of its ways of organising life owe more to the 19th century than the 21st., so progressive moves like the upcoming all female contest for the job of mayor of Paris are to be widely welcomed.

A contest of another kind has just taken place in Cannes, the annual film festival. Once famous for the starlets photographed on the beach, that kind of publicity has long since become old hat. But this year, hardly anyone can remember what films were on offer, but instead, this year's Cannes film festival is going to go down in history for the two audacious jewellery heists that took place during it. There's also been intense speculation and comment about the new partner of Dominique Strauss-Kahn, the former md of the International Monetary Fund, once considered the front runner for role of French president, before scandal overtook him. He appeared at the Cannes Film Festival with his new partner, Myriam L'Aouffir. It turns out that she is of French Moroccan origin and she is the head of online communications at France Télévisions. Strauss-Kahn and his long suffering wife, Anne Sinclair, along time presenter on French television, and fabulously wealthy in her own right, divorced in March of this year. Anne Sinclair is now the editorial director of the Huffington Post in France, run in association with Le Monde. Her new partner is Pierre Nora, an historian. It's all bit of a merry-go-round in the best French tradition.

Meanwhile, a great loss to popular French culture came with the demise of Georges Moustaki at the age of 79, described as one of the great voyagers of the French chanson. He created a whole string of hit songs, including Milord, which he wrote in 1958 and which became a favourite piece for Edith Piaf. She was buried in the Pere Lachaise cemetery in eastern Paris in 1963 and George Moustaki is buried just metres away from her. Moustaki's life is a great illustration of the often multi-cultural make-up of France. He was born in Alexandria, Egypt, to Jewish parents who had emigrated there from Greece. His birth name was Giuseppe Mustacchi and even though he had lived in France for most of his life, he only became a naturalised French citizen in 1985.

Finally, if you're looking for something uplifting to do in France this summer", no better place than Normandy. It's an excellent part of France, with a fine historical and cultural tradition and has just as much to offer as the south. The Festival

Normandie Impressioniste is taking place until the end of September, highlighting the Impressionists' involvement across five départements. Museums such as the Musée des Beaux-Arts in both Caen and Rouen are having big exhibitions on the subject, while the Musée André Malraux in Le Havre is depicting the relationship between the painter Pissaro and the Normandy ports. Then of course in Giverny, between Paris and Rouen, the Musée des Impressionists is showing off its wares, ust beside the remarkable gardens at Giverny, restored by Monet, and one of France's prime tourist sites. It's perhaps appropriate in what looks likely to be a rather wet "summer", that the water-based delights of Monet's garden will be so much a key part of this festival of Impressionism.

June 5, 2013

Mum's the word!

I t's most extraordinary here in Ireland, but now that the property tax has come into effect and the time has come for people to pay up, he whole episode has been characterised by a remarkable silence on the part of the people of Ireland. Normally, people here are quick to protest about perceived injustices, if this property tax had been put in place under the old British regime, pre-1922, we'd have seen no end of protests and complaints. The silence and complicity this time is extraordinary.

Already, there's 80 per cent compliance with the new tax and all the protest movements that were promised have turned out to be little more than piss and wind—there's simply no substance to them. No doubt, the powers-that-be are delighted and are now busy thinking up new taxes and charges for the forthcoming budget in three months time. The property tax is inequitable, because it's based on the value of people's homes, not on their disposable income, so that a pensioner could live in a house in Dublin with a comparatively high valuation, yet have little disposable income with which to pay the tax. Even people with disability benefits are going to find a certain proportion of their income from the state taken at source to pay their obligations. Yet people in Ireland have just let this new tax roll over them with scarcely a murmur, which is enough to let those in government think that they can repeat this exercise ad infinitum and that no-one is going to create a fuss.

There have been all kinds of suggestions about this remarkable docility, even a suggestion that since Ireland is the only country in Europe to still put fluoride into its drinking water that this has somehow softened people's brains. Maybe they are right! It all proves that in present day Ireland, people will take any old crap, most obligingly, without a murmur of protest! he situation is not helped by most of the media, which seems determined to follow the government line, without any questioning. But then one has to ask how relevant is much of the media to people's everyday lives? It's not just much print media but broadcast media too that finds it easier to serve up pap rather than ask any hard questions. And it's not just media in Ireland that's to blame; the other day, I was scrolling through the BBC Radio 4 programme listings for this week and they are just desert territory. Literally one or two interesting and relevant programmes and that's about it, even allowing for the fact that swathes of Radio 4 listening on long wave is given over to that ultimate absurdity, cricket. There's another interesting current example of media docility in the UK. The other day, it was reported that the Tory party was about to be engulfed in another love scandal (it's famous for those!) but that for legal reasons, no names could be published or even any details of the case.

Has the British press gone totally soft post-Leveson? Papers just haven't bothered to follow up this latest scandal, which is a pity!

The media in France can be just as bad. But fortunately, over the past few days, at least the weather in France has been improving, while in central Europe, floods are ravaging several countries, including Switzerland, Austria, the Czech Republic, Slovakia and Germany. After a slow start, the great floods of the 'summer' of 2013 are being well reported on media outlets like the BBC news website. But if you look for details in many French newspapers, you'll look in vain, because they have scarcely bothered reporting them. So the question must be asked: how useful is the media? Can the social networks provide a better understanding of what's going on?

One of the interesting facts about the central European floods has hardly been reported outside the Czech Republic. Last time there was a big flood in Prague, in 2002, immense damage was caused to the zoo, the lower parts of which are close to river level. A lot of lessons were learned and this time round, all the animals at risk were safely evacuated to higher ground and the only casualty was a flamingo that broke its leg.

Despite all this negativity of feeling about what the media reports, and how, there are signs of positivity. One interesting development has been the signing of an accord between the authorities in Ireland and France responsible for electricity transmission to explore the possibilities of a 600 km long submarine cable with a 700 MW capacity to link the electricity systems in Ireland and France.

There's also the Tour de France starting on June 29.This is the centenary of the great cycling race, which has survived despite all the doping scandals. This year, it's going to start in the tourist resort of Ponto-Vecchio in Corsica, the first time that the race has come to Corsica. The only time that the Tour de France has been stalled was during the two world wars. It provides great TV coverage as well as continuous coverage you can follow on your tablet or PC, resulting in the finish of the race on the Champs-Elysées on July 21. The race has always provided great excitement, if not entirely good clean fun.

This week, I've been thinking a lot about eastern France, not least because of all the dramatic photos of the high water levels on the Rhine, which at this point separates France and Germany, passing by Strasbourg en route. Further up the Rhine, at Basle, close to where France, Germany and Switzerland meet, the photos of the Rhine waters have been truly dramatic.

One place that has come to mind in eastern France, Seine et Marne to be precise, is Provins, which is 89 km from Paris and easily reached by train. We found it a most delightful medieval town, with extensive old ramparts and the Tour César, from the top of which are splendid views over the town.

In the Haut-Rhin départmente, the village of Eguisheim is vying for the title of the most beautiful village in France. It's a picture postcard wine village, with half-timbered houses bedecked with flowers, an entrancing sight. Eguisheim is a member of Les Plus Beaux Villages de France. The Haut-Rhin départmenteis well placed, with a total of five villages in the organisation. Alongside Egusheim are other delights, such as Riquewhir, which is the one everyone thinks of when they consider wine making in Alsace. The only snag with Riquewhir as we found for ourselves was that the day we were there, a few thousand other tourists had the same idea and the centre of the village was bedlam! If you want to see some of the entrancing wine villages of Alsace, you're much better of going for the lesser-known ones.

Finally, this week, I must recommend a book about French village life, even though it describes an era long since vanished. Over 60 years ago, an American professor, Laurence Wylie and his family, lived for a year in a village in the Vaucluse in south eastern France, between Avignon and the famed Mont Vaucluse. He called it Village in the Vaucluse. The book came out in 1957 and the third edition, of which I bought a copy, was published in 1974. Despite the passing of time, this Harvard University Press book is still readily available. For anyone who wants a blow-by-blow account of what French village life was really like before the advent of widespread industrialisation and the immense social changes of the past three or four decades, this is the book to read. It's sociology with a human face and it's absolutely riveting stuff.

June 12, 2013

Managing Monet

The wonderful Monet gardens at Giverny, 80 km north-west of Paris, have a new attraction in the form of Le Jardin des Plumes hotel, a mere 10 minutes walk from the gardens. The gardens at Giverny are easy to reach; if you're driving from Paris, it'll take about an hour, whereas if you take the train from the Gare St-Lazare to Vernon, it's a 45 minutes journey. hen you have to take a 15 minute bus transfer. It's all too easy to reach the gardens, which are open from the end of March until the beginning of November. Monet lived in Giverny from 1883 until his death in 1926 and apart from the many delights of the water-based gardens, you can also see such gems as his original studio. Nearby is the Musée des Impressionists, which replaced the Musée d'Art Americain in 2009.

There's only one snag with the gardens at Giverny; they are an absolute magnet for tourists, who pack the place all summer, helped by numerous cruise ship passengers from ships that have docked in one of the Normandy ports. In fact so many tourists descend on Giverny, about half a million a year, that the whole exercise is self- defeating. However, there's one way to beat the tourist scrum: explore the gardens as soon as they open in the morning. With this new hotel, this can be done very easily, since it's only a 10 minute walk from the hotel to the gardens, an ideal stroll after breakfast.

The new hotel is the creation of a local chef, Eric Guérin, who already owns an hotel on the Atlantic coast of France. He has turned a 1912 manor house into a sumptuous hotel, a charming place to stay, and not too expensive, either. The room rates run from €180 to €320 a night.

Talking about sumptuous places to stay reminds me of the glorious summer of 1976, when a heatwave scorched much of western Europe in June and July that year. It was a wonderful time, recreated briefly in Ireland last week when we had a week of true summer weather. Anyway during that summer of '76, my wife and I were on one of our frequent visits to the Champagne region, guided by a great friend, Colonel François Bonal. He was a great character, who had given great service to the French nation during the dark days of the Second World War. After retiring from military service, he found a new occupation that was much to his taste, in charge of the publicity for the Champagne Growers' Association in Épernay. He was a great raconteur and in the best French tradition, a great womaniser. He was also a prolific author and wrote several definitive and massive works on the history of Champagne, which we still have at home. He was also a great traveller and well into his 80s, we would have cards or letters from him, sent from all kinds of obscure places round the world. He died in 2003, but we still have fond memories of his enthusiasm for life and in particular, the world of Champagne. In Épernay, a street near the Champagne headquarters has been renamed in his honour.

On that particular trip in 1976, we stayed in the Royal Champagne hotel, which is about eight km outside Épernay. It's the last word in luxury and the guest rooms are particularly pleasant, almost like town house apartments, looking out on the endless vineyards. The hotel is very historic; just over 200 years ago, any time Napoléon and his entourage were on their way to Reims, this was where they stayed. It was also where we set a personal drinking record. One night at dinner, having been told by our hosts that we could have whatever we liked, three of us, my wife, myself and a wine trade journalist from Glasgow, and we got through nine bottles of Champagne, followed up by lage brandies each, just to top things off. Yet next morning, when the sun was already blazing hot at 9am, we were out in the vineyards, totally unfazed by our boozy experience the previous night.

Épernay itself is a pleasant town, more agreeable to walk round than the larger Reims. The star attractions of Épernay include of course several Champagne cellers, including most notably those of Moët and Chandon. Other sights not too far from the town include the famous Verzenay windmill, from where there are panoramic views of the vineyards. But I must admit, even though the classy Champagne cellars are a sight to behold, a visit to a small, artisanal Champagne house in a small village near Épernay was much more interesting, because of the great characters we met, not least the man who ran the place and treated the workers like family. But during that trip, one note jarred. We were taken on a tour round the great cathedral of Reims and we felt very discommoded because a funeral was going on at the same time. We felt as if we were intruding, unwisely, in an event that was deeply personal for the people attending and it highlighted the stupidity of so much present day mass tourism, often an idiotic and vacuous pursuit.

Still, France always managed to keep producing something new, as in the brand new museum that has just been opened by the waterfront in Marseilles. It has an unlovely acronym that sounds like something you'd clear from your nose, MuCEM, short for the Museum of the Civilisations of Europe and the Mediterranean. The modern glass fronted design of the museum is absolutely breathtaking and from the top of the museum, you can take a walkway across to the historic Fort St Jean and then on into the city itself. While all the experts have praised the design of the museum, some critics have been less kind about the way the museum, which cost €191 million to build, is organised. However, one small section devoted to photographs of cities in the region it covers that have been shattered in recent history sounds most interesting. It includes Smyrna in 1922, Barcelona from 1936 until

1939, Marseilles in 1943, Jerusalem in 1948, Algiers in 1962 and within the past two decades, Sarajevo and Beirut.

Otherwise, it's business as usual in France, in other words, President Hollande has put his both feet in it again. The other day, on the first French presidential trip to Japan since 1996, he managed to call the Japanese people Chinese, not wise, considering the long enmity between the two countries. But then, he's not alone. On a recent trip to Paris, German Chancellor Angela Merkel greeted the French President, calling him François Mitterand!

Talking about presidents, I heard a story the other day about a former Irish president, Mary Robinson, who devotes so much of her time to the developing world. She's a remarkable woman, but an impeccable source told me that from the variety of official jobs she's had over the years in Ireland, she now allegedly manages to collect no less than five pensions! Great work if you can get it.

On the subject of extravagance, I was intrigued by the fact that the Greek government has just closed down the ERT, the Hellenic Broadcasting Corporation, describing it as a haven of waste. The plan is to eventually reform it into a much small smaller organisation. The old ERT employed about 2, 800 people, not dissimiliar to the numbers employed in RTÉ, the State broadcaster in Ireland.

All of which brings me to the places in France that we've least liked and there are just one or two. We hated Le Puy-en-Loire, in the Haute-Loire départmente. True, it has some fine buildings, like the 12th century cathedral and the tiny chapel perched high up on a pinnacle of rock, but I think that its overwhelming religiosity told against it. Another place we thought was absolutely ghastly was Alès in the Languedoc-Roussillon region, 40 km north-west of Nimes. It was once a big place for mining and metal-bashing industries, but our only amusing memory of it is of the guesthouse where we stayed. The curtains had to be kept drawn all day, because of the heat of the sun, and the loo in our suite was perched high up on a kind of throne, so that we literally felt we were sitting on the throne! Mind you, Nimes, even though it's chock full of Roman ruins, such as the great ampitheatre, still used for bull fighting and concerts, and the Maison Carrée, one of the best preserved Roman temples anywhere, it just didn't appeal. Nimes has other attractions, too, like Les Quais de la Fontaine, embankments to the spring that once provided most of the city's water, and which were turned into the first civic gardens in France, way back in 1738. Nimes also has the 1986 Norman Foster-designed Carré d'Art, a museum of modern art.

Nimes has made many contributions to history and heritage, not least the fact that the word denim is derived from the Serge de Nimes textiles that were once made here. Yet despite all its history, we just couldn't get to like Nimes, so it has gone on our fortunately very short list of places we can't stand in France. However, one of the great ancient architectural wonders of France, the Pont du Gard aqueduct, is a mere 20 km distant from the city, so that is sufficient consolation.

Just as I'm concluding this blog, the sun has re-emerged. Who knows, perhaps after all, we may have a summer that may challenge that of 1976, although I can't promise to emulate that earlier Champagne drinking epic!

June 19, 2013

Never mind the rain!

Some extraordinary images are circulating this morning of the violent storms and inondations in the south-west of France, where the grotto at Lourdes is currently under about two metres of water. It's not just the south-west of France that's getting this stormy weather; an orange weather alert is in place for similar weather in the eight départmentes that make up the Ile de France.

Despite all this very unseasonal weather, I'm tempted by some islands in France, starting with the Ile St Louis right in the heart of Paris. It's a wonderful small island in the Seine, right beside Nôtre Dame and a welcome antidote to the masses of tourists at the cathedral. In earlier times, there were two islands in the river here, the Ile de Nôtre Dame, with the cathedral, and the Ile des Vaches (Cow Island), where cattle were grazed before being sold at market and where wood was stockpiled. These two islands were once so isolated that in the days of Louis IX in the 13th century, he used to escape to the Ile de Nôtre Dame to read and pray, away from the hordes at court on the Ile de la Cité.

In the 17th century, during the reigns of Henry IV and Louis XII, the Ile de Vaches was mapped out, in one of the earliest examples of urban planning in France. The island was quickly built up, so that by 1660, it was largely inhabited, by a variety of merchants, artisans, entrepreneurs and others, who lived along the two new thoroughfares in the centre of the island. The aristocrats and wealthy bourgeoisie who came to live on the island preferred to live along the quays.

Today, the island of St Louis has changed comparatively little, with quiet residential streets and the occasional grand house, such as the Hotel Lambert at Number 2 rue St Louis en l'Ile. This great mansion was built in 1639 for Baptiste Lambert, who held important positions at court, including as secretary to the king. The island has no Métro station and only a couple of bus stops. But it also has a variety of art galleries, small specialist shops and a handful of booksellers, as well as restaurants and the headquarters of Glaces Berthillon, the luxury ice cream makers, whose ice cream is considered the best in Paris. However, the population of the island has fallen quite dramatically. In the 1950s, about 6, 000 people lived here, but now, the number's around half that total.

It's easy to get to the island, which is connected to the 'mainland' of Paris by five bridges, from the right and left banks, but it remains a wholly delightful oasis of calm in the midst of the city bustle. While the Ile St Louis is a natural island in the Seine, another island further downriver, the Ile aux Cygnes, in the 15th and 16th arrondissement, is artificial. This island is 850 metres long and a mere 11 metres wide; it's noted for its quarter sized replica of the Statue of Liberty.

Elsewhere in France, off the west coast, one favourite holiday spot for French people, during the peak holiday months of July and August, is the Ile de Ré. It's a lovely unspoiled island, close to La Rochelle. It's 30 km long and five km wide and at its highest point is only 20 metres above sea level. It's very easy to get to, thanks to the 2. 9km bridge that was opened in 1988. Before the bridge was built, the sea crossing could be quite rough and arduous. But the bridge makes access much easier; nearby La Rochelle is easily reached from Paris, on the TGV train which takes three hours. However, I remember vividly one trip we did between La Rochelle and Paris, which took all of seven hours in sweltering heat, as the train broke down en route, not the most pleasant of experiences!

However, back to the Ile de Ré. The island has much natural beauty, as well as small coastal villages and salt pans, where sea salt is dried. The villages, usually with whitewashed houses, bedecked with flowers, are choc full of restaurants, mostly specialising in locally caught fish; the island has a long tradition of local fishermen selling small quantities of their catches, on the quays, when they arrive back home, so that they'll have enough money to go for a drink or two. The island is ideal for such sporting activities as swimming and surfing, horse riding and tennis. One of the man-made attractions is the Museum Ernest Cognacq, in St-Martin-de-Ré, which was named after a native son of the village, Ernest Cognacq, who founded the famous Parisian department store, La Samaritaine.

The island has long attracted the famous. Jean Monnet, considered the father of the European Union, was a devotee of the island, as has been Princess Caroline of Monaco in more recent times. Lionel Jospin, who was prime minister of France from 1997 to 2002, retired to the island when he left political life. Performers, too, ike Charles Aznavour and Johnny Depp, have also been devoted to the island. But it's not all sunshine and sea spray. Last year, family from New Zealand who had settled on the island had to leave after a whispering campaign and vendettas against them by some of the notoriously insular local people.

In winter, the settled population is about 20, 000, while in summer, the number of people on the island soars tenfold. So if you are heading towards the Ile de Ré, far better to avoid the main summer months and go out of season. September's an ideal time to visit.

Also in this part of western France, there's another big island, the Ile d'Oléron, slightly bigger than the Ile de Ré, which makes it the second largest island in France after Corsica. The Ile d'Oléran is also reached by bridge from the mainland. This island too is a popular holiday destination and offers the same kind of attractions as the Ile de Ré. The Ile d'Oléron has eight communes and its villages have many interesting old buildings. So if you want a tourist island that's not quite as chic, and therefore, not quite so packed, it's a good place to head.

Sandwiched between these two islands is the tiny Ile d'Aix. t's very small, just over a square kilometre and can only be reached by ferry from the mainland. We' ve made the trip and must admit we found the small village there quite delightful, even if the Napoleonic museum wasn't quite so interesting. Napoléon had fortified the island in 1808 and the commander's house is now the museum. This is the island where Napoléon spent his last days on French soil after his defeat in the Battle of Waterloo in 1815, and his subsequent exile to St Helena.

Something I was reading this week about French technical history, on the BBC website, was equally fascinating, the first telegraph network in the world, developed in Napoleonic France, 200 years ago. The Chappe system, named after its inventor, Claude Chappe (1763- 1805), used a series of towers, just over 500 in all, to send semaphore messages all over the country. It meant that messages could be dispatched from Paris to the most distant parts of the country in a matter of hours; previously, dispatch riders on horseback had taken days to make the same journeys. But the system was relatively shortlived. By the 1840s and 1850s, railways were being built throughout France and alongside them, a new invention, the electric telegraph, was installed. The new style telegraph quickly ousted the Chappe system, which fell into disuse. Most of the stations disappeared, although enthusiasts have rescued a few of them from oblivion. The fate of the Chappe system is reminiscent of the uniquely French Minitel system, which has itself been made redundant by the development of email, the Internet and social networking.

The Minitel system of videotexting using the telephone network, only began in 1978, but it was once a huge success, with most homes in France having a connection. But it was made redundant last year; this precursor to the Internet had outlived its time. It was also introduced to other countries; it was launched in Ireland in 1988 but failed to make any lasting impact.

Still, another French invention has come to market. A wine marketing company, Winestar, is putting AOC wines in cans for the first time. These 187ml cans sell for around €2. 50 and the aim is to get away from the bad reputation of wines in non-traditional packaging, such as wine boxes. The marketing company also wants to promote good quality wines to younger drinkers, who have often abandoned wine in favour of beers and spirits. The cans are also 100 per cent recyclable. In Germany, the market for canned wines is big, about 60 million cans a year, so hopefully this trend will catch on in France.

Another example of French heritage and tradition has also been promoted; windmills and dovecots. Around 1,500 events were organised at traditional windmills and dovecots up and down the country and you can see more detail of what happened on the website for the event, www.patrimoinedepays-moulins.fr

Meanwhile, back at the ranch here in Ireland, another developing trend is what is beginning to look like a property bubble mark two. The collapse of the first one, around five years ago, was the main cause of the great Irish economic collapse and it seems that the powers—that—be have learned little from the first fiasco. They don't even appear to notice the building up of a strong boom in residential property in Dublin, ith all its fatal consequences if it's uncontrolled. Property is one of the strange obsessions of so many people in Ireland; the only other European country with a similar addiction is Spain, where a similar collapse of the property bubble also left that economy in ruins.

So what can you do, except send for another can of AOC wine and drown one's sorrows!

June 26, 2013

Heating up?

P erhaps after all, the summer is heating up. In Strasbourg last week, the tram service had to be put on hold temporarily because the weather had got so hot. The air temperature had soared to 38 degrees Centigrade, which meant that the temperature of the rails on which the tram system runs had heated up to between 60 and 70 degrees Centigrade. We know all too well what Strasbourg is like in the middle of a very hot summer, darned uncomfortable. Trudging round this city, a strange mix of medieval quarters, a wonderful cathedral, lots of rundown areas reminiscent of Ireland in the 1950s, and the ultra-modern facilities of the European Parliament, in temperatures nudging towards 40 degrees Centigrade, is a decidely unpleasant experience. Mind you, it's almost worth putting up with the heat there in August, because all the Eurocrats have disappeared on holiday and it's easy to get into other wise unobtainable luxury hotels. At all other times of the year, these are packed out with MEPs and other Euro fat cats enjoying their hefty expenses.

Elsewhere in France, the weather has been dreadful, again. In the Côte d'Or region in central France, a mini-tornado struck last week and destroyed about 60 houses. Going over towards the north-west, in the Indre-et-Loire department, this year's crop of grapes in the Vouvray wine region was practically wiped out by hailstones. Vouvray may not be to everyone's taste, because it's on the sweet side, but still, it's one of the iconic fine wines of France. It's described by veteran wine writer Hugh Johnson as being sometimes so intensely sweet that it's almost immortal. Two of the ancient vintages he recommends are 1921 and 1924; if one ever got the chance of tasting wine that old, it would certainly be a memorable experience.

Down in the south-west of France last week, orrential floods wrought enormous damage, including to the town and grotto at Lourdes. The underground part of the basilica was flooded, yet despite the scale of the disaster, and thanks to an enormous voluntary effort, the facilities at Lourdes partially reopened after a few days. And talking of storms, he darkened skies over Paris last week produced some spectacular photos of black rain-laden skies in the middle of the day.

In Geneva and the Suisse Romande, in western Switzerland, the weather situation was even more dire and dramatic. Last Thursday afternoon in Geneva, the Calvinist city was battered by a violent hailstorm and winds of up to 130 kph. In this delightful French part of Switzerland, much of this year's crop of grapes was wiped out by hailstones the size of eggs. A national gymnastic event was being held in the city of Bienne, not far away, and it too was wiped out by a storm that injured close to 100 people and blitzed tents and other equipment. Altogether, between the floods in central Europe and all the storms in France, it's been a pretty dramatic summer weatherwise in Europe—who knows what is still in store?

At least, France, as always, has loads of events on that will surely appeal to tourists. In Nice, not my favourite among French cities by a long way, despite the Promenade des Anglais, the original seaside walkway, plenty of events are taking place to commemorate the 50th anniversary of the opening of the Matisse museum in the city. Beyond a doubt, Matisse was one of the great 20th century painters in France. He died in 1954, aged 85; in the early 1900s, when he was a young, vibrant painter, he created the Fauvism movement, with its bold patterns and vibrant colours.

Matisse used this new style to great effect in his still lifes, portraits and nudes, most especially with his controversial Woman with the Hat work in 1905. Interestingly, one of the big influences on his work was Islamic art, so he was way ahead of his time in this respect too. One of his last works is the truly inspired stained glass in the Dominican chapel at Vence, that idyllic hillside town not far from Nice. In Nice itself, all through the summer, until September, you can see special exhibitions at the Matisse museum and in a total of eight other locations throughout the city.

In Brittany this week, from this Thursday up until Sunday, you can enjoy the Entre Terre et Mer festival beside the Baie de Morlaix. Much emphasis will be placed on local produce, from the land and from the sea and you can find more details on: www. tinywl.com/Cnx-terre-mer

Also in the west of France this coming Sunday, there's an interesting event as some of the top athletes from France and elsewhere will race to beat the incoming tide as they attempt to cross the four km long causeway between Beauvoir-sur-mer and the Ile de Noirmoutier, in an event called Les Foulées du Gois. You can see more details on: www.lefouleesdugois.com

Meanwhile, a trend that's long been popular in Japan seems set to come to Paris. In Tokyo, the small size of apartments makes it impossible for people to keep cats or other pets. So the idea of Neko cat cafés has taken root; people can go in for a coffee or other non-alcoholic refreshments and make temporary friends of the cats there. Space problems also mean that lots of people in Paris who would like to own a cat can't. In France as a whole, close on three-quarters of the population are favourably inclined towards having a cat as a pet, but in the Ile de France region, only a mere 11 per cent of the population actually have a cat. An enterpreneur called Margaux Gandelon is planning to open the first Japanese style cat café, in the Marais district of the third arrondissement, in August. That month is of course the time the normally logical French all decide to go on holiday at the same time, causing enormous bottlenecks on the autoroutes, all very illogical of course. But don't be deterred from going to Paris in August—you'l l still find lots of places open and a certain spaciousness to the city that you won't find at all other times of the year.

Of course, if you prefer a seaside holiday, then France is richly endowed, not just on the south and west coasts, but along the north coast, too, Brittany through Normandy. Coastal towns in northern France, such as Calais, Le Touquet, St Malo and Granville, all have lots to offer. Down south, in the Côte d'Azur, you don't have to go to the big name places, like St Tropez, which are bedlam in high summer. Other coastal places like Cavalaire and the town with the delightful name of Six-Fours-la-Plage, are a little bit off the beaten track and therefore more enjoyable. Two inland towns that I can strongly recommend are Annecy beside the lake of the same name and Aix les Bains, close to Lac le Bourget. On the French side of Lac Léman, usually known to Anglophiles as Lake Geneva, there are such delightful places as Evian, yes Evian of spring water fame and still with a touch of the Marcel Proust era about it.

But back to sordid reality. The ratings of the French president fall month-by-month. In May, M. Hollande's approval ratings were a miserly 30 per cent, but this month, they have fallen to 26 per cent. How low can they go? In a small example of how out of touch he is, there were photos last week of him visiting flood—stricken areas of south—west France. He was wearing elegant shiny shoes, all covered in mud; surely, he sensible thing to have done would have been to wear wellies, which is what other leaders like David Cameron or Angela Merkel would have done in similar circumstances.

A priest in Madrid has found himself on the receiving end of much abusive tweeting, because he bears such a strong resemblance to François Hollande. Javier Alonso Sandoica is the priest in question and a few days ago, he appeared on a Catholic TV channel in Spain, 13TV. Apart from the fact that he has an enormous mop of black hair—the sheer quantity of his hair reminds people of Boris Johnson, the Mayor of London—but otherwise, he's a spitting image of M. Hollande and it hasn't done the popularity of the priest any good.

The other day, I got a glimpse of the future, when I saw for the first time a 3D printer, which can make all manner of objects by building up layers of plastic. In America recently, there was great rumpus when someone started using the technology to make guns—all the bad consumer and social trends seem to start in the US, so this will probably be the latest. But anyway, one of the big technology forecasting groups said recently that of the 12 new technologies, mostly derived from the Internet, that will change the future and in the process, wipe out work, one was 3D printing. In time to come, there will probably be no limit to the size of objects that can be printed off—print your own car, at home, in your own time. Seeing this 3D printer in Dublin gave a strange sort of feeling, what someone might have felt when they saw a steam locomotive for the first time, or got their first glimpse of television.

The truth is that much of current technology will soon be irrelevant, as technological change is happening so quickly. How much of the technology we are currently using will still be relevant in five years time? An even more pertinent question is how people can continue to access archived material, given that the systems they are using are becoming obsolete so quickly?

And to finish, I can't resist a joke I read the other day: " Dear me, I'm late again for my cocaine awareness course. Talk about cutting it fine! "

July 3, 2013

Bamboozled by its own farts

I really enjoyed a news video the other day from France; it was totally stupid and therefore, all the more hilarious, showing a Gallic bulldog that had a rampant fear of its own farts, running around in small circles, chasing its tail, just like a typical politician. Why should all this remind me of President Hollande?

Well, for starters, he's running in fear of the French electorate. In May, his approval ratings were down to 30 per cent, but in June, they fell even further, to 26 per cent. No new president in France—and Hollande has only been in office just over a year—has ever had such low ratings. Apart from that, the ruling Socialist party is in a state of turmoil and upheaval. Yet while the great French public has so little confidence in President Hollande, neither is there much appetite for the return of that great swashbuckler, Sarkozy. Another recent poll showed that 60 per cent of the French electorate would issue a resounding "non" to any idea of him ever returning to power.

President Hollande looks so worn out these days that inevitably, there must be speculation as to whether he is actually going to see his term of office through to the bitter end. In the US, where similarly, President Obama has promised much and delivered precious little, there's a lot of speculation that he won't complete his second term of office.

In France, the slump in approval ratings for the president comes amid increasing economic gloom. The recession is getting really serious, but it's a sign of how generally useless the mainstream media is at reporting what's really going that the state of the French economy merits little if any coverage. An exception to this rule is the Daily Telegraph in London, which with its EU sceptical bias, does deliver some excellent news coverage of what's really going on in Europe, including France.

The Cour de Comptes, which is the watchdog for French government finances, says that over the next two years, the country will need an extra €28 billion in cuts, targeting such areas as unemployment benefits, pensions and family support. Those projected cuts are about twice what is proposed for government cuts in the UK in 2015 and 2016.

Ambitious plans to double the size of the high speed rail network over the next two decades have been scrapped and places like Normandy which had hoped for a TGV service, will now have to put up with a slow, conventional rail service for goodness knows how many years to come. The only new TGV line to survive these massive cuts is the extension of the new Paris to Bordeaux line, already under construction, to Toulouse. Hardly surprisingly, the French data office, INSEE, has said that consumer confidence in France is at its lowest level for 40 years.

More fury was generated last autumn when Libération, that left-wing organ of the media, published a commentary piece that said that France was a decrepit, overcentralised gerontocracy, stating that if young people in France wanted to get on in life, the best thing could do would be to leave the country. The basis themes of this piece were repeated in a feature the other day in the New York Times. Yet unlike countries like Ireland, where qualified young people continue to leave the country by the planeload, there's little tradition in France of this kind of mass emigration, unless you count the big exodus in recent years to London. In terms of its French population, London can now be classed as the sixth largest French city!

French consumers do not take attacks on their well-being lying down; the stage is being set, through the massive decline in consumer confidence and its economic woes, for much social unrest, which the French do all too well. Whereas in Ireland, people have taken all the austerity measures like sheep in doze mode—scarcely anyone raises a voice in protest—the French are all set to become very vocal indeed on the subject.

In Germany, an Anglo-Saxon term has become very popular, among all classes, and is even being used by the Chancellor, Angela Merkel, yet is not even raising an eyebrow. It's very expressive: shitstorm. Who knows, its French equivalent, merde orage, may be about to happen!

At least, there's one piece of good news from Paris. An old mansion at number 5 bis, rue de Verneuil in the 7th., was home to Serge Gainsbourg in 1969. He was perhaps the most iconic performer of his generation in France. For the past 40 years, the wall outside has been plastered with graffiti. Now comes news that for the first time, Charlotte Gainsbourg, who owns the house, the daughter of the singer and of Jane Birkin, has authorised a renovation of the graffiti wall. There are also plans to open a Gainsbourg museum inside the house; meanwhile, as from September, small groups of people will be able, for the first time, to have a look round the interior of the old Gainsbourg abode.

But one should always be highly sceptical about over-wrought hyperbole in the media. I had an excellent example of this the other day when I went to see a screening of the Renoir film by young French director, Gilles Bourdos. The film is set in Cagnes-sur-Mer, in the south of France, in 1915, and shows the great painter Renoir in the last stages of his life (he died in 1919). Into the picture comes one of Renoir's sons, Jean, as well as the woman who was the last of Renoir's models, Catherine Hessling, born Andrée Heuschling. From the Champagne-Marne region, she had escaped wartime Paris and gone to to the Côte d'Azur, when she stumbled into the job of model for Renoir. When the film opened in the US earlier this year, reviews of it in major media outlets like the New York Times and the Wall Street Journal, were positively gushing, making it out to be almost the greatest French film of all time. It just shows how even the big media brands in the US can get it wrong!

I found it was boring as hell and all I became interested in was how much time was still to elapse before it ended and I could leave the cinema and get some fresh air. It gave little if any appreciation of what life was like on the Côte d'Azur in 1915, while in north-eastern France, the first world war was being waged ferociously. The characters were two rather than three dimensional, so that one cared little for them. Directors often think that nudity and sex in a film will cover a multitude of sins, but that simply isn't true.

The lead actress in the film (how I hate the use of that word, actor, for both sexes!) was Christa Theret, born in Paris in 1991. She was excellent, however, and what's more she has a lovely body, seen to full naked effect in the film. But all her displays didn't remotely compensate for the boredom that had already set in.

It wasn't until the last half hour of the film, where Jean Renoir comes into prominence, that the film started to come alive. He had recovered from his war injuries and announced he had signed up again, this time, as an aviator. He forms a relationship with his father's model. The most interesting part of the film came with text at its very end, where it outlined what happened later to Jean Renoir. He and Catherine got married and during the 1920s, when Jean was beginning his film career, Catherine was his lead actress. Up to the end of the 1960s, Jean Renoir made more than 40 films, becoming one of the greatest ever film directors. But he and Catherine had split up in 1930, although they didn't divorce until 1943.

After the split, Catherine appeared in a few more films, then disappeared from public view, but always living in Paris. For the rest of her life, she maintained a monastic silence. Jean Renoir died, in California, in early 1979, a feted figure in the movie industry. In September, 1979, Catherine died, an impoverished and totally forgotten old lady. This part of the story has the makings of a much more interesting film, but whether the French film industry in its present state, Is up to the task of making such a film is a very good question.

Somewhere with vestiges of French culture that's well worth exploring, the Channel Islands, came to mind when I saw the latest offerings on the Internet from the tourist board for Guernsey, Herm, Sark and Alderney. I must say that I've always found Guernsey by far the most appealing of the two big Channel Islands and I made my first trip there, aged seven, which is rather a long time ago. The other big island, Jersey, has never appealed as much to me; It always seems more of a honky-tonk, nouveau riche (very rich) place.

Guernsey on the other hand is full of flowers and lovely lanes and beaches. Its capital, St Peter Port, is much more interesting than St Helier in Jersey. One place in St Peter Port that's particularly fascinating, despite its gloom, is Hauteville House, where Victor Hugo lived in exile for 15 years, up until 1870. The house in the Marais, in the 3rd arrondissement of Paris, to which he returned, is even gloomier!

But apart from Victor Hugo, Guernsey has lots to offer and through this summer, It has all kinds of events, including the famous Battle of the Flowers and a parade of islanders in traditional costumes. There's even a scarecrow festival on August 3 and 4, while you can also enjoy outdoor cinema on the island during the summer. During seven Sundays through the summer, St Peter Port seafront is closed to all traffic, to give free rein to pedestrians and all kinds of markets. All in all, Guernsey is a wholly delightful place, one that I can wholeheartedly recommend. But even though the original culture of the islands was French, these days, you'll find only vestiges of it left, including the local patois.

If you take a very short boat trip from the harbour in St Peter Port to the tiny island of Herm, you'll be mesmerised. There's little to do on Herm except explore the vast sandy beach. The island has a lovely hotel, the White House, where you can really get away from it all. A two day package, half board, including flights from the UK, starts at £330, a little bit expensive, but well worth it to escape from the woes of the 21st century.

Sark is the only Channel Island I don't know and I'm not tempted to go there, since the place seems bogged down in acrimonious land disputes. The Barclay Brothers, whose business interests include the Daily Telegraph and Sunday Telegraph, live offshore from Sark. The other Channel Island, Alderney, I wouldn't particularly recommend. We found the atmosphere round the harbour really oppressive, with almost a feeling of evil in the air. It wasn't until later that I discovered that during the second world war occupation of the Channel Islands by the Nazis, dreadful atrocities were carried out on Alderney- the spirits of the departed must haunt the harbour.

And just to end on an Italian note- I'm currently engrossed in a new book called Italian Ways, by Tim Parks, who has lived in Italy for many years. He explores Italian railways and uses them to paint an all too realistic portrait of Italy. It's gripping reading and as I know from my own experiences over the years, it may be a delightful country, but when it comes to mind crushing bureaucracy, the Italians can really put the French in the shade! And that's really saying something!

July 10, 2013

Why not try Beauvais?

I f you're flying to Paris this summer, why not try Beauvais rather than Roissy? The latter airport, opened in 1974 and named after General de Gaulle, is so vast and cumbersome that negotiating check- in and boarding queues, or even getting in and out of the place, can be so time consuming. On the other hand, Beauvais, which is 85 km north of Paris, is much more traveller-friendly.

Should you be flying to Paris with Ryanair from whatever take- off point in Europe you're travelling from, you'll arrive in Beauvais. It's all so much more manageable than Roissy and even though there's no direct rail link from Beavais airport to Paris, the capital is easily reached by bus or taxi. Ryanair is often criticised for flying to airports that are some considerable distance from named destinations, but in this case, there's much to be said for using its services to Beauvais.

And once you get to Beauvais, there's much to be said for exploring the town itself, which is full of fascinating historical places. For starters, the cathedral of St- Pierre in the town centre dates back to the 13th century; it lost its spire in the 16th century, but that doesn't detract from its wealth of Gothic architecture. On the outside of the cathedral is the Horloge Astronomique and it's well worthwhile seeing the procession of figures as the hour strikes.

The whole area around the cathedral, the medieval quarter of Beauvais is full of intriguing small streets, all drenched in authentic historic atmosphere. Not far away is the national tapestery museum; Beauvais and tapestry- making have been synonymous since the 17th century. The tapestry factory was founded in 1664 and was nationalised during Napoleonic times. For anyone interested in fabric design and making, this is a wonderful place to tour.

If on the other hand, you're fascinated by aviation, Beauvais is a good place to start. The Beauvais- Warluis aviation museum, just south of the town, has a great collection of old aircraft, displays and documentation. Its treasures include a display on the D Day landings on the Normandy beaches in 1944 and a restored V1 bomb from the second world war. The other aviation museum, also on the southside of Beauvais, is even more intriguing. It's the Musée des Dirigeables, devoted to airships. It's a small, privately funded museum and the facade of the museum looks like an ordinary house. But inside this wonderfully eccentric collection, there's loads of stuff about the old airships.

One tragedy in particular is well commemorated. On October 5, 1930, the R- 101 airship was on its way from England to India, when it came down in bad weather just three km from the site of this museum, and burst into flames.

So, lots to do and enjoy at Beauvais, quite apart from using its airport to make an easy access into Paris.

Mind you, we're coming right into the peak holiday months of July and August, when the Bison Futé, the route planner, will indicate horrendous traffic jams on the main autoroutes, especially to the south. The French are so logical about so many things, so it has always amused me that they totally refuse to think laterally about their summer holidays. Everyone insists on going on holiday at the same time, with the result that holidaying families often spend endless hours stuck in traffic jams. The sensible thing would be to stagger holiday times, but this is evidently a logical step too far.

I was struck by the futility of going to popular places during the French summer holidays when I saw just how many people go in mid- summer to Belle Ile, a delightful and quite large island off the south coast of Brittany. It's a 14 km sea journey from the Quiberon peninsula and the island has some lovely small vilages, harbours and beaches, all idyllic looking. In the 1870s and 1880s, Claude Monet was so struck by Belle Ile's beauty that he started doing paintings of its rock formations. When they were shown in Paris in 1887, they created a sensation and laid the foundations for the island becoming a haven for artists.

The island has a permanent population of about 5, 000, but during the peak tourist season, from July 15 to August 15, something like 35, 000 tourists, mostly French, can be seen on the island each day in search of solitude on the beach! Yet as I know myself, if you pick the right time, you can really enjoy the tourist sights of France.

One August, we spent a week in Paris, and despite the fact that many facilities were closed because their owners had decamped to holiday in the traffic jams on the way to the Côte d'Azur, we still found plenty of places, including restaurants, open and not nearly as busy as during the rest of the year. Paris that August was so memorable that I would almost recommend exploring Paris then in preference to any other time of the year.

One of the places well worth seeing in Paris during the quiet season is the Musée Jacquemart-André, in a splendid late 19th century building on the Boulevard Haussmann in the 8th arrondissement. It has an extraordinary collection of rare furniture, tapestries, objets d'art, you name it, you'll find it there. It's owned by the Institut de France, connected to the five leading French academies, and it's run by Culturespaces. That organisation runs other such sites as the train and car museums in Mulhouse in Alsace and the battlefield of Waterloo in Belgium. The reason why the Musée Jacquemart- André was in the news recently was because it was the venue for a Swiss company, Savelli, to launch the world's first luxury smartphone designed for women.

A strange makeover befell the Grand Palais the other day. Karl Lagerfeld was staging a show for Chanel and just for the day, the interior of the Grand Palais was transformed into a ruined theatre. Why anyone should want to see a fashion show in such surroundings beats me, when there is so much real- life destruction going on in other parts of the world, especially Syria.

But people in France often love a show like this that's slightly over the top, just as they love any suggestion of scandal, preferably involving a well- known personality. A former call girl, Zahia Dehar, fits this particular bill perfectly. She was born in Algeria in 1992 and in 2010, just before the French team took part in the World Cup football series, some of its players were involved in a scandal involving under -age call girls. The case against two of the players was subsequently dropped because they said they weren't aware that Dehar was 16 at the time. Her involvement in this and other scandals, heightened by her posting indiscreet photos on Twitter, have earned her the nickname in the French media of la scandaleuse.

She subsequently became a fashion model and launched her own range of lingerie and a perfume named after herself, which she did in collaboration with Karl Lagerfeld. Now she's opened her own fashion and cake shop in Paris- all the publicity and notoriety hasn't done her the slightest bit of harm!

But at least, the French had a fashion anniversary to celebrate the other day. July 6 was the 67th anniversary of the invention of the bikini by a Paris fashion designer Louis Réard. For years, of course, not such much the bikini as the monokini has been the norm on French beaches. Going topless on French beaches has been de rigeur for so long that no- one takes the slightest bit of notice- very sensible!

Another recent scandal has really got the French going. Carla Bruni- Sarkozy recently went on a trip to New York and Air France not only covered the €11, 000 cost of her return flight, but even the €500 airport taxes involved. It just so happens that the chief executive of Air France, Alexandre De Juniac, once worked as an aide to her husband Nicolas, until last year,

President of France. At the moment, Air France is cutting €2 billion from its costs, which means shedding loads of jobs, so the special treatment that Carla received has gone down very badly with the French public at a time of increasing austerity.

Talking about airlines, I can't see the French media or media elsewhere in Europe being as

inventive as the Washington Post. Last Saturday, July 6, an Asiana Boeing 777 aircraft crashed as it came in to land at San Francisco airport. The next day, as part of its reportage, the Washington Post had the tape of the conversation between the control tower and the plane's cockpit crew in the minutes before the crash, up on its website, for anyone to listen to. All fascinating stuff, but when will the European media ever be so ingenious?

Mind you, something else has just come to light that will demolish traditional views of France as a tourist destination. France is still the most popular country in the world for tourists and one of its attractions is that whether you are in a big city or a tiny village, you'll be able to enjoy a meal that has been carefully prepared and cooked on the spot. Now, a survey that has just been done by the national union of workers in the hotel, restaurant and café sectors, has found that a third of all restaurants in France admit to using factory- prepared dishes that have been deep frozen, as a means of saving a lot of time and money. Restaurant owners says that the proportion of establishments taking this short cut is actually much higher.

This really undermines one of the main reasons for going to France, enjoying traditional food that has been prepared in time-honoured traditional style by a chef slaving over a hot stove. Now, it looks as if the traditional image of French dining out is all one big sham! These days, you might as well save money, stay at home and enjoy a factory- produced meal straight from the chill or frozen cabinet in Tesco!

One piece of music, incredibly popular, that I was listening to the other day brought in unexpected recollections of the Latin Quarter in Paris, the Concierto de Aranjuez is one of the most popular of all Spanish pieces. It was written in 1939 by Joaquín

Rodrigo, who had been blind from the age of three. He and his Turkish- born wife, Victoria, a pianist, had moved to Paris after the start of the Spanish civil war and it was while they were living in the Latin Quarter that Rodrigo composed the famous piece. It was long thought that the haunting slow movement was a tribute to the massacre at Guernica, but no, it turns out that Rodrigo was inspired to these haunting melodies by the miscarriage his wife suffered in her first pregnancy.

As for the piece itself, it had its first performance in Barcelona in 1940. Years later, in 1974, Rodrigo transcribed it for harp and orchestra. In 1999, the king of Spain elevated Rodrigo to the Spanish nobility, making him the 1st Marquis of the Gardens of Aranjuez. Rodrigo died in 1999, after reaching nearly 100, and he and his wife Victoria are buried in the cemetery at Aranjuez, while the title passed to their daughter. It's an intriguing story behind a wonderful piece of music and it all has a specific Parisian connection.

Finally, this week, a little cause for celebration with one of my own books. Earlier this year, a book was published that I did on the history of Achill Island, Ireland's largest island, and which contained many old photographs. As soon as it was launched, the grapevine went into overdrive, helped by Twitter and Facebook. So despite the irrelevance of so little coverage in the traditional mainstream media, the book just took off. It's now sold out and is in the process of being reprinted, just a small indication of how and why the social media have become so important.

July 17, 2013

Bastille Day- come and gone

It's all over for yet another year, that wearisome celebration called Bastille Day. This year, few people in France have felt there was much to celebrate. The country seems on a perpetual downward spiral, despite rather absurd claims by President Hollande in the course of his July 14th address to the nation that the country is actually on the path to economic recovery.

Graphic accounts have been published of the slide in business at the Marché aux Puces, the great antiques venue in Paris, where photographs show near deserted alleyways at a time of year when the place should be packed with buyers. The sellers complain that consumer spending has fallen off the proverbial cliff this year; people just don't have the money to spend on fripperies like antiques and other knick- knacks. Just in time for Bastille Day, Fitch, one of the big international ratings agencies, decided that France should lose its triple A rating. Hardly any wonder that this year, Paris got a cut price Bastille Day parade, although the Patrouille de France, with its red, white and blue jet trails, did make its customary mark on the sunny skies above Paris.

Quite apart from France, other troubles pile up in the EU. Luxembourg has just lost its long serving prime minister Jean-Claude Juncker, in an unlikely spy scandal in this tiny country that's little more than an adjunct to Belgium and the Netherlands.

Until his resignation, he had been the longest serving PM in the EU. In Spain, prime minister Mariano Rajoy is fighting off serious corruption charges, as the recession in Spain continues unabated. Troubles continue in France. On Wednesday of last week, one of the grand mansions on the Ile St Louis in central Paris caught fire during building work- funny isn't it just how many fires break out in the middle of reconstruction or refurbishment work? The Hotel Lambert on the Ile St Louis is one of the great houses on the small island in the middle of the River Seine, close to Nôtre Dame cathedral. The house had been bought five years ago by the Emir of Qatar- Middle Eastern money is as evident these days in Paris as it is in London- and a multi- million restoration project was under way at this national monument when a fire started underneath the roof.

Then came the train crash last Friday at Brétigny- sur- Orge, just south of Paris, when a Corail Intercity express from the Gare d'Austerlitz to Limoges came off the track as it was going through the station. It all seems to have been an entirely preventable accident and even President Hollande commented that SNCF should put more money into the maintenance and upkeep of non-TGV services. The TGV lines have attracted plenty of investment money over the years, which is only right and proper, but not correct if it has been at the expense of other railway operations. France still has a massive railway network and there are few parts of the country that one can't reach by train. Train crashes in France are fortunately very much a rarity and in the 32 years that the TGV has been operating, no passengers have been killed or even seriously injured. It's an impressive record. Yet I have scary memories of the time we were travelling from the south of France to Paris on a TGV. Just hours before we had caught the train, several bombs had exploded at the main railway station in Marseilles and there was always the possibility that more could have gone off on the train, but thank heavens, they didn't and we arrived safely at the Gare de Lyon, only to be met by a typical French experience. There weren't enough taxis at the station and we had to wait for an hour in the taxi queue.

The disaster on the Paris to Limoges express was horrendous-I've been in a train crash, so I know exactly what it's like, a shock to the system that one can never forget. Yet such is the nature of modern media that for a couple of days after the crash last Friday, the story was all over the media, both in France and internationally, then disappeared totally off the radar. Neither was there a word about the octogenarian couple from the town where the accident happened; they had the misfortune to be on the platform when the train derailed and were both killed. Not a word more about their fate- just one more example of how utterly useless the mainstream media often is at reporting what's going on. So many newspapers these days, both in their printed and online versions, are so utterly irrelevant, reporting on stories that are of little use to their readers and completely omitting to report stories and trends that would be relevant. I often say that having a gossipy conversation with a neighbour about what's going on in the district is often far more revealing and relevant than anything one reads in a newspaper.

One should always read behind the headlines- what's the real story. Much public relations noise in France at the moment about the tourist figures for last year. It turns out that in 2012, 83 million tourists visited France from all over the world, making it yet again, the world's most popular tourist country. The figures were even up on 2011, when 81. 4 million tourists visited. It means a great deal to the French economy, about €35 billion annually, but as one cynic (realist?) pointed out, it's hard to understand just why so many people come to holiday in France. The country is grossly over- priced (other countries like Spain offer much better value for money) and the whole idea of customer service is a nasty American invention that can never be allowed to sully the French way of life. I remember once going to the SNCF desk at Roissy airport, only to find that the workers were on a go- slow, and even though they didn't have any other customers to deal with, I t took the best part of an hour before they deigned to answer some fairly straightforward queries. Stories of similar poor customer service still abound across France, so I always find it amazing that so many tourists continual to travel there regardless. But at least I found one piece of good news this week. As readers of this blog know, I have a particular soft spot for the artistic seaside town of Collioure in south- west France, close to the frontier with Spain, Barcelona next stop. Having been to practically every seaside resort on the coast of mainland France, Collioure remains our number one choice. When we were there, we stayed at the Hotel Mediterranée, on the road that leads to the station. At the time, it was a fairly basic structure, like walls in the bedrooms made from undecorated breeze blocks, yet even in its basic state, it was perfectly adequate and very reasonably priced. Now I see that the hotel has just done a big makeover on itself and the transformation is astonishing, with all the rooms now looking very chic and comfortable, with all mod cons. Yet the prices are still very reasonable, with a room for two people starting at €100 a night and breakfast at €10 a person.

In recent years, Collioure has started to make its mark winewise, with some excellent vintages from the vineyards on the hillsides around the town. Marks & Spencer is just one of the wine retailers that's now selling Collioure wines. Talking about wines, the results of a recent blind tasting of blush wines in London made for interesting reading. It was found that lighter rosé wines from outside Provence, from wine regions like Bordeaux and Sancerre, more than held their own against darker rosé wines from Provence. The latter region is the traditional home of rosé wine making in France and while to be fair some of its offerings just can't be bettered, it's good to know that other regions can do as well, if not better.

And on another agricultural subject, this time rather more down to earth, natural fertiliser. Britanny in north- west France is renowned for its seaweed, which often creates a nauseous smell for holidaymakers in the region. Brittany produces about 80 per cent of the seaweed harvested in France and half of the production in Brittany is in north Finistere. A new factory has opened in this part of Brittany and it claims to have made huge reductions in the smell factor. The seaweed it processes is used by local farmers. In several parts of Brittany, what were once small villages for seaweed gatherers have now been converted for tourist use. In one such village, Le Meneham, what were once sturdy houses built for customs officers in the early 19th century, complete with slated or thatched roofs, are now used for tourist accommodation. They feature the traditional Breton box beds, the lits clos. Nearby, the village inn features a harvest of the sea menu. Brittany is one of the best places in France to get close to and explore the heritage of the sea.

Talking of heritage reminds of the one left by a French banker, Albert Kahn, who made untold millions for himself, as bankers tend to do, at the end of the 19th and the beginning of the 20th centuries. Yet unusually, he was also a philanthropist and internationalist. He spent vast sums of money financing photographic expeditions around the world. Teams of photographers went to more than 50 countries around the world, often photographing places that were on the cusp of great change, from predominantly rural communities to 20th century mechanised societies. The photographers ventured as far as Mongolia and Brazil, and brought back an amazing collection of images, 72, 000 in all. Nearer home, in places like France, England and Ireland, the images from just over a century ago, are equally fascinating to look at. What made the project even more interesting is that this was the wide scale use of colour photography. The images from the first world war are made even more realistic and gruesome through the use of colour.

His mansion at Boulogne- Billancourt on the outskirts of Paris now houses the museum that preserves the photographic work he financed. Kahn himself was only photographed formally on one occasion; the image shows him outside his office on the rue de Richlieu in Paris in 1914. By 1929, Kahn was still one of the richest men in Europe, but the Wall Street crash that year wiped out his fortune and put an end to all the photographic expeditions he had been financing. Kahn died in 1940, just as the second world war was set to engulf France itself. At the museum, ou can also explore the eight hectares of gardens, which show what gardening techniques and designs were like in the early 20th century. The museum is easy to reach by public transport, Métro, bus and tram. It's at the end of the Number 10 line on the Métro, at Pont St- Cloud and the entrance fee to the museum is astonishingly easy on the pocket, a mere €4 for the full entry fee.

All this treasures are just one reason among countless thousands as to why so many people still come to and enjoy France. The Albert Kahn museum itself is an unforgettable experience.

And I can't miss the opportunity to end on a slightly cynical note, as is my wont! During the conclusion of a trial in Scotland, this week, a woman who ran a multi- million pound vice empire based in Edinburgh was convicted and sent to prison for five years. Her manager suffered a similar fate and it turned out that he had plenty of financial expertise- he was a former bank manager! Nuff said.

July 24, 2013

Hot, humid and sticky

Right now, the weather in Ireland is very warm and very humid, marked with plenty of downpours. The sticky weather is far from pleasant but all the same, a big improvement on the five months of miserable weather we had from January to May this year. In France, it's even worse, as temperatures have soared and today, an orange alert for storms is in place for many départements across the country. Expect absolutely torrential downpours! A friend of mine had to drive the other day from western Brittany to north of Paris; the temperature was 35 degrees Centigrade and since his car has no air conditioning, it made for very unpleasant driving conditions.

Meanwhile, the temperature is likely to heat in another direction, too. Planet. fr is a French news website that has just run a photograph of a very pregnant Duchess of Cambridge lookalike showing someone very like Kate in the nude. However, it is quite tasteful and doesn't show anything it shouldn't, apart from what is portrayed as the royal bump. The photo looks like a good example of Photoshopping and was originally published in the Huffington Post but many inside and outside France will wonder if nothing is sacred any more.

Planet. fr is typical of a new generation of news websites that owe nothing to the newspaper business and take a far edgier approach to the news, taking risks and making comments that websites allied to traditional newspapers simply won't do. Here in Ireland, there's an excellent digital only newspaper, journal. ie, that's renowned for a similar approach. It enlivens its output with some exceptionally good photography and an offbeat approach. It has just run a piece about the best jokes about the new royal arrival; they are all in good taste, if not particularly funny. However, there was one that made me laugh out loud. Buckingham Palace had put an announcement of the royal birth on an easel outside the palace but on the journal. ie website, this has been changed to read that the palace has just released the name of the new royal baby: Dave. It takes a lot to make me laugh out loud at something I've read online, but this did the trick!

Sport is very much on everyone's minds at the moment, especially with the Tour de France once again an English triumph. However, I was slightly staggered by something I saw on The Guardian website. The other day, I t said that the last stage of the Tour de France was from Versailles to Paris and that it stretched for 133. 5 km. How they managed that, I m not quite sure, since Versailles is merely 15 km as the crow flies from central Paris. Given the Guardian's old notoriety for typos, one wonders: surely this was shome mistake? Talking about mistakes in the media, when the Montreux Jazz Festival in Switzerland was planning the publicity for this summer's event, they inadvertently used a photograph of the Grégory boy without realising who it was. Grégory was the little boy who was murdered in the Vosges region of eastern France way back in 1984. The murder caused such outrage that even after all these years, it still has the power to shock in France and his family quickly won an abject apology from the festival organisers in Montreux.

Still on sport, I see a delightful event is coming up in the next few days in Paris. It's on Sunday, July 29 and it's the fifth traversée de Paris. That rather pedestrian title doesn't give any clue to what it's all about, a procession of 650 old vehicles, vintage and veteran cars (yes, there is a difference between the two!), buses, vans, lorries, tractors even motorcyles. This procession will make its way from the Château at Vincennes to the Observatory at Meudon. It starts at 8am on Sunday, French time, and will make its way through the place de la Concorde, past the Grand Palais and through the place des Invalides before reaching its destination at 12h00. There are even limited seats available on a 1930s bus, or €5 each. Further details on the website: www. vincennesenanciennes. com

It would be very hard to get nostalgic for present day vehicles, all computer- designed, but as for the old style transport, well that's a different matter entirely and one could even get interested in seeing old style buses. Still it's an improvement on all the traffic jams currently being reported by Bison Futé, at the height of the holiday season. Last Friday afternoon, the péripherique motorway that encirles Paris was described as being almost one continuous tailback. In the current heat, that's no fun at all, even if you do have air conditioning in your car.

But of course, you could also chill out on the beach in Paris. For the 12th time, the plage de Paris has been created on the banks of the Seine in the vicinity of the Ile St- Louis and the Ile de la Cité. Some 5, 000 tonnes of sand has been dumped to create the illusion of a beach and besides all the deckchairs, lots of different activities aimed at holidaymakers of all ages, are in full swing, everything from pétanque to beach volleyball with a music festival thrown in for good measure. The beach will be there until August 20 and this year, the idea has been extended to a second location, the Bassin de Villette on the north side of Paris. The only snag is that the road closures in Paris for the city's summer beaches mean long detours for motorists, but who in their right minds would want to be driving in Paris anyway?

Artificial beaches have also been put in places at many other places around the country, including Amiens, Clermont- Ferrand, Dijon, Lille, Reims, Rouen and Toulouse. Bordeaux has its seasonal beach, too, but it's pretty real, since it makes use of the banks of the Lac de Bordeaux. It's interesting that so many of this year's artificial beaches are in Alsace- Lorraine and just released statistics show that this fascinating region of France is the best place to go if you are looking for sunshine.

The picturesque, flower- bedecked town of Colmar, between Strasbourg and Mulhouse, and close to the River Rhine, has recorded 184 hours of sunshine this month, with another week of July still to come. This makes Colmar the sunniest place in the whole of France, for instance beating Cannes on the Côte d 'Azur hands down; it has had a mere 148 hours of sunshine this month to date.

Still, some people aren't able to enjoy the south coast sunshine this year. Jacques Chirac, the former French president, used to spend part of every summer at the villa in St Tropez owned by a great friend of his, François Pinault, but not this year. His health means that Chirac has to stay at home in the Corrèze with his wife Bernadette. He's too unwell to travel much these days and his public appearances get more and more infrequent. Yet when the current President, François Hollande, was in the Corrèze recently, he visited the Chiracs and found his predecessor alert and good company. During his time as president, Chirac did little that was ground- breaking or innovative, but the country motored along, and compared to the present state of France, the Chirac era seems in retrospect almost like a vanished golden age. Chirac himself was known in France as "four minute Chirac". He was notorious for his many swift seductions and he was so speedy that he was renowned for consummating his seduction, having a shower and making a quick exit all in four minutes flat!

One of the star political figures from another recent golden age in France, the Mitterand era, was Jack Lang, the culture minister. He was incredibly innovative and go- getting with two long periods in office between 1981 and 1992 and France's present cultural patrimony owes much to his vision and energy; beyond a doubt, he was the country's best culture minister since André Malraux in the late 1960s. Lang's daughter, Valérie, has just died, from an unspecified long term illness, at the young age of 47. She had made a good career for herself, first as a comedienne, then as a film star and she was scheduled to play Phedre in Paris next January. Alas, it is not to be, a sad demise at a young age for someone so talented.

All of which brings me back to my first trip to France, back in pre -history, in 1958, when I was little more than a child. Knowing my sense of direction, I'm still amazed that I was then able to do so much on my own. Starting off from Birmingham, where we then lived, I took the train to London made my way across London to Victoria to get the boat train to Paris and then managed to navigate my way across Paris to the Gare de Lyon. One thing that sticks in my mind from those far- off times was the primitive public payphone system, where you had to use jetons to make a call. It's sometimes had to realise just how much mobile phone technology has changed people's lives in the past 20 years. I can still remember seeing one of the first mobile phones to arrive in Ireland, the best part of 30 years ago. It was meant for car use, but the instrument itself was the size of a car battery!

That's digressing! I did the 460 km journey from Paris to Lyon in 1958 by train, which in those days, took about seven hours! In more recent times, I've done the same journey by TGV in just two hours.

I've vivid memories of Lyon then, a mere 15 years after the end of the second world war; it looked a bleak and desolate city, a complete contrast to the present day Lyon. The city had barely awakened from that wartime nightmare. But I remember vividly the cathedral, Nôtre Dame de Fourvière, the Tour Metallique, the funicular railways that run up the hill to the cathedral, and the riverside quays. Lyon is at the confluence of the Rhone and the Saone rivers and the riverscapes alone are well worth seeing. These days, Lyon has a fine airport named after that great aviator and second world war poet, Antoine de Saint-Exupéry, while it has four Métro lines and six tramway lines, not to mention trolleybuses. These days, Lyon is hailed for its incredible gastronomic heritage, but in those far off days at the end of the 1950s, it hadn 't even been created!

The little village I stayed in during that trip was close to Maçon, that great wine centre, and what struck me then and in retrospect, was how empty the village was of cars. People by and large just didn't own cars in those days, so the village was an oasis of calm and quietness. But I remember very clearly going to the village cinema one night- few people had television in those days- and seeing a dramatic black and white newsreel of the assassination attempt on de Gaulle. It was the first of 31 assassination attempts on his life; in 1958, he had once again become the leader of France, firstly as prime minister, then six months later, as president.

It was a time of deep unease in France, with the ongoing Algerian war, not ended until four years later.

But in that small, very rural village, I was blessed with another discovery. The family I stayed with had no English at all. They were a rather large family, with a dozen of them sitting down to a lengthy dinner every night. It did wonders for my French- it was a case of sink or swim at the dinner table! By the end of my month's sojourn, I had become fluent in French, to my own astonishment and those of my schoolfriends and it was the start of a lifelong affection for France and its people, yes even Parisians, whose haughty uncaring image is in my experience totally untrue. But you do do need to speak at least some of their language!

Meanwhile back here in Ireland, the government promises that the next budget, in October, will be the last of the tough ones. Sounds like a lot of bullshit to me! Politicians' promises are nearly always totally unbelievable. In the general election in Ireland in early 2011, the two parties that now make up the Coalition government in Dublin, made all sorts of grandiose promises that they have since been quite happy to bin, so much so that these days, no- one believes a word of promises they make. It's rather like RTÉ, the State broadcaster in Ireland, which was recently forced to admit that a third of its television schedules are repeats. In many cases, the programmes are repeats for the second, third and fourth times.

July 30, 2013

Eiffel Tower's a hit!

I f you were in Paris last Friday evening or have seen photos or footage of lightening striking the Eiffel Tower during the dramatic electrical storms that hit Paris on Friday and Saturday last, you could not help but be mesmerised. The bolts of lightning were incredible; some hit the very top of the tower, while others struck further down. The net effect was astonishing and what was even more incredible was that since the tower is made of iron, it acts like a conductor. As a result, the lightning from the tower turned the night sky an extraordinary shade of blue.

Talking about the Eiffel Tower, police in Paris have seized 60 tonnes of miniature sized Eiffel Towers that were destined for sale on the black market, taking sales from authorised vendors and depriving the state of the tax from the sales. These days, you can get fake everything, even Hèrmes scarves. On one occasion in Paris, we were walking along the quays in central Paris when a shifty looking guy, who turned out to be Italian, approached us and asked us if we'd like a load of coats! His car was full of them. At first glance they seemed to be reasonable quality but it was immediately obvious that these were fakes and that for some reason or other, he wanted rid of them, no matter how much he lost on the transaction. We immediately sniffed something highly suspicious about the whole matter, made our excuses and beat a very hasty retreat!Funny things happen in Paris!

Elsewhere on the weather front, down in south- west France over the last few days, there have been a spate of drownings, as people on beaches in the Herault region have ignored warnings about not going swimming in the sea. Ferocious winds have whipped up the normally calm Mediterranean into a frenzy. In central France, violent hailstorms the other day did a huge amount of damage to the impending grape harvest in a prestigious part of the Burgundy wine region, one of the most important wine areas of France, after Bordeaux. In the area close to Beaune, several key wine growing villages such as Pommard and Volnay, have had crops virtually wiped out by torrential downpours and hail showers. In some cases, several years work put in by wine growers was wiped out in literally a few minutes. Lots of the Burgundy region wasn't touched by this bad weather, but some of the most prestigious wines will suffer badly this year. Exactly the same thing happened last year, so for some growers, it's bad news two years in a row.

One more fascinating weather- related story from France was all about Mont Saint Michel. The island, with its eighth century abbey, has been connected to the mainland by a causeway, which was built in 1879. Just the other day, during an exceptionally high tide, the island was cut off from the mainland for a mere 20 minutes, the first time this has happened in 134 years. The island is an intriguing place, but best seen either very early in the morning or very late at night; especially at this time of year, when it's absolutely jam packed with tourists. We once spent a night there in one of the hotels on the island and waking up in the middle of the night, when all was total silence, and seeing the sea stretching away to the mainland, was indeed memorable.

Another disaster of a totally different kind was remembered the other day- July 25 was the 13th anniversary of the Concorde crash at Charles de Gaulle airport in Paris. When the plane was taking off, it hit a metal part on the runway that punctured a fuel tank, leading to a fuel spill. Within seconds, the plane was a dramatic sight, still taking off, but enveloped in a blanket of flames. That one crash effectively spelled the end of Concorde.

We made one trip on Concorde, from Dublin to Paris, and such was its top speed, twice the speed of sound, that in order to reach its full speed, it had to fly out across the Atlantic. We were a good way to New York before the plane turned and headed towards its destination. At its maximum speed and altitude, far above earth and most of the atmosphere, the views of inner space were quite incredible. Our flight souvenirs include an inflight cartoon of my wife and I done when we were both fairly intoxicated with Champagne- fortunately the cartoonist wasn't in the same state! I always remember that one of our fellow passengers was a young dj called Gerry Ryan; he went on to become one of the top presenters on RTÉ. He was found dead in his Dublin apartment just over three years ago; drink and drugs had done their worst.

Another trip that comes to mind, from far longer ago, was the time I went to Rome while the Olympic Games were on in 1960. Once at the Olympics was plenty for me- I've never had the slightest wish to ever attend another Olympic Games! But the best part of that trip was getting there. I took an overnight train from Paris to Rome and as dawn was breaking, the train was just past Ventimiglia, the first town in Italy past the Côte d'Azur. The line goes through the Italian Riviera, mostly very close to the sea, so sitting in the dining car having an early breakfast and watching the sun come up, was a literally dazzling experience. I'd never seen sunlight that strong before and even after all those years, that experience is imprinted indelibly on my mind. Quite incredible, totally intoxicating!

Talking about waste reminds me of the scandalous amount of taxpapers' money that was spent building a charity website for Carla Bruni- Sarkozy when her husband was still President of France. Between 2011 and 2012, some €410, 000 was spent on building the website, a job that could have been done for a mere €4, 000 and the end result was complete chaos. La Cour de Comptes, which looks into public finances in France, investigated the case recently and hardly surprisingly, a petition has been started calling on Carla Bruni- Sarkozy to repay the state the money, ie taxpayers' money, that was used to create the shambolic website.

Another well- known public figure who's under renewed fire is Dominique Strauss- Kahn, the former ceo of the IMF. He's being charged with pimping, over what has become known in France as the Affaire du Carlton, after the luxury hotel in Lille where he and various other well- known business figures attended sex orgies alongside various prostitutes, all the while proclaiming their entire innocence. But then what is the IMF all about but international financial pimping on a grand scale?

With all the bad news around these days, I wasn't a bit surprised to hear the other day about the wealthy man who lives in the 17th arrondissement of Paris where a lot of other very wealthy people live. This particular gentleman has an aversion to two things, newspapers and television. He neither reads the former nor looks at the latter! Funnily enough these days, digital only news websites can be a lot more edgy, unconventional and informative than many websites that are derived from newspaper content. Here in Ireland, I'm thinking of the excellent journal. ie website and in France, the equally iconclastic planet. fr website. These days, so many newspapers are getting so jaded; even the i newspaper, which used to be almost essential reading, is these days becoming just a little boring and predictable, a fatal combination for any newspaper.

All of which brings me to the Code de Travail, the 3, 200 page long manifesto that governs employment in France, everything from the classification of jobs to firing staff. If a firm in France takes on an extra worker, the cost of all the extras, such as national insurance, will be almost the same as the amount paid in salary. Making people redundant is very expensive, so firms are reluctant to take on extra people, even in good times, which is most certainly not the present state of affairs. A good example of how industrial sectors have been decimated in France comes from the textile industry. Three decades ago, over a million people in France worked in this sector but such is the cost of doing business in France that these days, employment totals in textiles are a mere tenth of that figure. In fact, French firms are said to have the lowest profit margins of anywhere in the EU. Whether that situation is ever going to change is a good question indeed!

Having said all that, there's a brilliant example from Ireland of how state- sponsored austerity can be utterly stupid and self-defeating. The general hospital in Letterkenny in Co Donegal in the north- west of Ireland is on a hillside, with lots of housing further up the hillside at the back of the hospital. It turns out that drains and gullies around the hospital hadn't been cleaned out for many months, because of budgetary cutbacks. Then last weekend, an enormous storm hit Letterkenny and water poured off the hillside into the hospital. It was badly flooded and since the water was badly contaminated with sewage, the hospital itself has been so compromised that it's been put out of action. Repairing all the damage is going to cost millions of euros and the hospital is going to be out of action for months. If the drains and gullies had been cleared, at minimal cost, the excess storm water would simply have run off! But doing something as simple as that is just too straightforward in these times of state sponsored austerity!

I was reading recently about an astrologer in the US, full of dire warnings, as these people usually are. After all, it's how they make their money. This astrologer predicted that if the Pope continues doing what he was doing in Brazil recently, dispensing with his security, sooner rather than later, someone is going to take a fatal pot shot at him. St Malachy was a 12th century Irish saint, a one time Archbishop of Armagh. He wrote a whole series of prophecies about future Popes, work that wasn't discovered until about 500 years after his death. Many of his Papal predictions were remarkably accurate and he predicted that the current Pope will be the last, as well as signalling the end not only of Rome the city but Roman Catholicism itself. But back to that American astrologer; he said something even more significant, that he thinks that the spirit of another Hitler is in the cosmos, waiting to manifest itself. Goodness knows, the conditions are perfect, especially in many parts of southern Europe, thanks to the crisis created by the euro, for a new Hitler to emerge.

One future source of much conflict could be the Senkaku islands, as the Japanese call them, and the Diaoya islands, as the Chinese name them. China claims most of the South China Sea and its islands, which not just annoys Japan but other nations, too, including the Philippines and Vietnam. The situation with the Senkaku/ Diapoya islands is becoming so serious that the Chinese Army has designed a computer game that lets players fight Japan for the islands. Yet the situation is hardly mentioned in the media in this part of the world!

There's even a claim going round in the US at the moment that the US is making plans for a pre- emptive nuclear strike on China. A friend of mine here in Dublin said something rather astonishing the other day. We were talking about weather around the world and I mentioned how much hotter it has been in New York than even the hottest parts of Europe. " New York", he scoffed, " I can 't stand the place and besides, it's yesterday's town". At the rate China is advancing, he may well be right!

Still, amid all the gloom and doom, lets wrap up with a quick look at some of the delightful happenings around France over the next few weeks, when the country will be awash with festivals. At the same time, Paris will be so deserted by so many of its inhabitants that this is the best time of year to visit the City of Light.

In the village of Sare in the French Basque country, from August 6 to 20, there's a great Basque festival recreating many of the old customs of the region. In Beziers, in Languedoc-Roussillon, from August 14 to 18, the Feria de Beziers will draw a million visitors to the town, to see such events as the traditional Corridas in the arena. The Recontres Musicales in Vézelay in Burgundy from August 22 to 25 will bring in some of the best European ensembles to perform sacred music in the town's unique basilica. Then from August 23 to 27, the Russian Art Festival in Cannes will celebrate the innumerable facets of Russian culture and the innumerable cultural links between France and Russia. It's now largely forgotten that in the early 1920s, huge numbers of Russians settled in France, escaping from the consequences of the

Russian revolution. Around 40, 000 came to Paris, while in the rest of France, close on 100, 000 arrived.

With so many spectacular festivities planned throughout France during August, it will be a great month to be on the road- but please, let there be no more hailstorms, deluges of rain, violent gusts of wind or lightning around the Eiffel Tower.

August 6, 2013

Athlone calling

T his week, the focus is not so much on France but on Athlone, right in the very heart of Ireland, midway between Dublin and Galway. Mind you, there's one similarity with France; while I was in Athlone the other day, the rain just bucketed down, as it has been doing and continues to do, right across France.

Athlone is a very old established town, absolutely steeped in historical resonances; the castle, which in many ways is the focal point, dates back to the 13th century. In 1690 and 1691, Athlone was under siege during the Williamite wars, but it managed to survive all that while the castle itself survived a plan by the local council to demolish it. Local councils have the happy knack of coming up with crazy ideas like that, but people in Athlone mobilised in such strength that this kooky plan was soon thrown out the window.

Of the galazy of personalities that the town has produced over the years, none was more famous or widely regarded than Count John McCormack, born in a humble household in the centre of Athlone in 1884. He had an incredible tenor voice and was arguably the most famous and memorable international singing star ever produced by Ireland. A special section of the town's new museum is devoted to this most famous son of Athlone.

With such a wealth of history, it's hardly surprising that the town has produced this delightful new museum, called The

Little Museum of Memories Athlone, with the aim of preserving recollections of bygone days in and around Athlone for present and future generations. There I met some of the people who are so dedicated to seeing the museum prosper, including Maria Gillen, who has a great interest in everything historical in both Athlone and Achill, Ireland's largest island, and Carmel Feeney, a photographer by profession, who has produced lovely colour postcards of Athlone for the museum, Deirdre Brennan, Laurna Carey and Mairead Brannigan.

The museum started a couple of years ago and had temporary premises before finding its present permanent home, at 1 Lloyds Lane, which is right in the centre of Athlone. The building it's in was previously a medical centre named after Dr Steevens, whose family had strong connections with Athlone.

The Rev John Steevens had been made rector of St Mary's church in Athlone about 1660, when his son, Richard, was a young boy. The Steevens' family lived in Lloyd's Lane, two doors down from the present museum. Richard Steevens qualified in medicine at Trinity College, Dublin, and thereafter, practised medicine in Dublin. When he died, he left a substantial amount of money to his sister Griselda, who founded the renowned Dr Steevens' Hospital in Dublin, nearly 300 years ago. Incidentally, the fine building of what was once the old hospital, which closed down almost 30 years ago, is still in use by the Health Service Executive, and it's right beside Heuston station, from where trains depart to Athlone.

So the committee behind the new museum now have the premises and a wealth of material to draw on. To date, they've put up countless photographs showing many aspects of life in Athlone over the years. There's a photograph of the famous Athlone radio transmitter being built; it opened in 1932 so as the broadcast the proceedings of the Eucharistic Congress in Dublin that year. The word 'Athlone' soon became synonymous with Irish radio far beyond the shores of Ireland. For years the old twin radio towers were a welcoming beacon for Athlone folk coming home; their red lights could be seen from miles distant.

There's a whole host of other photos, showing old buildings in and around the town, while an important part of the collection is devoted to the host of well- known personalities the town has produced over the years, starting with McCormack. Another character was John Broderick, who wrote some well- regarded novels in between running the family bakery business, known as Broderick's Sunshine Bakery. A present day singer of renown from the town, Louis Brown, is also featured, as is Brendan Shine, a big name on the 1960s showband circuit and still performing (Do You Want Your Oul Lobby Washed Down?) Athlone has also long been the hub of the amateur drama movement in Ireland, with its annual festival devoted to the subject.

Athlone, like everywhere else in Ireland, once had a profusion of local characters, and some of these can be seen in the photo collection. These days, t seems that everyone is too busy walking round glued to their iPhones and iPads to notice the present day characters. But Ireland being Ireland, we're still producing the characters, except that they don't seem quite as prominent or memorable as in earlier days.

So much has happened over the years in Athlone and the town has produced so many great characters and personalities that the new museum has an incredible dazzle of riches from which to draw. Sport, too, plays a big part, and one photo that intrigued me dates back to 1975/ 76 and the UEFA cup competition that saw Athlone Town FC compete against A C Milan. Jail history and Army history are also important facets of Athlone life that also feature in the museum. Railway history is also important in Athlone, since the first station opened in 1851 and this is another aspect of the town's history that the museum wants to develop.

One corner of the museum is dedicated to the garden shed and a variety of old utensils, I spotted included an elegant looking watering can that was made years ago by tinkers. Before widespread mechanisation and the diy stores that sell everything you need for the garden, tinkers had a great reputation for making and repairing all kinds of utensils for the home and garden, a skill that has now vanished. Something else that attracted my attention in this part of the museum were the two old- fashioned hot water bottles, made from steel, and known informally as ' pigs', that had to be filled with boiling water and were then used to heat the bed.

In between looking at all the old memorabilia on Athlone-and that includes a few mock skeletons, which the kids seem to find particularly fascinating- a young lady called Laurna Carey picked up an old accordeon and played some very tuneful melodies. We could so easily have had an impromptu ceili there and then; all the contents of the museum would put you in the humour for celebratory jigs and reels.

The house that now has the museum is quite spacious, with plenty of rooms on two floors. One of the aims is to set up facilities so that people, including schoolchildren, can research local history and family history. There are also plans to dedicate a room to the famine and the local workhouse. When this section was in the museum's previous, temporary, home, children seemed to get a lot out of this subject, so there's keen interest in developing this particular aspect.

It's all very enterprising and I was interested to hear that since the museum receives no government funding, everything depends on their own fundraising efforts, including donations from visitors and the entrance fees paid by them. But of course there's an upside to not having any government funding, which can disappear on a whim. There's much to be said for self-sufficiency and this the new museum has it in spades.

Once visitors have spent time in this engrossing museum, they can then buy lightweight gifts, easy to transport, as a permanent reminder of Athlone's heritage. And in case you need any more info about the museum, which is open every day, except Mondays, the phone number is 089 8040202.

The museum will also have a role in the upcoming Luanfest in Athlone, which runs from August 10 to 18, and which will feature many family events as well as heritage and cultural happenings that will also reflect the central role played in the life of the town by the River Shannon. The museum's contribution will be an exhibition of Shannon photos.

Just in case you're wondering about the name of the festival, it comes from the Irish name for Athlone, Baile Átha Luain, the ford of the Luan on this strategic part of the Shannon. These days, visitors can take a Viking boat tour up the Shannon to Lough Ree or down to Clonmacnoise and it's all a fascinating cruise experience.

Somewhere I went to during my recent visit to Athlone was Seán's Bar, located in the shadows of Athlone Castle. It was founded in AD 900, a fact confirmed by the Guinness Book of Records. A framed exhibit on the wall of the pub contains some of the original wattle wall from the pub's inception. John's bookshop, right next door, has an intriguing mix of collectable books and all kinds of memorabilia, a perfect example of how Athlone folk are so proud of and determined to preserve, their amazing heritage.

In short, Athlone and district has a great variety of tourist attractions and plenty of good quality hotels and restaurants to keep visitors in comfort. The new museum is already becoming yet another very good reason to visit and explore this fascinating town, a great destination for tourists looking for interesting things to do and see.

Meanwhile, in France, just as in Athlone, the rain keeps pouring down. Over the last 10 days or so, violent storms have struck right across France and a lot more rain is forecast for the end of this week. Near tornado conditions in Nice last week did a lot of damage, especially along the seafront, while last Friday, storm conditions that extended from the Dordogne right across to the Gironde estuary produced hail stones the size of ping pong balls. Over 4, 000 hectares of vines in the Entre- deux- Mers region were wiped out, yet another natural catastrophe this year for French wine growers. This summer has been an unlovely mixture of rain, lightning, hailstones and heatwaves. Another abnormality this year is the number of jewellery robberies on the Côte d'Azur. Cannes has seen some spectacular heists this year and one of the most recent, of €40, 000's worth of jewellery, took place at the Grand Hotel in Saint- Jean- Cap- Ferret, just the other day.

All this bad weather coincided with all the traffic jams we expect in France at this time of year. Last Saturday, August 3, is the worst day of the year for traffic, called the annual chassé-croisé, or crossover day, when all the July holidaymakers return home and the August ones set out on their vacations. The end result was that by midday on Saturday, France had 828 km of traffic jams, the equivalent of virtually the whole length of road from Paris to Toulon on the south coast being one traffic jam!

Curiously enough, while the beginning of August has long seen Parisians abandon their city, It hasn't happened nearly so much this year, because the economic situation is so bad. This year, about 40 per cent of people in France, and that includes Parisian city dwellers, just are not going anywhere on holiday. Even President Hollande isn't going any further than La Lanterne, an official residence of vast scale in the grounds of the palace of Versailles, and that's only about 15 km from Paris.

Still, the bad economic situation in France is producing some quirky side benefits, as can only happen in France. The latest big hit on the fashion scene is a rather expensive cashmere pullover, which sells for €285; it has one word inscribed on it- chomeur, or "unemployed".

An old tourist sight in Paris has just opened up to visitors. The Tour Saint Jacques dates from the early part of the 16th century, and it stands just at the back of the rue de Rivoli, right in the city centre. It's an extraordinary tower, that has had all kinds of uses and which has inspired many literary connections. The tower has been extensively renovated over the last years, as has the surrounding park, which was opened to the public four years ago. But not until now has the tower itself been opened, but from now until mid- September, small groups of people can climb upwards to explore the insides of the tower.

Another brand new innovation in Paris that's well worth exploring is the new 2. 3 km walkway that runs beside the River Seine, close to the Eiffel tower.

Yet another really fascinating item about Paris has just been launched. J. H. Engstrom arrived in Paris from his native Sweden in the late 1980s and spent the next 20 years taking photographs of the seedy, down- at- heel parts of working class Paris that are far removed from all the tourist clichés we see so often, of the Eiffel tower, the enormous tourist boats on the Seine, and all the rest of the multimillion worldwide tourism industry- after all, France and especially Paris are still the number one destination worldwide for travellers. But Engstrom kept snapping away, right up to 2012, and he has produced an enormous variety of truly fascinating photos of the down- to- earth Paris that tourists rarely see. A selection are in a newly published book, A Sketch of Paris, published by Aperture. It's pricey, at just over €50, but for anyone who can afford such extravagance on a book, it's well worth the expenditure.

As for August in Paris, we have many fond memories of holidays there at this special time of year. Our favourite hotel, the Quai Voltaire, is on the quays, facing the Louvre, one of only two riverfront hotels in Paris. In years gone by, the hotel attracted all kinds of artistic types, from Wagner to Oscar Wilde. These days, it's all tourists, and despite having a makeover in recent years, it's still very reasonably priced. For much of August, a room costs €82, but those room rates can go up to around €160 a night.

August is a great time to see this part of Paris, the 7th arrondissement. Nearly all the government ministeries are there and of course, during August, there's a mass exodus of civil servants. Mind you, when they are in residence, it's all very civilised and it's amusing to find that in the restaurants that are popular with them, they often manage to prolong some very vinous lunches until 15h30, which I reckon is a great way of ensuring that the French civil service comes up with some very well thought out and sensible solutions to problems. I hate to think what the reaction would be if the staff in the Department of the Taoiseach decided to follow the French way of doing lunch! We'd never hear the end of it!

The seventh is noted for its many museums, most especially the Musée d'Orsay, home to so many Impressionist paintings. But there's a lot more to the seventh, including Serge Gainsbourg's place in the rue de Verneuil; the high water mark at the top of the rue de Bellechasse, which marks the great floods that swamped the centre of Paris in 1910; the Pagoda cinema, built in the 1920s like a pagoda and above all the church of St Clothilde. One of its organists was the great composer César Franck (1822- 1890), while from 1945 until 1987, ts organist was a blind maestro, Jean Langlois. Even today, to sit in the church while an organ recital is being given, or while a choir is singing, is a magical, enchanting experience.

The rue de Grenelle in the seventh, just beside St Clothilde, is also home to our favourite restaurant in Paris, which isn't French at all, the Grenelle de Pekin. It's a wholly delightful Chinese restaurant with a lovely, welcoming ambiance, almost next to the mairie of the seventh.

So even though the seventh at first glance seems to full of government ministeries, there's much more to it. We've been going there for so long that all kinds of little rituals have built up. In our earlier days in the seventh, we stayed in the Hotel de Bellechasse in the street of the same name. But it happened to be almost opposite the old railway station that was transformed into the Musée d'Orsay, so the hotel was given a big makeover and gentrified, with prices following suit. But when we used to stay in that particular hotel, when we were arriving from the airport, we'd get off the Métro at Solférino. Even now, the klaxon on the Métro trains has a resonance that so much symbolises Paris. We also used to go, on arrival, to a brasserie overlooking the great junction of the boulevard St Germain and the boulevard Raspail, where inevitably, a favourite was consumed, an oeuf dur or hard boiled egg. Even this tastes very different in Paris!

It's hardly any wonder that some people in Ireland, through letters to a national newspaper, have been suggesting that the answer to Ireland's woes is for the country to become an overseas département of France. We would benefit in all sorts of ways, not least that everyone in Ireland would enjoy more official holidays. We would also benefit greatly from the French cost of living, which is about 30 per cent cheaper than the Irish. Recently, friends of our took their estate car to France on the ferry for a few days break. The weather in France was lousy but at least they were able to fill up their estate car with loads of French food, wine and other essential household items. They reckoned they saved so much that those savings paid for the entire cost of the fares over on the ferry! So roll on another great idea for the constitutional convention!

To conclude for this week, I've been fascinated by the turmoil in the US newspaper industry, decimated by the Internet. Just 20 years ago, the New York Times bought the Boston Globe for $1. 1 billion. I well remember the days when the Globe was such a huge newspaper, packed with ads, that it was almost impossible to hold it, the paper was so heavy. It's just been sold to a local sports mogul, John Henry, for a mere $70 million. Now comes the news that the Washington Post, famed for its Watergate revelations 40 years ago, I s being sold to Jeff Bezos, the founder of Amazon, for $250 million. The Graham family owned it for the past 80 years and the latest member of that family to run the paper, Katharine Weymouth, is to stay on as publisher and chief executive. Rather embarrassingly for the New York Times, which I find a bit passé these days, it ran a lengthy profile of Katharine Weymouth a couple of days before the Amazon announcement, with ne'er a hint that such jaw- dropping news was about to be revealed.

Truly, we live in times that are built on shifting sands, but Athlone and Paris will always be there to captivate people's interest and create so much enjoyment of their surroundings.

August 14, 2013

Under guard

~~~~~~~~~~~~~~~~~~~~~~~~~~

I don't have to go very far in Dublin to find something unusual, even provocative, a different way of doing things and when I went to Clarendon Street church just off Grafton Street, the city's main shopping drag (and shopping is such a drag!) the other day, that's precisely what I found.

On my way into the church, I was astonished to see a security guard sitting at his desk keeping a close eye on all the churchgoers, exactly the same type of security guard you'd see in any shop. I presume that he was keeping a lookout for thieves trying to rob people while they are at Mass. The way things are going, it can't be too long before the guards at the entrance to churches will be armed! One other depressing piece of news from Ireland, Crowleys, a music shop that was going for 90 years in Cork city, and which supplied Rory Gallagher with his first guitar, is going out of business, partly because there's so much competition from online purchases. Online has so many advantages, but it's very depressing that it's wiping out so much of the traditional retailing environment.

Of course, they have exactly the same problems in Paris, as well as the gross problem of widespread thieving. As many as half a million Roma gypsies from Bulgaria and Romania are now living in France, most of them in encampments on the fringes of Paris. Many of the gangs of thieves now plaguing Paris are drawn from this community. During August, when the normal city life of the city slows down, making it even more ideal for the 16 million tourists who throng to Paris every year, long queues of them form outside all the main tourist attractions. People are also very inclined to sit outside cafés, especially the famous ones along the boulevard St-Germain. All these tourists vulnerable to the gangs that make their living by robbing visitors to Paris.

It's a very serious problem and one that's very difficult to solve. But this influx of Roma gypsies and other immigrants to France has created a racist backlash in French political life. The other day, I had a look at the new look website put up by Marine Le Pen, leader of the Front National, in time for her 45th birthday on August 5. The photo of her on the website is immensely seductive, showing her in a harbour setting, stroking a fantastic looking cat. It all looks very appealing, until people stop and realise what the real aims of the Front National are, very right wing and very anti- immigrant. One of its policy platforms is the withdrawal of France from the single European currency and that's just one of its more respectable ambitions. Predictably, given the state of the French economy, it's hardly surprising that the Front National is heading towards the top of any forthcoming political opinion poll.

Still, France being France, despite the desperate political situation and the extreme right wing gaining ground at a rate of knots, helped by an enfeebled president, there are always beacons of hope. I was very struck by an article in the New York Times the other day praising the town of Uzès in the south- west of France, not far from Avignon and Nimes. Uzès is a small town, with a population of around 8, 000, dating back to Roman times, with a maze of fascinating small, narrow streets, markets and historic buildings, such as the cathedral. It was always a strongly Protestant town, especially during the wars of religion in the 16th century, which wreaked so much damage on the Languedoc. It was this very Protestantism that caused the New York Times to hail Uzès as a centre of liberality, a certain free floating spirit that makes the place so attractive for ex- pats, American and otherwise, to settle in.

Talking about the south of France, Bono, his family and friends have been enjoying their usual summer vacation there; the U2 star and his family have a mansion retreat in the mountain region of Eze. Just the other day, Bono, who recently received France's highest honour, becoming a Commander of the Order of Arts and Letters, was pictured with his wife and friends in St Paul de Vence. The place is jampacked with celebrities in summer.

This is a marvellously historic and appealing small town, only about 15 minutes inland from the coast, midway between Nice and Cannes. The hilltop town attracted such artists as Chagall and Matisse and one of its famous hotels and restaurants, La Colombe d'Or, has many works by Picasso. St Paul de Vence has long attracted celebrities, going back to the film actress Simone Signoret in the 1960s. One of its most famous residents was the American writer James Baldwin, who died there in 1987. St Paul de Vence is also noted for the Maeght Foundation, an amazing collection of 20th century art works.

Incidentally, if you're in the seventh arrondissement of Paris, peep into the Maeght shop and gallery at 42 rue de Bac. It's run by Isabelle and Yoyo Maeght, grand daughters of the man who set up the Maeght Foundation in St Paul de Vence. The Paris gallery is small but delightful and the vernissages there (wine fuelled show openings) are also very special, as we can testify!

But back to St Paul de Vence; it's a very attractive town, but best seen out of season when there aren't so many celebrities clogging up the place and helping push up the prices. Close by, just four km away, is Vence. It's a much larger place, with a population of about 20, 000 or about five times more than St Paul de Vence. Vence also looks a much dowdier town, although it has lots of small, narrow streets and markets, as well as the Chapelle de Rosarie, which has stained glass and other fittings created by Matisse. Vence also appealed greatly to the English writer, D. H. Lawrence, another big plus point in its favour.

But if you are determined to see both towns, don't do what we did. When we were there, we decided the best way of getting from St Paul de Vence to Vence, since there was no handy bus at the time, was to walk there along the main road. It turned out to be a nightmare, of cars going at breakneck speed and thundering great lorries, with no safe bits to step into on the verges of the road. That was one French experience we won't be repeating in a hurry!

Otherwise in France, there are lots of bits and pieces happening on the tourist front. There's a big row going on in Paris that involves the legacy of Picasso. From 1935 until 1955, he lived in one of those grand mansions for which Paris is famous, more precisely the Hotel de Savoie, on the rue des Grands Augustins in the 6th. It's said that Picasso painted his famous Guernica artwork here in 1937. For years, a private arts organisation has been based in the mansion, rent free, but now it seems that the owners want possession, so that they can renovate the crumbling building. The appeal against the legal judgment upholding the eviction order is due to be heard by the Paris Court of Appeal next month.

Meanwhile, the renovation work at the Picasso museum in the 3rd drags on and on. The new look museum was meant to be reopened this summer, but now that opening has been put back until at least the end of the year.

But at least another prime museum is set to reopen, on September 28. The Galleria Museum in the trendy 16th, opened in 1895 and since 1977, it has been dedicated to archiving and presenting French fashion, from the 18th century to the present day. It's going to reopen, following extensive refurbishment, with an exhibition devoted to the work of couturier Azzdine Alaia.

Talking about heritage, something well worth looking out for, also next month, are the Journées de Patrimoine, being staged right across France on September 14 and 15. Lots of historic venues will be open, as well as numerous exhibitions and for many museums, entry on those two days will be free.

There's also a brand new way of taking a look at Paris, from the air. For the first time, a tourist Zeppelin has taken to the skies above Paris, floating serenely and sedately along at an altitude of 300 metres. The company running the trips is based at Pontoise, to the north- west of Paris and its tours include an overview of Versailles, Paris itself and the magnificent Parc National du Vexin Française, just to the west of Paris. The Zeppelin carries 12 passengers and trips cost from €250 to €650 each, depending on the duration of the flight.

And despite all the recent horrendous weather in France, there's news now that sea temperatures around the coast have hit record levels. In Corsica, a sea temperature of 27 degrees Centigrade has been recorded, while even along the French side of the English channel the water is quite warm now, between 15 and 18 degrees Centigrade.

As for Corsica, once again it's in the news, as the president of the executive of this beautiful but deeply troubled island, Paul Giacobbi, has called for residency restrictions on outsiders and that includes people from mainland France, buying properties on the island. He says that if someone can buy land in Corsica as easily as buying a bar of chocolate in a supermarket, then the island will face catastrophe. Giacobbi is calling for measures like five year residency to qualify for property purchase, in order to deter non- Corsicans from buying up the island. But since what he's suggesting is against EU law, he has opened a whole bucket full of worms and created a lot of controversy.

But France being France, there's always a light side. Gérard Depardieu, absolutely no stranger to controversy, is now looking for an Algerian passport! But cinema goers can rest easy- it's only in his latest film role, Les Invincibles, a comedy with Algerian themes. And then there was the online ad posted last week by a 28 year old woman, a trained nurse, who lives in one of the suburbs immediately to the west of Paris and who says that she is very healthy.

She has offered to rent out her breasts for €100 a day, to breast feed young babies. She aimed the ad specifically at gay couples who've adopted very young children and who for obvious reasons can't undertake the necessary themselves. The whole issue of gay rights, and especially gay marriage, has raised enormous controversy in France, where a substantial proportion of the population is firmly opposed to such rights. But at least, the breasts for rent saga has brought a little light lightness to a very heated and often acrimonious debate.

President Hollande himself even managed to bring a little light relief to an unemployed woman, Nathalie Michaud, who although 50, is still living at home in La Roche- sur- Yon. Last March, when the president visited the town, she berated him for the difficulties in finding a job. But now, it seems that she has been offered a job working with the website of the Europe 1 radio station. However, there are catches, inevitably. The job on offer will only pay €500 a month, not enough to enable Nathalie to leave home, and it's only for a year, so the whole episode is beginning to look like a mirage. A poll the other day asked French people whether they believed the president's claims that he was going to make dramatic reductions in the unemployment rate by the end of the year; nearly 90 per cent were disbelieving. They've turned out to be exactly right!

The present era seems to be producing some very lame duck leaders. President Hollande is berated on every side in France, while President Obama in the US is being called the ultimate wimp in his second term, such is the level of disappointment. Someone even said the other day that Obama makes Jimmy Carter seem like Theodore Roosevelt.

One issue in which the Americans are deeply involved is the saga of the Fukushima nuclear reactor in Japan destroyed by a tsunami two and a half years ago. The plant was an American design and many people are now saying that a massive cover- up is going on, with the authorities pretending that if the problems are ignored long enough, they will go away. The wrecked plant is 300 times more radioactive than Chernobyl, pouring 300 tonnes of badly contaminated water into the sea every day. Many nuclear experts fear that before long, there will be a massive explosion at the plant, which would contaminate much of the northern hemisphere with radiation.

Environmentalists often say that in terms of planning ahead, you have to consider the needs of seven generations ahead. But with nuclear power, you have to look 700 generations and more ahead. So the immediate problem of Fukushima is sitting there, not going away any time soon, and likely to get a lot worse.

Another mystery, much closer to home, is catching people's attention. In mid- July, Allison Benitez and her mother suddenly disappeared from their home in Perpignan. Then in early August, the father and husband of these two women, Francisco Benitez, a member of the Foreign Legion's elite army unit, was found hanged in his barracks, a suicide note proclaiming his innocence. Then it turned out that nearly 10 years ago, he had been questioned over the disappearance of his Brazilian mistress, who like the other two women, hasn't been seen since.

La Belle France, as always, comes up with some great mysteries, all the while, beguilingly intriguing and captivating. All that never changes, for which we must give great thanks.

August 21, 2013

August-a very wicked month

A ugust has a bad reputation; everyone thinks of it as a quiet month of summer, although it's actually the start of autumn, but there's been an amazing propensity for world- shaking events to happen during this month.

Just consider some of the events that happened during previous Augusts, like the death of Princess Diana in Paris in 1997- if you're in the 8th arrondissement of Paris, it's worth going to see the entrance to the Pont d'Alma underpass. There's a memorial in place to the flame of liberty, even though most people think it commemorates Diana, it doesn't. You can't go and explore the Ritz Hotel because it's in the middle of a big renovation programme.

Something else that happened one August was the outbreak of serious trouble in Derry in Northern Ireland, in 1969 which saw the arrival of British troops to try and quell the unrest, the precursor of decades of the ' troubles". As always in these situations, the politicians promised it was temporary (a bit like the imposition of income tax over 200 years ago), but the arrival of the troops was anything but temporary and their coming did little except make matters a whole lot worse. It took nearly 30 more years for the 1998 peace agreement to be concluded and even today, matters are far from settled.

On a lighter note, he Woodstock Festival took place in the US during August, 1969, and this too was a groundbreaker, but in a much more endearing way- peace loving joint smoking hippies, free love and all that.

But what really strikes a personal chord is the 45th anniversary today of the arrival of Warsaw Pact troops in Czechoslovakia, in August, 1968. I happened to have been in Prague for a week that month, leaving just a day or two before the invasion. I was working for a business magazine in Dublin and the unlikely idea had come up of doing a supplement on trade between Ireland and Czechoslovakia. My job was to go to Prague, organise all the editorial and bring back all the material for the State advertising that was to go into the supplement. The work part of the trip was easy enough and fortunately, I found that for most of the week I was there, I could be a plain old fashioned tourist.

All the sights of this wonderful city were waiting to be explored, the Charles Bridge over the River Vltava, Hradcany Castle on the heights above the city and next to it, St Vitus cathedral. Then not too far away from the cathedral, the church with the Child of Prague statue. At one time, practically every Catholic home in Ireland had a miniature replica of this statue, but these days, that notion has disappeared into the mists of time. Prague has such an unbelievable abundance of fine buildings and sights; to name a few more, the astronomical clock in the Old Town, the Mozart museum in the Bertramka, the Rudolfinum concert hall, home of the national symphony orchestra.

Typically me, I nearly managed to miss my flight there, from Heathrow, but despite being last to board the plane, I settled down, only to find that since the plane was a Soviet built jet, all the signs in the passenger cabin were in Russian. The announcements from the cockpit were in Czech, so I was little the wiser as to what was going on. But eventually, the plane touched down at Prague's main airport, now renamed in honour of former president Vaclav Havel. I took a taxi into the town centre and before long, the taxi driver confided that he had once been a university professor whose political views didn't coincide with those of the Communist regime. Subsequently I met up with a journalist working on the economic newspaper, still going today, Hospodárské Noviny. He told me that during the 1950s, which was after all, only the previous decade, the government had a unique way of dealing with journalists who didn't toe the party line- they were sent to work down the coal mines. A spell underground soon softened their cough. Lets hope the present Coalition government in London doesn ' t hear about this little ruse when it thinks of how it's going to deal with Guardian journalists! Czechs, I soon found, have a very sardonic view of life, which I found most appealing; they are great at seeing behind facades.

The place I stayed in was amazing, a b and b place on Narodni, which is the main street in the centre of Prague. The woman who ran the place spoke not a word of English and my knowledge of Czech was minimal to say the least, but we got on fine, and once she had organised breakfast every morning, I was free to wander round the city I met many strange characters, including a guy who was a nightclub artist after dark, but who during daylight hours, would stand at a particular street corner juggling a whole series of balls, whispering to anyone who was interested that he would change money for a very good rate. I'd taken US dollars with me and the exchange rate was such that day- to- day expenses in Prague were practically nothing.

This was all long before Prague got a very efficient Metro system, but even then, the trams were excellent for getting around. However, one really irritating feature of that trip was the length of time it took to get service in a restaurant. In one particular restaurant one night, dinner took a full two hours for a very modest meal, simply because the waiters took so long to deliver the courses. The banks were the same- vast slow moving queues and huge amounts of paperwork, typical of an old style Communist state. These days of course, now that the Czech Republic is a EU member and a fully paid up member of the European free market, things work a lot more efficiency, but at a price- plenty of corruption. You can even do a tour of the city to see some of the places associated with the greatest recent Czech corruption scandals.

One place I was in that trip was a jazz club just off Wenceslas Square. They had a radio set there tuned in to one of the long wave stations in France and it was clear from listening to the news bulletins that a huge build- up of Warsaw Pact troops, with some exceptions, ike Romania, which had opted out of the invasion, was going on close to the borders of Czechoslovakia. No-one knew how imminent the invasion was; all that was clear was that there was no way that the Soviet Union was going to tolerate the mild reforms that Alexander Dubcek has initiated only the previous April.

I was booked to travel back to Dublin just before it all happened, so I took the Pan Am flight from Prague to Brussels, a flight which went through a tremendous and perhaps symbolic storm en route. The last night I was in Prague, I had gone to the National Theatre, just across the Street from where I was staying, to see a performance of the Janacek opera, The Cunning Little Vixen. The curtain came down on a memorable performance, since all in the cast were obviously hyped up over the dramatic situation. Then the invasion happened. You'll be interested to know that the supplement, while postponed, did eventually appear. The following year, I managed to get a visa. But after that one return visit, it became impossible to get a visa.

But eventually, as always, history changes and within 20 years, Communism had started to crumble in eastern Europe. The invasion of Czechoslovakia 45 years ago was really the beginning of the end of the USSR and of its Communist satellite states in eastern Europe. An amazing experience, never to be forgotten!

Everything goes in waves, even religion. I was struck by that on August 15. This is the Feast of the Assumption and years ago in Ireland, it was a big religious holiday, when the seaside towns would be absolutely packed with trippers. These days of course, I'd be surprised if many younger people even knew about the feast day.

This August is of course living up to its name, with all the dramatic and tragic events in Egypt. The Egyptian Embassy in Dublin is just down the road from where we live and normally, it's a very sedate place in a very quiet suburban road. But over the past few days, crowds of pro-Morsi protesters have gathered outside and the other afternoon when I drove past, the crowds seemed so angry that if there hadn't been lines of police in the front garden of the embassy, the crowd would have been of a mind to burn the place down. It all reminded me, obliquely, of the time we were having an excellent vinous open air lunch in one of the restaurants close to the Tuileries Gardens in Paris. We glanced around at some of our neighbours, only to see the Egyptian actor, Omar Sharif, there, almost beside us, enjoying the same lunchtime pleasures. He made his name in the Dr Zhivago film way back in 1965 and I see that this year, and now in his 81st year, he has been working on his latest film, Rock the Casbah. He lives most of the time now in Cairo, so I hope that he's OK there- a great character and what's more a fantastic contract bridge player!

I've also had a good illustration in the past few days, in a very small way, of the differences in European efficiencies. For a book I'm working on at the moment, I wanted to find out when the first diplomatic missions opened in Dublin after the Irish Free State came into existence, in the early 1920s. I got on to the German embassy and with typical thoroughness, they sent my request through to the Foreign Ministry in Berlin. Within a short time, they came back to me with the exact date on which their mission to Dublin opened, and where, with its exact location.

I tried the same exercise with the French embassy and I'm still waiting; I even got on to the Quai d'Orsay, the headquarters of the French Foreign Ministry, only to be sent a mass of material that was completely irrelevant to my query. All I can say is that no wonder the Germans are top dog in the EU- they really are running the whole show, while the French slip steadily down the scale.

Another amusing tale of French official incompetence came up the other day. A civil servant in the prime minister's office in the Matignon was keying in some details to an official website of a new French plan to combat Al- Qaida. What happened? Twitter followers were instead given the directions to a sexy clothing website called Forplay!

So given all this, how much credibility should be given to the predictions for 2025 that President Hollande ordered all the members of his cabinet to make. Le Point magazine managed to get hold of the predictions and of course, the tame French media (no Guardian or Independent equivalent among French national newspapers!) made a meal out of it. Good quality housing for everyone and full employment were just two of the predictions for the year 2025, but such predictions usually turn out to be absolutely useless.

In the meantime, consumers in France are putting up with some dramatic rises in the price of fruit and vegetables, thanks to the awful weather last spring. It seems that fruit prices have gone up by 14 per cent, while vegetable prices have soared 17 per cent. Courgettes have gone up in price by 32. 6 per cent, while pears have increased by nearly as much. Only one item of fruit fell in price, cherries, down by 12. 42 per cent. And like everywhere else, organic fruit and veg- one of the great luxury items in any shopping basket- are much dearer in France, where consumers can expect to pay about 70 per cent more for organic compared to conventionally grown fruit and veg.

But at least you can now find out where to get the cheapest cup of coffee in Paris. A new map, available on the Parisdata website, shows 164 cafés in the city and their coffee prices. The cheapest cup turns out to be in the 17th arrondissement, where the Petits Frères des Pauvres (Little Brothers of the Poor) café is selling cups of coffee for 45 cent each.

So at least some good news for travellers in Paris, in the midst of a month that sees dramatic news from around the world, not least in Egypt. But if you think back, how much media coverage the 1968 invasion of Czechoslovakia generated at the time and how little coverage there is in today's media, August 21, 2013, of what was after all, a world-shaking and world- changing event.

August 28, 2013

Preparing for war

This week seems oddly like the last week of August, 1939, when the world was preparing for war. Now, it looks as if it could all happen again, if the US, the UK and France press ahead with their plans for limited military attacks on Syria.

There's no doubting the morality of what they might do; no-one could possibly excuse what happened during the chemical attacks in the suburbs of Damascus last week, but the real politik of the situation is entirely different. The Syrian regime is backed by Russia, China and Iran, three formidable foes, so who knows what an attack by the West might generate.

The consequences cannot be foreseen, if those three western nations press ahead with these very foolish plans. It could well be the Suez fiasco of 1956 all over again, but on a much bigger scale. For months now, many experts on the Middle East, and not just the off- the- wall doomsday pundits that seem to swarm in the US at any hint of a disaster, have been warning that Syria could be the fuse that ignites the third world war. To quote a word that has just made the online Oxford English Dictionary for the first time, Syria could be the genesis for the mother and father of an omnishambles.

So on that sombre note, lets remember a special anniversary at the end of August, the liberation of Paris in 1944. On August 26 that year, General de Gaulle led the Free French forces in a joyous liberation march down the Champs- Elsyées. Two days previously, the liberation forces had reached the Paris suburbs and on August 25, both eastern and western parts of Paris had been liberated. Paris had surrendered to Nazi Germany on June 14, 1940, a month after the Wermacht had invaded France. The liberation was indeed a joyous moment after four years of Nazi occupation and as for de Gaulle himself, he went on to be a very striking and strident President, from 1958 to 1969. If you walk around Paris these days, you'll often still see plaques set into walls that commemorate members of the resistance who had fallen during the liberation of the city. But it's well to remember how long the Nazi tyranny lasted in comparison with the length of time since the US invaded Iraq on false premises.

If the attacks on Syria go ahead, we could be facing another interminable period of strife and upheaval, possibly something much worse.

Another and much more interesting anniversary took place at the end of this month; on August 26, 1936, the BBC launched the world's first television service, based at Alexandra Palace in London. It lasted until the outbreak of World War II, but in the short time in between, my uncle Basil, a great character indeed, had performed some of his jazz repetoire on the station. Good to know that somewhere in our family tree, we have a TV star hidden way!

Still, these days, one wonders just how useful the television revolution has been; I agree with a letter writer to today's Irish Times who says that so much utter rubbish is being produced on Irish television that people would be much better off if it all closed down. It would also prevent the powers- that- be feeding the populace so much electronic pap to keep them quiet and docile.

Not even the once mighty BBC is free from errors these days. The other day, I swear I heard a BBC announcer say that this August was the 34th anniversary of the assassination of Lord Louis Mountbatten. If I heard the announcer correctly, he said that Mountbatten was killed at Warrenpoint in Co Down; that was totally untrue. He was killed off the Co Sligo coast in the West of Ireland, while on the same day, 18 British soldiers were killed in a bomb attack in Warrenpoint. Just recently, when I heard the BBC describing the bomb attack on the Air India plane that blew up over the Atlantic in 1985, the plane was said to have come down in the Irish Sea. It didn't; it came down in the Atlantic, off the coast of south- west Ireland. But then so much of the BBC's output is questionable these days; if it can't get the small things right, how is it going to fix the big picture?

When you look for instance at the Radio 4 programme schedule, your initial reaction is that there's plenty on but when you fine tune it and listen to some of the programmes, you soon change your mind! The trouble with the BBC, as someone pointed out the other day, it that it is dominated by people who come from a white middle class middle England background, just about the worse source you can imagine for creativity!

Still, the elite as always have their own troubles. In the Bernese Oberland in Switzerland last week, a Spanish adventurer and TV star called Álvaro Bultó was killed when he was involved in a base jumping accident. He had a close liaison with the daughter of the King and Queen of Spain, themselves never far from trouble these days. And on a lighter note, did you see the recent photos of Prince Albert of Monaco in his bathing togs? He's really developed a very unseemly and very unhealthy paunch- there must be plenty of profits to eat in Monaco! But talking of elites, I loved the story about the teenager in Italy who wrote to the Pope. When the teenager was out one day recently, the phone rang and someone left a message on his voicemail to say he'd call back again. And sure enough he did, for an eight minute call. " Pope here", announced the caller- the new Pope does seem a wonderful, down- to- earth kind of person.

Talking about eminent people in the entertainment business, I was reading a very interesting piece the other day about the Greek singer Nana Mouskouri, who is now 78, more or less retired from singing and certainly retired from her duties as a Greek MEP. She's lucky in that she and her husband live outside Greece, in Switzerland. But I remember when we went to a concert given by her in the National Concert Hall in Dublin. It was a wonderful concert, but utterly spoiled because some stupid woman who was sitting right in front of us had drenched herself in perfume that was as intoxicating as toilet cleaner. The smell wafted out over the auditorium, making quite a lot of people feel quite nauseous. Mentioning public performances reminds me that one of the theatres in Dublin has a good show on at the moment, Cats, but when I found out about the price of tickets, they turned out to be €50 each. Add on taxi fares, drinks in the interval, etc, and you're talking about €150 for a night out. That would almost add up to a year's TV licence so that you can spend every evening of the year watching a load of mostly rubbish!

So on to Paris! Last week, there were some really spectacular photos of a fire in the 7th., close to the Hotel des Invalides, not far from the Eiffel Tower. A hotel was being renovated and as so often happens in these situations, the whole place caught fire, sending up plumes of smoke that could be seen all over the city. Still a good friend of mine was telling me the other day about their trip to France this month. Taking their car on the ferry from Ireland to France, an overnight journey in each direction, they drove all the way to Provence and back, just for a week's stay there, but they had a wonderful time, remembered in a stack of bottles of wine nestled on their bookshelves. Who couldn't have a wonderful time in Provence, an enchanting part of France, especially away from the big cities on the coast.

One of the places in the South of France where the residents feel under siege is St Tropez. It's home to Bernard Arnault, who runs LMVH, the world's largest owner of luxury goods, with over 60 major brands to its name, everything from Christian Dior to Moët et Chandon champagne. Arnault is worth €21 billion and is the richest man in France and the 10th such person on the planet. But locals in St Tropez fear that he wants to turn the town into a gigantic bazaar for LMVH brands, encouraging the super rich, who anchor their mega sized yachts offshore or else squeeze them into the harbour, to spend lavishly on his products.

If you go to St Tropez between June and August, it's hell on earth, as the population of the town soars from its permanent level of 6, 000 to 150, 000 and prices go sky high accordingly. But if you go out of season- we visited one December- it's a wholly delightful place, with a small harbour area, fronted by lots of interesting restaurants. It has a fantastic market twice a week and you can visit nearby vineyards, as well as inspecting L'Annonciade, the local musuem, which has paintings and other art works by such artists as Matisse who fell under the spell of St Tropez, which was once a shipbuilding town, back in the 18th century. The town of course is famous for Brigitte Bardot, still resident there, but these days, devoted to a noble cause, animal welfare. The medieval hill village of Ramatuelle is only about 30 minutes drive away and it too is enchanting. But take my advice and don't even think of going to see the place during the peak summer season. The Bakerloo underground line in London is less packed at rush hour!

Back to Paris. A campaign is under way by the tourism board for Paris and the Ile de France to make what is often perceived as gruff service to tourists much more gracious. I've also been a little puzzled at the notion that people in the tourism industry in Paris are less than welcoming; true, there's been the odd incident of standoffish behaviour or less than efficient service, but generally speaking, I've never had any complaints in Paris and have always found the inhabitants of the city perfectly easy to get on with! Perhaps I'm missing something! But it has to be said that sometimes, tourists themselves are to blame. A lot of American tourists just shout, or don't say hello, and don't know a word of French, and then complain that the French treat them rudely.

Another interesting trend about Paris. The Guardian ran an interesting feature the other day about how some hotels in Paris are using their literary connections, very successfully, to market themselves. I take to heart what Marcel Proust once wrote, very tellingly: " The real voyage of discovery consists not of seeking new landscapes but of having new eyes".

In the rather grubby 10th, near the Gare de l'Est, Le Marcel hotel makes the most of its namesake and has named its rooms after the most famous characters that Proust created. In the next door 9th., Les Plumes hotel is devoted to literary lovers, George Sand and Alfred de Musset; Paul Verlaine and Arthur Rimbaud and Juliette Drouet and Victor Hugo. The original literary hotel was of course L'Hotel, a posh place in the St Germain district, where Oscar Wilde died in 1900, having said that either he or the wallpaper had to go. The hotel is still very interesting, despite having been gentrified so much. And of course I should mention our favourite hotel in Paris, the modest Quai Voltaire, opposite the Louvre, where not only Oscar Wilde but other creative characters such as Wagner, once stayed.

It's all a long way from the story of something funny peculiar that happened to us once in Luxembourg once. We had been in Germany for a while and travelled there by train only to find an unusual surprise when we went to check in at the hotel we had pre- booked some time previously, before we had left Dublin. When we walked into the hotel, we could see very clearly into the bar, which was adjacent to the lobby. On closer inspection- you always have to check out these things very carefully!- I was amazed to see some very scantily dressed women, young and not so young, sitting at the bar. A careful recce revealed that the hotel was in fact one of the local brothels, no doubting servicing many of the personnel who work in the various EU offices in Luxembourg!I n the best traditions of tabloid journalism, we made our excuses and left and soon found a modern hotel right opposite the railway station. It had all the usual hotel facilities but after the previous establishment was so dull!

Still, we found Luxembourg city itself rather enchanting. Its old fortifications are a UNESCO heritage site and the city is full of gorgeous gorges, as well as a splendid twice weekly market in the place Guillaume, the cathedral of Nôtre Dame was once a 17th century Jesuit church, while the 16th century ducal palace, where the royal family lives, is equally interesting. Certain parts of it are open to visitors, but only until the beginning of September.

Outside the capital, we found the wine district along the banks of the Moselle very interesting and went to a vineyard in Remich for some delightful tasting of some Germanic- style wines. Then on a wet Sunday afternoon, we found ourselves having lunch is a very old hotel, full of character and characters, in the centre of the steel making town of Esch- sur- Alzette, n the south- west of Luxmebourg. We also satisfied our curiosity by taking a short stroll out of town and in France, with absolutely no sign anywhere of a frontier.

Luxembourg is a small country, with a population of just half a million, but despite being sandwiched between France, Germany and Belgium, I t retains a strong identity. Parts of the country are very rural, like the forested Ardennes in the north and Little Switzerland" around Mullerthal in the east. French and German are the main languages, but there's also the local dialect, Luxembourgish, although during our time there, we didn't see or hear much evidence of it.

I would strongly recommend Luxembourg as a delightful small place to enjoy a holiday, but do keep out of the brothels posing as hotels!

September 4, 2013

Heading home

There's no doubt about it, France is one of the best countries in the world for a retired person to live in. Recent figures show that while the average monthly salary of someone who is in work in France is €1, 735, the average income for pensioners is around €1, 500 a month.

A French economist, Henri Sterdyniak, says that pensioners are among the most privileged groups in the country, while younger people are much less well treated. In general, the gap in living standards between those who are still in work and those who are retired is only nine per cent in France, compared to 20 per cent in the UK.

The pensions that are paid to people in France have been steadily improving over the past 40 years. When the Sécurité Sociale was started in 1945, at the end of the Second World War, people reaching 65 could expect a pension that was 45 per cent of their final salary. By 1972, this figure had risen 50 per cent, but since then, the increases have been dramatic. However, in 1993, pensions started to be indexed to prices rather than to salaries, which meant that for some pensioners, the amount they got started to decrease. Today, although most pensioners in France are comparatively well off, there are still 10 per cent of pensioners who are on the basic monthly State pension of €787. Other European countries pay pensions equal to what's available in France, but where France scores is that compared with other European countries, ike Ireland, the cost of living is far cheaper. It costs 30 per cent more to live in Ireland than it does in France; in Ireland, the big mark- up in retail prices compared to other countries, like France and the UK, is still the order of the day. No wonder that big store groups from outside Ireland, that operate in Ireland, sometimes call the place "treasure island"!

One symbol for younger people in France is, however, creating a lot of problems- the love padlocks that have been placed over the years on the bridges of Paris. It's a demonstration of love that has become too popular; now, the city council says that there's a risk of love padlocks causing lumps of masonry to fall off some bridges onto the many tourist boats that ply the Seine. One bridge in particular has attracted people wanting to declare their love for their partner, the Pont des Arts, which is absolutely festooned with love padlocks. On this particular bridge, the sheer quantity of love padlocks is starting the damage the parapet, creating the possibility of bits of masonry falling onto boats below. So there are now reports that the city council is secretly removing as many love padlocks as possible from bridges at high risk and binning them. The whole trend of placing love padlocks began in Italy and there, the authorities are far stricter. On the Ponte Milvio in Rome, they are banned, while on the much more famous Ponte Vecchio in Florence, the local authority has removed them altogether. Here in Dublin, some landmarks are festooned with love locks, like the Ha'penny Bridge.

Another icon of France, especially for tourists, has also come a cropper. The Canal du Midi in south- western France was constructed in the 17th century and opened in 1682. It runs for 240 kms and it's so popular that 50, 000 tourists take boating holidays along it every year. One of the big scenic attractions has long been the plane trees that line its banks, but now, the ravages of a fungus are all too evident. When American troops arrived in France towards the end of the second world war, the munitions they brought with them were stored in wooden boxes.

These boxes contained an American fungus, ceratocystis platani, which was first spotted in the trees lining the Canal du Midi back in 2006. Already, about 15, 000 trees have either been felled, or are about to be felled, and the tree experts believe that all 42, 000 trees lining the canal will have to be cut down over the next 20 years.

It could cost up to €200 million to plant new trees, but recently, when the Voies Navigables de France, the country's inland waterways organisation, appealed for private donations in the absence of any national or local funding, to help the replanting programme, the results were derisory to say the least. The first three weeks of the campaign only brought in 30 donations, some as low as €20.

It's often said that when the French look for a scapegoat for their ills, they pin the blame on the Americans. In the case of the Canal du Midi, t is literally true. Which makes the support that President Hollande wants to give the US in punishing Syria for that country's government allegedly using chemical weapons, all the more strange. True, the French have a close interest in Syria, since it was once part of the French colonial empire, but most people in France, like those in the UK, are vehemently opposed to France helping to launch missile strikes against Syria.

Such missile strikes could literally open the Pandora's Box of the Middle East conflicts. President Assad of Syria wasn't so far off the mark the other day when he said that the whole Middle East is like a powder keg and that an American led attack on his country could well be the spark that causes the whole lot to blow up.

Just yesterday, September 3, I heard a clip from one of the most famous radio speeches of all times, that made by UK prime minister Neville Chamberlain, on September 3, 1939, when he declared that since Germany had ignored the ultimatum to withdraw from Poland, Britain was now at war with Germany. No matter how many times you hear this speech, I t still has a chilling effect, and the way things are going in the Middle East, we might well be hearing its present day counterpart any time soon.

It all reminds me of a very strange occurrence last Thursday morning in British Columbia, the far western province of Canada. There, in a normally sedate suburb called Terrace, residents were woken up by a strange noise coming from the sky, which they later said sounded like the trumpets of the Apocalypse. A local resident was woken up by the noise; she'd heard something very similar back in June, but not nearly as strongly. She got her video camera, went outside and recorded the whole phenomenon. It's been widely reported in the media in British Columbia, but doesn't seem to have caused any stir outside Canada. I've seen and heard the short videos and I must say I agree with the residents of Terrace and their description of the noise coming from the skies, that it sounded like the trumpets of doom.

There's damnation too facing France's winegrowers. This year is going to see the worst grape harvest for the past 40 years, because earlier this year, France had so much cold, wet weather, with lots of hail storms that caused immense damage to the vines. The end result is that this year's wine production is expected to be 43. 5 million hectolitres, well below average, making this year's wine production even worse than last year's. So cheers/ santé while you can!

Still, despite all the doom and gloom, the antics of French screen actor Gérard Depardieu are always good for a smile. He's just been made an honorary citizen of Belgium, having settled in his new home at Nechin, literally just across the border from France. The tax laws in Belgium are far less onerous than the proposed top rate of tax of 75 per cent in France, so many wealthy French people, like Depardieu, have decamped to Belgium. At the beginning of this year, Depardieu was also given honorary Russian citizenship and by now, the actor is thought to own passports from a total of eight countries!

This month sees the 70th anniversary of the first publication of the book about the Little Prince, by Antoine de Saint- Exupéry. He was a fascinating character, an aristocrat, a writer, an aviator, an inveterate womaniser, and even though this metaphsyical book for children is only 100 pages long, it has caught the world's imagination ever since it has published. By now, I t has been translated into some 250 languages around the world. The end of the little prince is almost a preview of the end of the writer himself, when his military plane crashed into the Mediterranean in July, 1944, ess than a year after his famous book was first published. Did the end of his life imitate the end of the little prince, did Saint- Exupéry have an inbuilt desire to reach the end of his life just the same as the little prince? We will never know, but the endless speculation continues.

If you go to the astonishing air and space museum at the old Le Bourget airport in Paris, there's a big permanent exhibition devoted to the book and the man who wrote it. There's also La Boutique du Petit Prince, at 57 boulevard Arago in the 13th., close to the Paris observatory. There's even an online boutique devoted to the little prince.

Still the tourists keep coming to Paris, the world's favourite tourist destination. Paris hoteliers have seen more visitors this year than last, with numbers up close on 10 per cent. However, elsewhere in the country, the news hasn't been so good. Tourist numbers are down by 10 per cent in Languedoc- Roussillon and 30 per cent in the Dordogne. But visitor numbers are up in Brittany and Normandy, on the northern coast of France, presumably mainly because of more visitors from the UK.

At least, the French judicial system has done something very favourable for the tourist industry. Plans to build four huge wind turbines 25 km south of Mont Saint Michel have been thrown out by a court in Rennes. The plan was to build these 140 metre high turbines on land that was 95 metres above sea level; on a clear day, they would have been easily visible from Mont Saint Michel, which attracts 2. 5 million tourists a year. Already, five other plans to build wind turbines around the bay surrounding Mont Saint Michel have been thrown out. The latest decision is very welcome, a contrast to the gay abandon with which wind turbines have been scattered across many landscapes in Britain and to a lesser extent, Ireland. The benefit of wind turbines in generating electricity is debatable;they are fine if they are "planted" in clusters at sea, but to destroy so many beautiful landscapes seems little short of daft. That court decision in Rennes was as sensible as the one in the House of Commons in London last week against British government plans to attack Syria.

I was reading the other day about another very sensible decision taken in Paris in the 1920s, not to proceed with a mad architetectural design. The Swiss architect Le Corbusier had come up with a grand plan to demolish most of the then very run-down 3rd and 4th arrondissements in Paris and built 18 enormous glass skyscrapers that would form a new business and government district. Those areas of Paris were then very delapidated and Le Corbusier called their inhabitants "troglodytes", which wasn't very diplomatic. He wanted to move them all to new garden cities around the fringes of Paris, although Le Corbusier wanted to preserve certain historical places like the Palais Royal and the place des Vosges. But very fortunately, nothing ever came of his grandiose plan, which was just as well!

One new book that's just come out about French history seems very interesting and I look forward to reading it. It's the story of the Huguenots, the French Protestants. Their expulsion from France was that country's loss and a great gain for other countries where they settled, such as the Netherlands, Britain and Ireland. The book is published by Yale University Press, whose publishing standards are legendary. There's also a very interesting sounding new French film out, called La Maison de la Radio, a documentary about working life in the great round building in the 16th arrondissement in Paris that houses the French state broadcaster, ORTF.

The past few days has seen an outpouring of grief and affection for one of the world's greatest poets, probably the greatest of the late 20th century, Seamus Heaney. It's telling that the last message he sent his wife from his hospital bed, minutes before he died, was a Latin text saying simply "noli temere"- don't be afraid. He was a man of tremendous personal moral integrity, quite apart from his genius as a poet, and he is now up there with the other Irish literary greats, including Joyce, Yeats and Beckett. In modern times, with all the available medical technology, Heaney should have had another 20 years writing ahead of him; poetry often does get even better as the poet gets older, but in the case of Seamus Heaney, we'll not now see this. We didn't know him at all, but curiously, we know his charming down to earth wife, Marie, well. One of the troubles with Seamus was that he could never say no, so that if he was invited to some interesting literary event, no matter where it was in the world, he'd say "yes" and pack his bags. It must have worn him out, literally. Sad to see another media great departing, at the same age, 74, Sir David Frost, who managed to keep his television career going at full throttle for 50 years. When I was a typical rebellious teenager, I really enjoyed Frost's first outing on television 50 years ago, with the programe, That Was The Week That Was. It was unheard of for the BBC so be so unstuffy, even anti- establishment, and it made for great viewing, even though by today's trolling standards, it was so tame.

I can't finish these musing without mentioning a case that has come up today, that illustrates perfectly the frequent absurdities and injustices of Ireland 's legal and administrative system. A well-known media figure here, John Waters, parked his car in a town just south of Dublin, one day in 2011, while he did some shopping. He paid for his parking ticket and when he returned to his car, he found that he still had four minutes left on it. This hadn't deterred a local jobsworth from issuing a parking fine. Waters quite rightly, refused to pay the fine for something he wasn't guilty of, but nevertheless, was found guilty. The whole saga ended yesterday when he got sent to prison; it turned out that he had to spend just 45 minutes in a cell before being released and of course today, he is making a meal out of this absolute legal farce.

But at least to end on a pleasant topical note. Too often, online advertisements are as boring and forgettable as their offline counterparts. But this week, some sections of the online media in France have been running really stunning ads for autumn holidays in the Auvergne. he autumnal colours are really brilliant and they do make one want to pack one's bags and head off! Lovely advertising and it really works!

September 11, 2013

September 11

September 11 is of course a day that will live on in history for its infamy, the attack on the twin towers in New York and as long as history itself survives, the many theories about the attack will continue, drawing lovers of conspiracy theories everywhere. This day also marks another anniversary, in France.

September 11, 1968, was the day that an Air France Caravelle en route from Corsica to Nice crashed into the sea off Nice with the loss of all 95 people on board. I was reminded of the tragedy by an In Memoriam notice in this morning's Irish Times. An Irishman, Arthur J. O'Connor, was on board and his death, is marked 45 years later by a memorial notice from his family who say in the notice that his loss still runs deep.

The Caravelle was quite an advanced passenger jet of its time, unique because passengers boarded from the rear, underneath the plane. But inside the plane was perfectly comfortable and I can testify to that having been on several Caravelle flights. But the reason for that 1968 crash has long remained shrouded in mystery. Then in 2007, the BBC's Radio 4 broadcast a programme about it, theorising that the crash had been caused by either a missile or a bomb and that subsequent French governments had suppressed the true cause of the crash. In May, 2011, a former high ranking official in the French military,

Michel Laty, confirmed these theories. He said in a programme on the TF1 television channel in France that the plane had been hit by a missile that had been wrongly fired during a test by the French army.

A contemporary piece of news about France, released over the past couple of days, is equally damning about the current state of the country. Le Figaro, the newspaper and website, used figures from the interior ministry to produce a chart showing how aggression and attacks by delinquents had increased dramatically in the 12 months from August, 2012 to July, 2013, on a département by département basis. The worst département was La Vienne, where the number of attacks was up by 32. 4 per cent. Many other parts of France have produced figures that are almost as bad. Les Hautes- Alpes are up by 17. 7 per cent, for instance, but the figures for Les Cotes d'Armor in Brittany (+ 14. 7 per cent) and La Manche (+ 14. 4 per cent) show comparatively modest increases.

All the while, the hapless Hollande, the underfire French president, has come under even more attack for his promise that France will support the US in any military attack on Syria. Polls show that close on two- thirds of the French people are opposed to any such move and Hollande has been attacked for being a mere lackey of the US. A satirical programme on French television the other day went even further.

It showed President Hollande visiting a school in the company of US President Obama. Hollande was depicted asking Obama: " S'il vous plait, monsieur le président, veulez- vous m' excuser. Je veux faire pipi". In other words, Hollande was asking permission to take a leak and the French public obviously lapped up the biting satire. I can 't see Hollande behaving like the admirable new Pope, who seems totally down- to- earth, determined to place the Roman Catholic church on the side of the people, rather than any elites. The latest news has him pictured driving around the Vatican in a modest 20 year old car that was donated to him by an Italian priest.

But talking of presidents reminds me of another shameful episode in French life. Before François Mitterand died in 1996, he had his last meal with a group of close friends. He was eating a traditional French songbird, the ortolan, which is an especially popular tradition in south- west France. The bird is cooked in Armagnac and when people eat them, they do so with a napkin over their heads so that they can savour all the aromas from the bird. It's also said that this hides their shame from God. I always thought Mitterand was an exceedingly politically astute president, who left a fine legacy, I ncluding the new national library in Paris, but when I heard about his last act, eating ortolans, I was absolutely disgusted. Maybe a lot of French people feel differently, but to me it totally degraded his legacy.

The ortolans are under serious threat and the German-run Committee against Bird Slaughter now alleges that the French authorities are colluding with poachers by not imposing the conservation rules and regulations designed to protect this seriously endangered species.

I felt much more positive about a property story from Devon that I read the other day. A couple who have a large house on a substantial estate in the Teign Valley near Exeter are selling up, because they are moving to France. But on the estate, every variety of animal that can be found in Devon lives on the estate, fallow deer, badgers, dormice, cats, pheasants, you name it, they are all there and all incredibly tame. The deer often come up to the windows and the badgers have races on the patio. That sounds my kind of place and if I had the odd million or so euro to spare, I'd be tempted to purchase!

But at least, one traditional season is fast coming up, which presents joyous occasions for people, including tourists, to savour one of the great traditions of France, its wine making. Wine fairs will be taking place over the next few weeks in all the wine regions of France to celebrate what is admittedly a very mediocre harvest this year. One of the most interesting celebrations will be coming up in the Montmartre district of Paris which has its own vinous enclave. Another long standing tradition in France is already under way, the 39th American film festival at Deauville. Many stars will be appearing, so there'll be all the usual publicity. But I must admit: I've never warmed to Deauville. It's so chic, so upmarket, and so fashionable that the atmosphere is icy. By contrast, its twin town of Trouville, with its fish market and Les Vapeurs seafood restaurant, is so warm and down to earth that it's an absolute delight. We well remember our time in Trouville and the small hotel we stayed in. The owner had a great love of cats, so there were plenty of them around. We had them all round us while we were having our breakfast!

Meanwhile, I see that a member of the journalistic profession has disgraced himself in Lugano, in the Italian- speaking part of Switzerland, to my mind, the most attractive part of Switzerland. It's the most easy going, with all the positive elements of Italian living combined with Swiss efficiency (you don't go to Italy itself in search of any kind of efficiency!). Anyway, the other evening, at the Meno Uno gallery in Lugano, one of those invited was a reporter from Radio Switzerland International, who was getting fired up on all the cocktails. He reached over for a canapé and in the process sent a priceless sculpture flying. It was a famous work done by the Italian sculptor Lucciana Fabro in 1962- 64, designed as an impression of planet earth. When the reporter accidentally knocked it to the floor, it smashed into thousands of pieces. The sculpture was said to represent the longevity of the earth, so if you want, you can read something deeply symbolic into what happened.

Back in France, as is so often the case, there and everywhere else, when the media should be reporting lots of serious stuff, I t concentrates on the trifling. Online news websites tend to push the boat out more than the traditional news media, so in that respect they are good. France has planet. fr but from time to time it goes seriously astray looking for fluffy news.

Within the last few days, t has run big stories on which male stars have small zizis and which female stars have managed to show their knickers in public, all very elevated if you're interested in that sort of story! It also ran a story about the model Zahia, who was previously famous for allegedly having under- age sex with some French football stars. Not long ago, she opened her own lingerie and cake shop in Paris and now she's had to deny an onslaught of rumours that she has had her breasts surgically augmented. Now she has gone public on Twitter, citing a letter from a surgeon who specialises in such matters to say that her breasts are 100 per cent natural. Excellent news!

Talking about the media reminds me of a big feature the other day in the New York Times all about the cultural attractions of Marseilles. The article was very comprehensive and stated quite rightly that the city has an outstanding array of old and new art centres, museums and other places devoted to the arts and culture generally. Down near the end of the article was a small paragraph saying "oh by the way, Marseilles does have a crime problem". That was an understatement to say the least; crime and Marseilles are synonymous and in a recent attack, the son of the sport director of Olympique de Marseille football club was gunned down. The 30 year old Adrien Anigo was running a brasserie in the city but had been questioned by police over a series of jewellery store robberies. He was shot dead in broad daylight as he drove his rented car. Marseilles may be full of cultural glitter, but more than 20 per cent of its residents live below the poverty line and some estates have over 40 per cent youth unemployment.

This particular article highlights a perceived failing in the New York Times; it's often seen as too pro- establishment, too complacent with the status quo and too often missing the real questions. Its new ceo is one Mark Thompson, a former director-general of the BBC, whom many believe to have been tainted by the numerous scandals in recent years at the BBC. In contrast, the Washington Post is much more sceptical in its approach and has solid news reporting. Ironically, it has been taken over by Jeff Bezos the online entrepreneur, the man behind Amazon, and his takeover might actually be good for the newspaper! A lot of people swear that the New York Times is the best paper in the

US, but I actually prefer the Washington Post because it's far sharper.

The process of debunking myths continues, however, in certain quarters. A new book has just been published all about Edith Piaf, which says that she came into the world in a hospital in the 20th arrondissement, not on the streets, as per the common myth; neither was she weaned on red wine! The author of Piaf, a French Myth is Robert Belleret, a former journalist with Le Monde, so his credentials are good. He also points that one of Piaf's great talents was spotting talent and she started the careers of such international stars as Charles Aznavour, Yves Montand and Georges Moustaki. It's also well worth going to see the small private museum about Piaf in the Ménilmontant district of the 20th, close to the Père Lachaise cemetery where she's buried.

This in fact is the only museum dedicated to the great chanteuse and it consists of two rooms in the fourth floor flat of Bernard Marchois, a long time Piaf fan. Entrance is free but donations are appreciated. The tiny museum is only open from Mondays to Wednesdays, from 13h00 to 18h00 and you have to phone in advance (4355 5272) to gain admittance.

September 18, 2013

New beginnings?

E very day, my email inbox announces all kinds of so-called "goodies" from providers of services and products in France. If I took up half of them, I'd be rich, thin and preposterously happy with a vast spread of consumer items around me! Normally, they are just deleted as soon as they come in, but one email I get from time to intrigues me a little. It's from a clairvoyant called Isabelle, living in Versailles and the strange thing about her emails is that they are remarkably prescient. She's always asking me to sign up for this that or the other package, an offer of course that I never take up. But I must admit that the email I got from her the other day was quite startling.

She said that over the next few weeks, events not only in France, but in Europe, indeed the whole of the world, will determine the future of world history. Perhaps there's something in all that. Perhaps dramatic events will happen shortly that will shape all our futures? Who knows? Perhaps Russia's extraordinary foreign minister, Sergei Lavrov, who's managed to run many rings around the West over Syria, has something else up his sleeve! But very often, in following world events, it's often as well to think outside the box rather than taking the often limited and conventional wisdom that's often pushed in the traditional mass media.

I had another instance of that this week, when the news came through from an amateur weather forecaster in New Zealand, Ken Ring. Working by phases of the moon, he provides forward forecasts of the long term weather in Ireland that are so accurate it's incredible. Back at the beginning of the year, he gave a forecast of the summer of 2013 in Ireland that in retrospect turned out to be 100 per cent accurate, as we enjoyed the best summer since 2006. His forecast for the weeks and months up to the end of this year is for reasonably mild weather, with no snow until December and certainly no snow on Christmas Day. What is particularly amazing about this particular forecaster is that he also predicted with great accuracy the terrible earthquake in Christchurch on New Zealand's South Island a couple of years ago. No- one has ever managed to accurately predict earthquakes before, so this was quite a revelation.

From this coming Monday, drivers in France will also get a taste of the future, the new EU driving licence. I got mine earlier this year and it's the same size as a credit card, with all the details included in a very small space. The plan is to have identical driving licences right across the EU and what has already happened in Ireland is about to happen in France. This small example of greater EU integration comes at a time when the Front National in France seems to be making big gains. Last Friday, in the centre of Nice, a Lebanese- born jeweller called Stéphane Turk was opening up his jewellery shop for business when he was accosted by two teenage robbers. He promptly pulled out a gun and shot dead one of his assailants, a 19 year old. The case has aroused enormous interest in France.

The Facebook page set up to support him had got close on two million messages for him by Sunday morning, making it the biggest ever online petition in French history. A former right wing French prime minister, François Fillon, has encouraged voters in next March's municipal elections to transfer their second rounds of votes to the Front National. Marine Le Pen, the leader of the party, says that the UMP party of former presidents Chirac and Sarkozy is imploding and that in the upcoming municipal elections, she expects her party to win 1, 000 council seats in south-east and north- east France, as well as gain a slew of mayorships in those regions. The Front National, apart from its "France for the French" ideology, is also highly sceptical about the process of European integration and wants to pull France out of the eurozone, which of course if it happened, would make the eurozone unworkable.

There were other unmistakeable signs of present day France as well this week, especially in the story about the Louvre. Standards entry tickets to the famed art museum cost €11. 60 and €13. 60, which are reasonable amounts. But it turns out that many visitors from Asia, especially China, have been unknowingly presenting tickets that are perfect fakes. In April this year, customs authorities in Belgium gave the French authorities the tip- off that they had discovered a substantial quantity of forged entry tickets to the Louvre en route to France. Nothing it seems is sacred these days!

We also had a vision of the future the other day when the solar powered boat, PlanetSolar, arrived on the Seine in Paris at the end of a 20, 000 km long scientific voyage. The boat had travelled from Florida and the Bahamas to track changes in the Atlantic Gulf Stream. It's the largest solar powered boat in the world and it proves that it's perfectly possible to use the sun as propulsion power for marine vessels.

Meanwhile, here in Ireland, there was another glimpse of technology that enthralled many people, myself included, the Flightfest last Sunday in Dublin. Some 30 aircraft representing every decade in aviation since the 1930s flew up the River Liffey at a height of about 240 metres. The star of the show was the new Airbus A380, capable of taking 800 passengers, and the largest passenger aircraft in the world, in the livery of British Airways. Ryanair as usual was cheeky; on the underside of its plane was the slogan: " You can't beat d Irish". Wags were also saying that this was the first time Ryanair had flown so close to a city centre! Dublin hadn't seen anything like it since Alan Cobham brought his flying circus to Dublin and Ireland and that was in 1933.

Meanwhile, the Lonely Planet has come out with some top places to visit in Ireland. It says that Mullaghmore Head in Co Sligo, on the west coast, is one of the best places in the world to go surfing, the waves are so spectacular. It also recommends Croagh Patrick mountain in Co Mayo, also in the west of Ireland, as an ultimate pilgrimage destination. The Lonely Planet also recommends Castle Leslie in Co Monaghan, for its horses, its historic house and its touch of eccentricity. One of its inhabitants is 96 year old Sir John Leslie, who still has a taste for night clubbing, discovered when he was a young man in his 70s! But like all stories, there's also a dark side behind two of these places, but then of course, tourist publicity never tells you about them!

Mullaghmore is today a fairly prosperous and well developed seaside holiday village but it was in the bay there in 1979 that Lord Louis Mounbatten was one of four members of a boating party who were killed when their boat was blown up by the IRA. Similarly, there's a dark story behind Castle Leslie, for it was there in 2002 that Sir Paul McCartney made his disastrous marriage to Heather Mills.

Sometimes, however, the most unexpected can provide good news. I've a good friend here in Dublin who specialises in antiquarian books He set up a bookshop about two years ago to put his passion for books into practice, but in the recession that has engulfed Ireland during the past five years, antiquarian books weren't anywhere near the top of shopping lists. All that has changed within the last couple of weeks. The unexpected death of that great poet Seamus Heaney has led to a surge in demand for copies of his books that were signed by himself and a welcome boost in trade for this antiquarian bookseller. As another bookseller friend of mine said to me the other day, it's an ill wind and all that.

But a couple of stories about the media here in Ireland show how much things have changed. In RTÉ, a reporter called Joe O'Brien did an excellent job for years in reporting on all matters agricultural and he managed to combine that job with reporting on security issues, especially with the Irish Army, a strange combination indeed! But Joe retired last November and since then, he hasn't been replaced. The station has finally admitted that it has no intention of replacing him, since it can't afford what's involved, despite the fact that the farming industry in Ireland is still one of its biggest sectors, and an indigenous one at that.

But sadly, last week marked the 21st anniversary of one of the great Irish newspaper editors, J. J. Walsh, otherwise known as Smokey Joe. For something like four decades, he owned and edited the Munster Express in Waterford, in the days when local newspapers could be voluminous. The amount of local news it carried was just as amazing. Smokey Joe himself was incredible, a great source of stories. One of the best concerns his toupée. It was long rumoured that he used to keep a salt cellar in his office and that when he went out to functions, he'd sprinkle salt on his collar to give the impression of dandruff!

Other stories about him are legion. He also owned a lot of property in Waterford and it so happened that many of his younger staff lived in flats and bedsits that he owned. Long battles went on when they wanted their pay raised, but eventually, with the help of the unions, he gave way, just a little. The delighted reporters would find modest raises in their pay packets, only to discover that a week or so later, their rents had gone up by an amount equivalent to their pay rise. Smokey Joe was a great character, very flamboyant, of a type that you just don't find in the present day media, so it was rather surprising to find last week that although his family still continues to own what is now a tabloid sized rather than a broadsheet newspaper, his annual In Memoriam notice had been airbrushed out of history. It simply didn't appear in the family paper. However, he was included in his wife's In Memoriam notice at the end of November. It was all rather reminiscent of what happened recently in France when President Hollande was having official photographs taken. One showed him grinning from ear to ear—what he has to grin about I'm not sure—but it didn't fit the official image and was promptly banned. Needless to remark that photo has since appeared all over the place and now it seems one of the American TV satirical shows is going to do a piece about it.

Still, looking back can produce some fine programming. The Reunion programme on the BBC's Radio 4 last week was compelling listening; a group of people from Jersey in the Channel Islands, who had been teenagers at the time, recalled what happened when Nazi forces overran the Channel Islands, especially Jersey, during the second world war. The accuracy of everyone's recall was amazing.

I also recall another telling moment in history, one that I experienced myself. In October, 1987, we were on vacation in Aix-es-Bains, a delightful small town beside Lac du Bourget, a mere 34 km from Annency in the south-east of France, close to the Alps and the Swiss border. Those two towns are delightful and well worth visiting, but what really struck in my mind was what I saw on Tuesday, October 20, 1987. That day, I took the train from Aix-les-Bains to Geneva. I was en route to Lausanne to meet a publisher for whom I was then working. It's what I saw when I disembarked from the train at Geneva that still astonishes me: the newspaper billboards at the kiosks in the station were full of the dramatic news that the day before, Black Monday, October 19, 1987, had seen the first of the great recent world financial crises, when the Dow Jones lost a quarter of its value in a single day. During our holiday, we had deliberately avoided all news, so I'd had no inkling that Black Monday had happened, until I saw those billboards in Geneva. It was a powerful reminder of the power of the press in those days and nowadays, I just don't think that the same frisson from breaking news could ever be repeated in these days of instant, online, digital news.

September 25, 2013

At last, purrfect news from Paris

I t's purrfectly believable, a new café in Paris where you can go to caress cats. It's a lovely idea, that originated in Japan, where apartments are generally too small for people to keep pets. The Parisian equivalent, the Café des Chats, opened last Saturday at 16, rue Michel Lecomte in the third arrondissement, right in the centre of the city.

Cat lovers can go and sup tea or chocolate, or nibble on patisserie, all the while caressing some of the numerous cats in the place. There's just one problem; the café has been a victim of its own success. The café can seat just 30 people, but hundreds have been turning up, hoping forlornly to gain entry.

Another good idea is about to come up in France, a two hour show devoted to the works of Edith Piaf, that legendary chanteuse, who died exactly 50 years ago, on October 10, 1963, in the Provençal perfume town of Grasse, just inland from Nice. She died from a ruptured aneurism, the result of excessive consumption of alcohol and morphine. But she was excessive in her talents, which flowed in abundance, and were well appreciated in her native France while she was still alive (there's little or no point in being appreciated after departure!) and she was the first French popular singer to break into the American market.

Recently, Francophiles in New York organised a retro concert devoted to her music and performed by leading contemporary artists; it was staged at the Beacon Theater in New York and the whole show was recorded for television. It's being screened on France 2 on October 5, then again on October 10 on TV5.

Meanwhile, a great chronicler of pop music has died suddenly. Gilles Verlant, a native of Brussels, was renowned in France for his telling portraits of musical legends. He began his career by working for RTBF, the State-run broadcasting network in Belgium, before moving to France. He wrote biographies of many leading players in the music game, including Serge Gainsbourg, David Bowie and Françoise Hardy. In 2010 he started a series for Radio France chronicling the scandalous history of rock, which was broadcast on the local stations of the France Bleu network and on France Info. That series continued right up to his tragic death last week at the comparatively young age of 56; the mortal accident that happened to him is something that 's all too easy to do. He fell down a flight of stairs at home, a sad end to a legendary teller of musical tales.

Incidentally, if you're flush with cash, plenty of it, and have a taste for nostalgia, you could have a look at the extraordinary apartment that's up for sale in the 16th., for a mere €6. 1 million. It was occupied in the late 1960s by Brigitte Bardot and the man to whom she was briefly married, Gunter Sachs. The place was a mini palace, with its own private disco, its own billiards room and a host of other features, all decorated in very dubious taste.

Brigitte's name has been taken in vain by a comedy performer, who calls herself Frigide Barjot. Her real name is Virginie Merle, born 51 years ago in Boulogne-Billancourt in western Paris. She made a name for herself as a humorist, a columnist and a political activist. In her younger days, she was renowned for her raunchy, bitingly satirical stage act. She was also a member of a band called Dead Pompidous and one of the two films she appeared in was called Make Love to Me with Two Fingers, in which she took off Brigitte Bardot. Incidentally her present punny stage name of Frigide Bardot means in literal translation, " frigid bonkers".

This year, her career has taken an abrupt turn that hasn't turned out well for her. She emerged as the leader of the many large scale demonstrations against gay marriage. She's also a ferocious opponent of giving adoption rights to lesbian, gay and transgender (LGBT) couples. Both these viewpoints are enormously popular in France, as was evident from the huge turnouts at all the demonstrations. What the government plans to do in the name of civil rights is clearly totally at odds with what many in the electorate believe. But it s all gone wrong for Frigide Barjot since she is now on the receiving end of much hate mail from the far right spectrum of the anti-gay rights and anti-LGBT adoption movement, so much so that she is now distancing herself from the whole phenomenon.

She's also been having troubles on the home front. Her husband is Bruno Tellene, also known as Basile de Koch. He was a speech writer for Charles Pasqua, a very right wing politician from Corsica. Anyway, Frigide and Bruno live in a a chaotic apartment in the 15th., and they've been appealing against an expulsion order. They had been letting the Societé Jalons, a group of students who organise humorous happenings, use part of their flat and the landlord considered that as a result, they had broken their tenancy agreement. So they've been busy appealing against this verdict and hope to get it overturned in the appropriate court in Paris.

There are fireworks of another kind under way at the moment, the natural autumnal fireworks that can be enjoyed in many landscapes at the moment in central and northern France. Some of the best displays of natural colours, as the trees turn, are to be found in the wine regions, such as the Loire valley, where the autumn colours are starting to flourish, or a few short but utterly magnificent weeks.

There's news too on the transport front, with another of the Métro lines in Paris due to have driverless trains. It's Line Number 4, which runs from Porte de Clignancourt in the north of the city to the Mairie de Montrouge in the south. The line has stations at the Gare du Nord and the Gare de l'Est and it runs beneath the lle de la Cité. This line also has the station with the fantastic name, Montparnasse Bienvenue, possibly the most onomatopoeiac of all Métro station names. The work on making this line automatic is due to be completed in 2019.

It's a long time of course since the first fully automatic line was opened, 2005 to be precise. It was the Météor line, from Gare St Lazare to the national library, named after the president who commissioned it, François Mitterand. In 2007, a major new extension of this line brought it to Les Olympiades, in the 13th., a resident town of skyscrapers built between 1969 and 1974 and noted for having Chinatown on its southern edge.

Also on the theme of transport, the 25th modern tram network in France was opened recently, in Tours. The 15 km long north-south line has 29 stops and it all cost €433 million to build. In recent years, the rollout of new tram networks, not just in Paris but in many other urban centres has been impressive.

I was also reminded this week of an impressive Irish restaurant in Paris, that we tried and enjoyed, many years ago. On BBC Radio 4, Myrtle and Darina Allen were talking about the famous Ballymaloe cookery school in Ireland; one bright idea was taking over La Ferme Irlandais in Paris, just over 30 years ago, as a showcase for fresh Irish produce. It was in the place du Marché St Honoré in the 1st and one of the best of the Allen ideas was staging Irish Sunday brunches, which became enormously popular. It popped up, long before anyone had invented the concept of pop-up restaurants.

Another reference to Ireland came up with all the news about Billy Connolly's illnesses. It's only a few short months since he appeared at the convention and entertainment centre in Killarney, Co Kerry, and made himself deeply unpopular. The centre has a resident photographer, a young woman who has won many awards for her outstanding work. In the middle of his show, Connolly spotted her moving around the auditorium taking photos of the event and to signal his displeasure he unleashed an absolute torrent of abuse against the photographer, using language that shocked even long time fans of his. He got absolutely no plaudits for that performance, but in retrospect, I t could be put down to his illnesses. Anyway, he is now saying that when it's time for him to go he wants his ashes scattered over Loch Lomond, while a plane is skywriting the infamous Brendan Behan quote: " Fuck the begrudgers".

It's also true to note that these days, there seems to be a law against everything and anything enjoyable and sometimes, it can mean depriving people of a long treasured tradition. We have a perfect example here in our part of Dublin. St Bartholomew's church has clocks on the four faces of its tower and up to recently, the bells rang out every quarter of an hour. Then someone complained that the bells were annoying them at night time, so rather than risk a big fine from the city council for noise pollution, the clocks and the bells have been stopped completely. Unless a resolution to this impasse is found, a 130 year old tradition in the neighbourhood is going to be stilled for good.

I must end this week's epistle with a delightful typo from The Irish Times. Very recently, it ran an article about how people in Ireland, thanks to better diet and healthcare, are now much taller than they used to be. The article concluded by saying that "the average Irish male, born in 1980, is now 1. 76 cm tall". Now you know why Ireland is called the land of the little people!

October 2, 2013

Carla forgets her words

A n embarrassing moment for Carla Bruni-Sarkozy, wife of the former French president. The other night, when she was singing at a gala function in Paris to raise funds for research into Alzheimer's disease, what did she do, but forget the lyrics of the song she was singing. All very cringe making and there's more embarrassment on the way. Cécilia Attias, the former wife of Nicolas Sarkozy, has written her memoirs, and already many people, including in the media, are salivating over the prospect of some very candid—and embarrassing— revelations from her about her former husband. Mind you, the French media is so tame, so inclined to lick the establishment's ass, that it's unlikely that too many of those revelations will make it in print or online.

In many ways, the French mainstream media is a reflection of the American media. I was very interested the other day to read a stinging denunciation of the US media in guess where, The Guardian. They quoted Seymour Hersh, a veteran investigative news journalist, whose career took off after his scoop on the My Lai massacre in Vietnam. He's been going strong ever since and now he lambasts the American media for being "pathetic". However, one New York paper, the Daily News, is today making up for that by printing a front page photo showing the "House of Turds", a not too subtle reference to the impasse in Congress that's brought US government departments and state agencies to their knees because they no longer have funds to run their operations. The whole episode is remarkably childish, for one of the world's largest democracies. Seymour also condemns in particular the New York Times for its ass licking approach to the Obama administration and says that it is getting away with lie after lie, which just aren't being challenged by the newspaper. Just to round off his diatribe, he says that more nincompoops than ever are running the world today. These eejitsare everywhere, at all levels. Just look at what happened the other day in the Ukraine. A couple who were pissed out of their minds decided that it'd be a great idea to make love on a railway line. The only snag was that a train came along and killed the woman.

Still, talking about turds at the top takes me right back to October 5, 1968. That was the day that in Derry, members of the RUC, the old police force in Northern Ireland, baton charged a march by civil rights protesters in the Waterside district of Derry. A cameraman from RTÉ was there and filmed what was going on. The footage was screened that evening and it went around the world. The event quickly went down in history as the moment when the troubles began in the North of Ireland. Today, seeing that seminal footage in retrospect, 45 years later, s like watching historical film, similar to the Odessa steps sequences in that Russian classic, the Battleship Potemkin, which presaged the Russian revolution. What happened in Derry that day wasn't just a spontaneous protest; the trouble had been brewing for years, because of gross discrimination against Catholics living in the North of Ireland. In Derry in those days, few Catholics even had the vote in local elections and discrimination was rife. The North had been badly governed for years, but in typical fashion, various governments in London, which had and still have, the ultimate responsibility for the region, not only hadn't a clue about what was happening, but were very reluctant to intervene in any way.

And when they ultimately did intervene, when the troubles started getting serious the following year, 1969, they only made matters worse. Fortunately, hese days, much of that dreadful history has been consigned to the place it best belongs—history. Derry is busy staging lots of cultural events this year, even if its title of UK City of Culture jars with many people—Derry is in the opinion of many people who live in the city, or who know it well, the most Irish city in the island of Ireland.

That afternoon in Derry in October was the third in a series of world shaking events that year, 1968. Earlier that year, a semi-revolution broke out in Paris, but eventually, the idea of any permanent revolution soon died out. In August that year, forces from much of the Communist block invaded what was then Czechoslovakia, an event that in many ways was the start of the breakup of the Communist 'empire' in eastern Europe and Russia itself. Then came Derry. That October day was memorable in another way, too, for on that weekend, I was in Belfast, so had reports of what was happening in Derry pretty much at first hand. I was staying with a couple of friends, people I'd known well since college days. After they left college, they got married. Anyway, that weekend I was staying with them and on the Saturday night, we were having a very civilised dinner for three at their house, discussing this that and the other, when something very strange happened. I'd always been great friends with the wife and she had always been reasonably flirtatious, but that's as far as it went. Then all of a sudden, she stripped off completely—it turned out she's been high on a mixture of medical drugs and alcohol-and I found her sitting stark naked on my lap, while her husband was as bemused as I was; she was busy whispering very indiscreet sweet nothings in my ear! As for the rest of the evening, I'll draw a discreet veil over proceedings but suffice to say that for two entirely unconnected reasons, October 5, 1968, was for me a truly remarkable day!

Meanwhile, back to France. One of the most memorable days we've ever had in Paris came one November 17. It's Saint Elizabeth's Day; she lived from 1207 to 1231, dying before her 24th birthday. In her short life, she devoted great love and compassion to the poor and the suffering and a few days after she died, Saint Elizabeth of Hungary was canonised. That day in Paris had absolutely perfect weather, calm and sunny and reasonably mild; we've never known such a delicious day in the city of light, and we've enjoyed many. But that particular day turned out to be very special for both of us, my wife and myself, and it has remained lodged in memory ever since. So look out for this year's November 17 in the hope that such a memorable day might be repeated!

I was also interested to read the recent results of a survey on travel to Paris done by a holiday rental site called Housetrip. Admittedly, all their results were based on travel to and from London, but they hold good for other European destinations. It looked at two day trips to France for New Year and then for St Valentine's Day, 2014. In the list of cheapest places to go for a trip, Nice came in at number four, while Paris came in seventh. In terms of the cheapest flights, Paris was third while Nice was fifth. Nice worked out as the third cheapest city to travel in once you'd got there, with a mere £1 or €1.25 the cost of getting round the city by tram. The third cheapest New Year destination was Nice.

So the survey proved that despite its reputation for being expensive, it's still possible to enjoy a budget break to France. Mind you, I wouldn't recommend Paris over Christmas or the New Year—there aren't too many places open and the weather usually isn't that good. But Nice is another proposition—in December and January, Nice is usually still quite mild, great weather for walking along the Promenade des Anglais.

Meanwhile, in terms of flying, it's interesting to see that the European Parliament has rejected the proposals for EU—wide consolidation of the hours that pilots work. British pilots who are members of BALPA were strongly opposed to these new measures, as reports came in of how likely pilots are likely to doze off when they are flying on auto-pilot. I was also very amused by a news report on the BBC, which said that following the rejection by the European Parliament, the present system, of what it called a dog 's breakfast of different regulations for pilots' working hours in all

28 EU member states. Surely, they should have called it a dog's dinner?

However, in another recent poll, France didn't fare well. The Independent in London did a poll of European honesty and posed the question: if you lost your wallet, in which European city would it most likely be handed in? Out of 16 cities listed, Helsinki was the most honest, where it was reported that 11 out of 12 wallets found would be handed in. Sadly, not one French city figured on this list, so the motto is "hang on to your wallet" there.

In the meantime, the idea of doing with drivers on public transport gains ground in France. Last week, I was writing about the extension of automatic Métro trains in Paris. This week comes news that a manufacturer in France is trying out a driverless bus, which is being tested in the grounds of a hospital in Clermont-Ferrand. This driverless bus carries a maximum of just six people and has a top speed of just 20 kph. If the experiment works, which I'm sure it will, the plan is to have a fleet of driverless buses running at the Michelin research centre in Ladoux, by 2015. Ladoux is 10km north of the Michelin headquarters in Clermont-Ferrand. La Rochelle already has a driverless bus scheme in operation, while Lyon tested a robot bus earlier this year. The real test of a driverless bus would be in the Paris rush hour!

Talking of public transport, I saw a sad sight on a tram in Dublin the other day. A young man was waiting near me for the tram and when it arrived, he sat down not far away. He was enormous and must have weighed the best part of 25 stones (180 kg) complete with an enormous belly. Yet the whole time he was guzzling non-stop, either sweets or white bread sandwiches. In that situation, one is always tempted to offer a word of advice, but that's just not the done thing—it's up to the medics, but having said that, it was a sorry sight to see someone like that literally eating their way into oblivion.

Another example of how high tech can work to visitors' benefit comes with a new exhibition in Paris. An exhibition called Lost in Paris is on view in the 11th arrondissement until January, with the aim of connecting design with tourism. Objects on display include an Eiffel Tower lollipop, a baguette bag and a tandem Vélib rental bicycle. The exhibition also has a series of ceramic containers, which contain a series of distinctive smells, capturing the pleasant sniffs associated with Parisian suburbs. In another part of the exhibition, images are projected of scenes that people can see if they are travelling on the RER network. As an example, when it comes to Le Bourget, once the main airport for Paris, a mere eight km from the city centre and now the home of an outstanding aviation and aeronautical museum, viewers will see an image of a plane coming in to land. The whole exhibition sounds very enterprising and innovative.

On the subject of high tech, now 4G is being peddled furiously, even though only about a quarter of people in France are interested. By the end of 2015, it's planned that all users, anywhere on the Métro and RER networks in the Paris area will have access to both 3G and 4G. Already, there's 3G availability at the Gare de Lyon, rail gateway to Provence, and at the Chatelet-les-Halles Métro station, while free wifi is available at nearly 50 Métro, RER and bus stations.

While all this is going on, controversy rages over possible changes to one of the most old-fashioned laws in France. Sunday trading in shopping centres and by big shops is unknown in France; the only exemptions are with tourist areas and with small, family owned shops. Moves are under way by the government to take a fresh look at updating the Sunday trading laws, in the hope of making them more suitable for present day lifestyles and helping the jobless. But already, one of the campaigns for keeping the status quo has come up with a striking slogan: "Ne touche pas à mon dimanche" -don't touch my Sunday. The seventh arrondissement is a perfect example of the totally outdated French shop opening regulations. In the evenings, after 6pm, and on Sundays, it's practically impossible to find a shop open, apart from some touristy ones and of course restaurants. But if you go to the far end of the rue de Grenelle, past the Hotel des Invalides, in the direction of the Eiffel Tower, you'll come to a delightful market like area where you'll find loads of small family run shops, just right for purchasing a bottle of wine in the evening. In general, the working class parts of Paris offer a much better chance for stocking up on essential food and wine in the evenings and on Sundays than the posh areas, which simply elevate their noses and close their doors.

The French should take a look at Ireland. What the French do with shop opening now is what happened in Ireland 50 years ago. The consumer revolution here in Ireland means that on Sundays, you can do whatever kind of shopping you want, whether it's in a department store, a shopping centre or a wine shop. All the big names, like Marks & Spencer and Tesco, are all open all day, so naturally, many people who can't do their shopping during the week are facilitated. Our local Spar supermarket is open day and night all week, except for about eight hours on Sunday nights—imagine that happening in France, the land of the closed shop!

October 9, 2013

Harvest time in Montmartre

t's harvest time again in Montmartre—the 18th arrondissement perched on a hill that's topped by the Sacré-Coeur. The space devoted to grape growing in Montmartre is so small—1, 556 square metres, enough for 2, 000 vines—that you could be forgiven for missing it, but it's there all the same, a respectable little plot full of vines, almost in the heart of Paris, a heart-warming sight indeed. At harvest time, the grapes are pressed in the basement of the mairie in the 18th and then the 1, 000 or so bottles are sold at auction. It's a timely reminder that the Romans began cultivating grapes for wine in the Paris region all of 2, 000 years ago.

Now that this year's admittedly poor grape harvest is being celebrated at fetes des vendanges in wine regions in many parts of France, Montmartre joins in the fun. It seems no time at all since last year' vendage but that's just the result of getting older! But the celebrations on the hill are as lively as ever and as always, Montmartre is putting on a good show. There's a great display of the work of artists working in the district, which is on until this coming Sunday, while this Friday evening at 20h30, there's a big ball in the Halle Pajol, which promises much lively music and loads of foot-tapping fun until the small hours.

France being France, of course, there are plenty of other festivals on all around the country. In Brittany, until October 19, the accordeon festival that's being staged in Rennes and the surrounding Ille-et-Vilaine will bring in star accordeon players from all over the world, as well as presenting all kinds of other music, such as jazz, rock and electro.

Meanwhile, life continues as usual and so too do the high profile robberies. The Côte d'Azur has been plagued with them this past summer, but now Paris has had one as well. The luxurious jewellery shop, Vacheron Constantin in the place Vendome was raided the other day by a gang of about a dozen men armed with axes and sledgehammers, who created mayhem inside the shop and got away with 20 watches worth in total €1 million.

Two of the raiders were caught minutes later; they were from eastern Europe. Ironically, the shop that was raided is very close to the Justice Ministry.

There was more of the usual in the Côte d'Azur over the weekend-rain. On Saturday afternoon, I had a quick look at a webcam on the Promenade des Anglais in Nice, only to find that the skies were leaden, the sea looked the same colour and the rain was lashing down. It was only mid-afternoon, but the cars and buses were driving along with all their headlights on. This year has seen much more rain than usual in many parts of France, one of the reasons why the grape harvest this year is the worst for 40 years. While I was looking at that Provençal webcam, I was enjoying the weather here in Dublin. It was a beautiful sunny day, just perfect weather, and the sun was almost splitting the stones, rather unusual for early October.

Something else I noticed during the week that isn't good news for any employees of Air France and SNCF; both organisations are planning to abolish the free ticket regime that gives employees considerable scope for getting free tickets to the destination of their choice. Meanwhile, Air France is currently celebrating its 80th anniversary and a French news website, planet. fr, created an interesting feature showing the uniforms worn by cabin crew over the years. In the old days, of course, these were the air hostesses, but these days, such as phrase is almost legally passé. So too is the age of glamorous flying, when going on a great adventure in the sky meant dressing up for it. Talking about airlines, KLM has just celebrated its anniversary; it was founded on October 7, 1919, and today, it's the oldest airline in the world still flying under its founding name.

There have also been strange things going on in the museum and art world. The north-eastern town of Douai, not far from Lille, has a renowned museum called the Musée de la Chartreuse. During the first world war, German soldiers removed about 250 paintings from the museum and took them to Brussels. About 250 paintings vanished and were never recovered. These weren't just works by the great and the good, but many paintings by lesser—known local artists. Now, Anne Labourdette, the energetic young director of the museum, is about to publish a complete list of the museum's collection as it stood in 1914. Whether this will help in unearthing any of those missing paintings is anyone's guess. During the first world war, the museum was largely destroyed and a photograph of it taken in October, 1918, it's thought by a British soldier, showed just one painting hanging forlornly in place. During the second world war, the museum was completely destroyed, complete with that one surviving painting.

An even stranger museum story comes from the museum in Rochefort in Charente-Maritime in western France. The other day, a case containing three African funerary statuettes exploded without warning. Various scientific tests were carried out to try and find out the reason for the explosion, without coming to conclusion, and now many people suspect that there must have been something supernatural at work.

At least, this week, we were given some hopefully good news by L'Express, which ran a feature on why there are 10 reasons for hope in France in 2014. It concluded that among the contributory factors will be a renewed dynamism in exports, improving business confidence, more consumer spending power and a stabilisation of unemployment. Lets hope they are right-la belle France could do with a whole lot of boosters right now. If France could have the Glastonbury effect, it would do the world of good. The other day, tickets went on sale for next year's Glastonbury

Festival and they were sold out in less than 90 minutes, which was rather amazing!

Another good news story from France was the victory in the legal battle by the 3, 000 independent booksellers in France over the likes of Amazon, huge online retailers. They have been discounting their book sales by a perfectly legal five per cent and throwing in free postage, but now they have to stop that little game, which has been so injurious to smaller booksellers. There was more good news for consumers, too, the other day when it was announced that petrol and diesel prices in France have fallen to their lowest level during the past nine months. A little surprisingly, diesel now accounts for 80 per cent of the fuel market in France.

Another sign of changing times came from the film industry, which is still vibrant in France, turning out about 300 films a year. But the number of moviegoers in France going to see French-made films has fallen by a third since the 1980s. The big winners in French cinemas are US-made films. Mind you, I'm not surprised. Up until about 10 years ago, there used to be a steady stream of new French releases that were worth going to see, very creative, often provocative and usually featuring big stars of the French cinema. But since then, the release of interesting French films has dwindled to almost nothing, at least here in Dublin.

Trying to look into the future is always fascinating and hazardous, to try and see what trends are going to take hold. The other day, I heard a recording of Harold Macmillan, once an enlightened British prime minister, who also used to run the Macmillan publishing empire. It was amazing to hear him say, in the early 1960s, when he was talking about how people would read books in the future, that many people would simply press a button and read books onscreen. How prophetic he was!

It's little wonder, that given people have so little confidence in the present government and president in France, that the Front National seems to be doing so well. A cantonal election the other day in Brignoles, in the Var department in the south of France, showed the Front National candidate taking slightly over 40 per cent of the vote, almost double what the candidate from the conservative UMP party got. A candidate from a breakaway faction of the Front National got almost 10 per cent of the vote, so in total, the far right got very nearly 50 per cent of the vote. It is taken in France as an indication of just how well the Front National is likely to do in local and European elections next year. Now, Marine Le Pen, the leader of the party, is saying that the Front National is the first party in France. Since one of its pledges if it comes to power is to take France out of the eurozone, we could be in for some choppy times ahead!

But it would be but a tiny blip compared with what's likely to happen if the US debt default goes ahead at the end of next week. With extreme Republicans in the US acting like a lot of spoiled children ready to throw all their toys out of the playpen, any kind of compromise between them and the Democrats in power seems rather remote. And if the US does default, it's going to be a huge shock to the world financial system Many people in France always think the worst of the US and reckon that bad trends in the world often start in the US, so once again, it looks like for them, this point will be proven yet again. Talking about the US, there's currently a lot of speculation that the Clintons are going to get divorced and no—one wouldn't be entirely surprised if Hilary got married again—to a woman. She's still in the frame to run as a Democratic party presidential candidate in 2016, but I'd be rather surprised if that actually happens.

I heard a wonderful story of longevity the other day that beats all the news from the political world. A solicitor in Bandon, Co Cork, here in Ireland, Edward O'Driscoll, has just decided to retire, at the age of 86. He's been working in the family law firm, that was founded by his father in 1898, for a staggering 65 years. Still very bright eyed and bushy tailed, the energetic Edward has decided that he now wants to devote himself to charitable work.

Another interesting news item is also about to emerge in Ireland. The Ryanair calendar always creates lots of media attention. Cabin crew volunteer to be photographed in either their lingerie or their swimwear—what there is of it—and the photos always create a great stir. All the proceeds go to charity, so at least, what some people might regard as a dubious event, does help good causes. But now a group of righteous minded consumers in Spain are taking the airline to court because they consider the calendar sexist and they have now won the case.

All of which reminds me of a trip to Brussels we did quite a time ago. My wife and I strolled along one of the streets in central Brussels where the ladies of the night (and the day) are seated in windows, displaying their wares. They were all so nonchalant about what they were doing and some were cheeky to boot but it was all something of a novelty for these two innocents from Dublin. The only thing that surprises me about the whole carry—on is that the bureacrats from Brussels haven't decided to impose VAT on the transactions!

Still it makes a change from the usual boring stuff from Brussels—I always connect the place now with endlessly boring committee meetings on behalf of some obscure EU obsession, surely the ultimate in boredom. The EU has become one vast bureaucracy, the ultimate in soul destruction. Just imagine if one had to spend each and every working day in one of those committee meetings!

And to end, just to reflect on the looming crisis day in US national finances next week, it's interesting to see how many of the world's crises through the course of history have often hinged on a mere chance, a sudden fateful happening that seemed so insignificant at the time.

I was reading some history of the early 1930s the other day when I discovered that one day in Munich, a car driven by an young Englishman ran over a man in a main street. The man fell under the car; luckily for him, but not for the world, the car driver was taking it slowly because he was unsure of driving the car and of his route. If he had been driving any faster, the history of the world could have been very different! The man who was run over was Adolf Hitler.

October 16, 2013

Storms on the way!

—————

This week in Ireland, the 2014 Budget was passed and a raft of fiscal measures hit young people, the poor, the sick and the elderly, while the wealthy escaped scot-free.

One of the measures passed was the abolition of the €850 bereavement grant, which is entirely appropriate in one sense, as the Irish Labour Party, which is part of the current government coalition in Dublin, is in terminal decline. Come the next Irish general election and it's quite likely that Labour candidates may win no seats at all. At that stage, the most sensible thing to do with this once proud political party would be to put it down. It's no wonder that in an opinion poll done the other day, nearly one-third of the Irish electorate said that politicians of all parties were such clownish incompetents that they wouldn't bother voting for them in any upcoming election.

Also in Dublin this week, I received a plaintive Twitter message sent out by a student in University College, Dublin, one of the city's three universities. She said that she had been at a maths event in the college the other day and while there, had managed to lose her laptop. She added, plaintively, that it contained her PhD thesis. What a heartbreaking situation to be in, especially if she hadn't backed up her work, so lets hope there's a happy ending to this particular story. Before I leave Dublin stories, I must mention something amusing I spotted in a local

Tesco Express store this week. I was looking for pepper, but it had neither salt nor pepper, but loads of Durex. Surely, they must have their priorities wrong!

Meanwhile, back in France, everyone's gearing up for winter, with a big drop in temperatures, especially in northern France, caused by Arctic winds coming in from Iceland. Much more rain is forecast and already in the Pyrenees, snow is appearing above the 1, 000 metre mark. Today, an orange flood alert has been issued for two Départements in the east of the country, Vosges and Meurthe-et-Moselle. Three rivers in these two regions are risen so much that they are in danger of bursting their banks.

It's also being said in France at the moment that the electricity grid is under such strain that if this coming winter is rigorous, one problem of maintenance in just one key location could throw the whole system into chaos. An energy specialist, Colette Lewiner, was quoted the other day as saying that to add to this sense of chaos, international gas and electricity markets are in a state of chaos themselves. Meanwhile households in France are gearing themselves for a 0. 5 per cent increase in gas prices in November.

A reminder that winter—and Christmas—are fast approaching came from SNCF the other day. From tomorrow (October 17), it starts taking seat reservations for the Christmas period. Tomorrow of course is also the deadline day in the US Congress for sorting out their finances, otherwise the US is at risk of defaulting on its national debt, with global economic repercussions. No wonder that the Chinese are now saying that the world should have a benchmark currency other than the US dollar—sadly, the US is no longer the reliable economic barometer it once was and it's amazing that the decline in American reliability and ratings is entirely home grown. It has nothing to do with outside influences. The long term historical view will probably show Obama to have been one of the worst US presidents in recent decades.

But at least there's some good news from France. An annual list compiled by the Thomson Reuter group ranks countries by their most innovative businesses and organisations. This year's list, just published, shows the US in top position, with 45 such listings, followed by Japan, with 28. France comes third with 12 listings. These include such companies as Alcatel-Lucent in telecommunications, L'Oréal (cosmetics), Michelin in tyres and Saint-Gobain (industrial) as well as the French National Centre for Scientific Research. One interesting fact about this list is that it doesn't contain a single entry from the UK.

Another listing, this time from Crédit Suisse, has more good tidings for France. Its Global Wealth Databook 13 shows that people in Switzerland are the best off in the world, with an average worth per individual of $513, 000.France comes in at Number 7, with $296, 000 per person. Interestingly, neither Germany nor the UK figure in the top 10.

Talking about Switzerland reminds me of an excellent news website, that of the Tribune de Genève: www. tdg. ch. It's really fast and on the ball for international news, as well as for news from home and from next door neighbour France. It also does some fantastic photo galleries and one the other day had some really appealing advertising posters, done about 100 years ago, and all using Geneva and Lac Léman as the backdrop. These posters were full of nostalgia for a time long since past and a huge improvement on what passes for advertising art these days. Personally speaking, I just ignore advertising these days, so much of it is just plain downright bad, banal and boring. And invariably, I find that if any company or organisation spends heavily on advertising, the reality never lives up to the expectation created.

It's not all good news, however, about France. Hugh Schofield, who's the BBC correspondent in Paris, wrote a damning piece for the BBC news website about the Champs-Elysées in Paris. It's turned into a really grotty Main Street, as he says "crass, styleless, naff and expensive". In the old days, Parisians would stroll beneath the plane trees, have a coffee, meet friends and window shop in the luxury stores. Now, no Parisian worth his or her salt would dream of going near the place. All that the present day thoroughfare is missing is an Aldi or Lidl store. Schofield also said that the other Sunday morning at 7am, when he was going to work in the nearby BBC Paris office, that he saw a young woman urinating in the gutter in the Champs-Elysées. How the mighty have fallen, especially when you look back on all the triumphant photos taken there immediately after the liberation of Paris in 1944.

Things change of course. This week saw the time honoured newspaper title, the International Herald Tribune, change its name to the International New York Times. The paper, in its various guises, has been an integral part of the American expat scene in Paris since the late 19th century, but I'm not quite sure now how long the printed version distributed around the world is going to survive. The type of person who reads the paper is much more likely to read his or her newspaper on a tablet or an app than any other type of consumer.

There's reconciliation in the air, too. Sarkozy's ex-wife, Cécilia Attias, has just published her book of revelations about her marriage to the former president. Despite the controversies these have generated, the two are now said to be reconciled. Maybe one day, France itself will become reconciled to Sarkozy. To many French people, he now seems a model of positive, dynamic efficiency ncompared to the present incumbent, M. Hollande.

The insults go on however in the Assemblée Nationale. The other day, a Green party deputy, Véronique Massonneau, was making a point or two, when she was rudely interrupted by Philipope Le Ray, a deputy from the UMP centre-right party. He started making clucking noises; in French, poulet, the word for chicken is also used as a term of abuse for women. The deputy was promptly fined €1, 300, so it was a rather expensive insult. There are also insults flying in France over Femen, the group of women from the Ukraine who stage political protests all over Europe by appearing topless. Allegations have been made in the past few days that one of their spokespersons in France, Eloise Bouton, has also been doubling as a high class call girl.

And in case you're wondering what OVNI means—it's all over the French news websites at the moment—it stands for UFO. They are busy reporting UFOs from all over the place, but funnily enough, none of them has popped up in France recently! There was also an amusing news story from Paris the other day, about two Chinese tourists who had been staying at an hotel in Bagnolet in the eastern suburbs of Paris. When they tried to pay their hotel bill with a pile of one euro coins, suspicions were aroused. However, they were soon cleared of any forgery suspicions. It seems that they knew people in the scrap metal trade in China. When old or wrecked cars are sent there from Europe for recycling, it seems that the object most often found is a one euro coin. As a result, the two Chinese tourists were discovered to have €3, 700 stashed in their hotel room, all in one euro coins.

In other international news, it was very sad to read about the sudden demise of Maria De Villota, the former Formula 1 racing driver, who was found dead, apparently from natural causes, in her hotel room in Seville the other day. It was great to see a woman entering the ranks of Formula 1 racing drivers, but in a crash in Cambridgeshire last year, she lost an eye, which ended her racing career. And it seems that the injuries she sustained then finally finished her off.

Also on the international front, it now seems that Berlusconi is going to do community service in Italy in lieu of prison for his tax fraud convictions. What type of community service? The mind boggles.

I also see on the international front that the movement for changing the name of the Czech Republic is gaining ground and we could soon be calling the country Czechia.

But back to France. Once again, the country has proved its good name in preserving its heritage by reopening the Eden theatre at La Ciotat, between Marseilles and Toulon in the south of France. The restoration job cost €6. 5 million and what is claimed to be the oldest surviving public cinema in the world is now back in pristine condition. It was at the railway station in La Ciotat that the Lumière brothers made one of their first films, the arrival of a train at La Ciotat when it was first shown in Paris in 1895, the audiences were terrified as they thought the steam loco was coming straight at them. Soon after, the Lumière brothers showed this and other of their early films made in the area at the Eden. The brothers for long had a summer villa close by. But the theatre/ cinema had been closed since 1995 but has now reopened in all its glory. We've been through La Ciotat station— it's a perfectly ordinary rural station—but it's amazing to think that the cinema industry really began there.

I'd also like to mention some interesting places in Paris. If you're in Paris and you have children to entertain, two places are strongly recommended. The Musée en Herbe was founded in 1975 by Sylvie Giradet and Claire Merleau as somewhere that young children could enjoy the world of art. These days, it can be found at Number 21 rue Hérold, which is in the Ist arrondissement, right in the centre of Paris. It advertises itself on its website as appealing to children aged 3 to 103. The other place where children can become absorbed in all kinds of absorbing activities is the new children's section at the Cité des Sciences in the 18ᵗʰ. The restyled Cité des Enfants is meant for children aged five to 12. They can take part in about 100 activities in six themed zones, including the TV studio, the garden and the factory. The whole Cité is a marvellous show of everything scientific for all ages, but the new look children's section has kept all the old favourites.

If you're an adult and you are looking for a little fun playing boules, then go to the place Dauphine on the Ile de la Cité. It's one of the oldest squares in Paris, although it is in fact triangular. It's not a particularly prepossessing square, although it's lined with restaurants where you can sit on the terraces. It's also used for boules and if you want to join in, then you can sign up for €25 to play for 90 minutes and learn some of the fundamentals.

Just to end this week on a couple of down-to-earth topics! In Cullompton in Devon, as in most villages, towns and cities, dog dirt is a big problem. So they've decided to spray dog mess on the streets a garish pink colour, in the hope that this will embarrass the owners of the offending dogs. All of which reminds me of what we saw in Belfast coming up to Christmas one year, a long time ago. A fine upstanding dog turd had been left on a pavement and someone had sprayed it with gold glitter! This was in a Protestant part of Belfast, so this was definitely Proddy doggy-doo!

And up popped a story about Winston Churchill that I'd never heard before. One day, he was in the lavatory when one of his aides told him that the Lord Privy Seal was on the phone and wanted to speak with him. Churchill, noted for his one line put downs, said: "Tell him I can only deal with one shit at a time! ".

October 23, 2013

Warm weather!

Yesterday afternoon in Dublin, the weather was so warm and sunny one could be forgiven for thinking we were still in mid-summer! The recent run of mild weather has been incredible and welcome; in two months time, we're probably going to be in the midst of a snowy winter!

In France, they've had other concerns, like earthquakes. The other afternoon, an earthquake measuring close to four on the Richter scale rumbled beneath Rennes in Brittany and was felt as far away as Quimper. The experts described this as a rare happening in that part of France. Just the other day, too, on the Côte d'Azur, a similarly sized earthquake was felt, but no-one took much notice. There, rumblings in the bowels of the earth are fairly frequent, although fortunately, it's been a long time since the last big one.

On February 23, 1887, a powerful earthquake measuring about six on the Richter scale hit the Italian Riviera and was felt as far west as Marseilles. In Menton, more than 200 homes were destroyed, while in the centre of Nice, many buildings collapsed and the esplanade was badly damaged. The death toll was substantial, about 2, 500 in all, with all but about 500 of those casualties taking place on the Italian side of the frontier. In Nice, it was all total chaos. At 06h00 the morning the earthquake struck, the centre of Nice was filled with tourists who had fled their hotels; altogether, about 12, 000 people left the city on the first available trains, many still dressed in their pyjamas.

An emergency of another kind struck the other day. An Air France flight en route from Paris to Nice was having problems with its hydraulic systems and had to make an emergency landing at Lyons, but fortunately, no-one was hurt.

All of which brings me to the events of late 1783, when the first balloon flights were made. On August 27 that year the first ever flight by a hydrogen filled balloon, with no-one aboard, took to the skies from the Champs de Mars in Paris and landed in Gonesse, 21 km away (the same spot where a Concorde plane crashed in 2000) and close to the site of the present Roissy airport. The first ballon flight with people on board took off in Paris on November 21, 1783, and in five minutes, flew eight km. A much more substantial flight took off at the beginning of December that year when a manned balloon reached heights of up to 550 metres and flew for just over two hours. It's amazing how far and how fast aviation has progressed since then.

Yet another piece of transport progression is coming to Nice. The centre of the city has long had a tramway system, but the plans to build a tramway from the centre ville to the airport, about 11 km, have been delayed by years of consultation and disagreements. Finally, however, work is starting on the line, which should be ready by the end of 2017. Nice airport is one of the most spectacular in the world, since some of the runways are built out into the sea, and when you're landing or taking off in clear weather, the views over most of the Côte d'Azur, with the mountains of the Alps as a backdrop, are truly staggering.

I was also reading a fascinating book about Paris the other day by British author Gillian Tindall. Her 2009 book, Footprints in Paris, A Few Streets, A Few Lives, gives a fascinating insight into what life was really like in Paris in the 19th century, dirty and dangerous. The strike last week by 50 employees of Cartier in the rue de la Paix in the 2nd, was nothing new in the life of Paris-industrial relations have often been fraught, but usually at more manual level. It was unusual to see the employees of a luxury jewellery and watch store manning the picket lines.

But back to the Tindall book. Among its revelations are the horrors that a former French president, Pompidou, inflicted on the city. His idea of modernity was to fill parts of the city with high rise tower blocks and cut swathes of motorways through Paris. It's fortunate for Paris that he died unexpectedly in 1974; after his death, all his grandiose plans were abandoned, although the Pompidou Centre remains as a testament to his grand follies. In building that centre, vast and historic areas of the 4th had to be levelled.

Gillian Tindall has written other excellent books on France. An earlier one, Célestine: Voices from a French Village, is an excellent and moving account of life in a remote French village in years gone by, before mechanisation and automation had taken over.

These days, of course, that process has gone too far and I was interested in the piece written the other day by Steven Erlanger. For five years, he was the bureau chief for the New York Times in Paris, before departing recently for a similar position in London. His opinion of present day Paris is that it has become too ordered, too antisceptic, too tightly policed by the politically correct for the city to have much of a louche life left, except for bourgeous adulteries. He said that beneath the mountain of clichés about Paris, the city has lost much of its ancient character. Even the great political battles between left and right seem tamer now.

Erlanger also made the very telling point that France seems like a country that has lost its way, tainted by Islamophobia and extreme right nationalism. Another blight is the rampant phobia against gay people and communities. It's telling that in her latest prediction, Marine Le Pen, the leader of the Front National, says that the European Union is going to collapse into pieces, just as the old Soviet Union did, and that Europe is going to re-emerge as a series of sovereign states co-operating closely with one another.

The New York Times correspondent, while pointing out that many people who live in Paris treat the place with studied indifference at best, contempt at worst, the present day inertia is evident in matters like street cleaning. Traditionally, the gutters in Parisian streets are washed down around six every morning. These days, that just isn't possible, because so often they are blocked with rubbish. The area around the Gare du Nord, the Paris terminal of the Eurostar trains, is another case in point. These days, the area around the station, which for so many people is their first glimpse of Paris, is filled with young male Roma prostitutes, female Tunisian prostitutes and under-age Muslim and black bandes des filles-girl gangs. All very offputting, but having said that Paris will always be Paris—one hopes.

Still, slip- ups aren't exclusively French. The other day, the Vatican issued a medal to mark the first anniversary of Pope Francis. It bore a literal—instead of Jesus, it had Lesus. Sloppiness is everywhere these days, even inside the Vatican!

There's no going back, however, to some mythical golden age. A case in point was the other day, when the 200th anniversary of the defeat of Napoléon at the Battle of Leipzig was commemorated. he French leader was defeated by the Prussians and their allies, who included the Russians and the Swedes. It was a turning point for Napoléon's European campaigns and two years later, in 1815, he was decisively defeated at the Battle of Waterloo. For the re-enactment of the battle, thousands of overweight middle age enthusiasts of military re-enactments from all over the world descended on Leipzig and refought the battle. The French leader was played by a diminuitive 46 year old lawyer from Paris. It was a devastating battle in 1813 that saw some 100, 000 soldiers killed. This time round, it was broadcast live on a local TV channel and several local clergy condemned the whole episode, saying that it was wholly wrong to recreate such carnage as a TV gameshow.

Needless to remark, the events at Leipzig 200 years ago went unrecorded in the French media, which instead chose to concentrate on the Battle of Ulm, fought between October 16 and

19, 1805, in which France was victorious. But my guess is that few people outside France have ever heard of the Battle of Ulm and it isn't exactly a household word inside France, either.

Meanwhile, the head chef in the Elysée Palace, home of French presidents, has retired. Bernard Vaussion was there 40 years, but he has now become the honorary president of one of the most exclusive clubs in the world, of chefs to heads of state. Vaussion revealed the likes of recent French presidents. Mitterand preferred seafood, while Chirac's gastronomic tastes were obviously in his boots—sauerkraut and Corona beer. Sarkozy, who was on a strict diet, banned cheese, except when Angela Merkel was in town. The current president, M. Hollande, is much more accommodating—he will eat anything and frequently does.

I saw another interesting news item from France the other day, a flat to rent in Reims, for a mere €220 a month. But it's only nine square metres and the one room contains everything, including the loo perched beneath the cooker and a shower beside the tiny kitchen. It's all in the one room, which even managed to contain a microwave. And the fourth floor flat is in a building that has no lift.

I also spotted another interesting news item the other day. In the town of Leeuwarden, 110 km north of Amsterdam, there used to be a hair dressing salon until the other day. It was called "Hari", because the building had been the birthplace in 1876 of Mata Hari. Unfortunately, the other day, the whole place burned down. Mata Hari was the lady who made a name for herself in the Paris of the early years of the 20th century by being an exotic dancer. In 1917, she was executed by the French on suspicion of being a German spy, a claim that has long been hotly contested.

Something else I spotted a couple of days ago was a piece on the Tribune de Genève website about the small village of Céligny, halfway between Geneva and Lausanne. It was here in 1984 that the great Welsh actor Richard Burton was buried; his grave is in the old cemetery. The new cemetery in the village has a very striking inscription over its entrance: Ici L'Égalité. We were in the village shortly after Burton's burial and I wrote a piece about the graveyard and about Burton for a magazine here in Dublin, complete with a photo of his headstone. It was all very evocative, but something else sticks in my mind about Céligny. That day, we stopped for lunch in a pub in the village and were served some foul concoction that included chicken. The meal was so disgusting that I can honestly say that it was one of the worst meals we've ever had out, I n any location, Switzerland or anywhere else.

Back at the ranch, here in Dublin, pensioners are on the march. The recent budget here cut a swathe through allowances for pensioners and it was all done without an ounce of compassion on the part of the government ministers involved. To them, it was all a mere book balancing episode. So yesterday the pensioners took to the streets in Dublin in an impressive and vociferous turnout. The present government in Dublin is, it seems, more than happy to make cuts that affect the poor, the sick, the disabled and the elderly, all the while leaving their rich supporters totally untouched. I was reminded of this attitude when I was waiting in a local café the other day for a friend. Outside, two policemen were busy taking every last details about someone who begs on the pavement there every day. I just thought to myself: if the beggar had been a banker, he would have remained totally untouched!

What's worse about all the cuts in the recent budget here is that the Irish Labour Party, which is part of the government coalition, goes along with all this. As someone noted the other day, the present day Labour Party in Ireland is far to the right of George W. Bush. There's much sympathy here in Ireland for the artist in Prague, who in view of the upcoming national elections in the Czech Republic, has created an extraordinary edifice which he has put in the middle of the Vltava River that flows through Prague. It's a model of a hand, about 10 metres high; it depicted a hand, nothing else, but one finger on that hand is pointed skywards. It's a very rude gesture not only for Czechs but many others and it sums up what people think of Czech politicians. It also has lots of resonance here in Ireland, since it sums up perfectly what people in Ireland think of their politicians.

October 30, 2013

Let it flow!

I couldn't help but noticing a reader's letter in the Metro Herald daily freesheet in Dublin the other day. The contents, as follows, were quite startling:

"I have worked in the city centre for 16 years and until now I thought I was unshockable. However, I came out of our offices at 5. 30pm to be greeted by a gushing sound from the other side of the very narrow street. The sight I saw was two 'ladies' squatting on the footpath peeing to their heart's content, and handing a loo roll to each other. I didn't know where to look. Shocked. Niamh Dalton".

As if that wasn't bad enough, another incident in Dublin was reported the other day. In one of the city's Georgian streets, a woman stopped a passer—by and asked her to look after her young child, while she squatted down on the steps of a Georgian house and let fly with a piss in full view of passers-by.

Rather sadly, this is what passes for 'normal' in present day Dublin and I guess it isn't any different in other capital cities around Europe. Just shows what a crude world we live in, where any kind of behaviour is considered ' acceptable ', as with Lady Gaga's performance in the Gay Club in London last weekend. It's hardly surprising codes of conduct have declined so much; we live in a truly Orwellian world, where words mean the opposite of what people think they mean. Political leaders here in Ireland have given renewed impetus to the concept of Orwellspeak, by saying one thing and doing the complete opposite.

When the leaders of the two parties currently in coalition in Dublin were in opposition, they were full of empathy for the plight of pensioners. Indeed, the man who is currently prime minister, Enda Kenny (on one occasion, the New York Times couldn't decide whether he was a man or a woman!) said that he wanted to make Ireland a place in which people could grow old gracefully. Judging by the recent Budget 2014, it now seems as if his government wants to change that word 'gracefully' to 'disgracefully', after all the cuts that have hit vulnerable old people so badly.

The junior partner in the present Irish government is the Irish Labour Party, that has become so supportive of extreme right-wing policies that it's now somewhere to the right of Attila the Hun. Yesterday, another well-known local politician resigned from the party, saying that it seemed quite content to pass all the previously unpassable boundaries of social justice. Come the next general election and the chances are that the party will find itself totally and utterly redundant, wiped out of Irish political history. Not so long ago, a vibrant Green Party was also in a coalition government, performing generally useful works, but after the 2011 general election, it was totally destroyed. And these days, if anyone is looking for the Green Party, it just doesn't exist any longer as a viable political force. Labour, it seems, I s hellbent on going the same route to self-destruction.

On a more positive note, I was looking again at a photograph taken in 1838. It was a daguerrotype taken in the boulevard du Temple, which is still there, in the 3rd., close to the place des Vosges. The exposure time was about 10 minutes, so even though there was a lot of horse-drawn and pedestrian traffic when the photograph was taken, none of it showed up in the photo. But at a street corner, a man stopped to get his boots cleaned and he and the man who was shining his boots stood still long enough to appear in the photo. This is the first known photo with people in it and it is also recognised as the first photo to appear of Paris.

It ' s fascinating stuff, but one thing it shows so clearly is just how scruffy and rundown Paris looked in those days, getting on for 200 years ago.

I was also fascinated by an anniversary mentioned on Radio 4 the other day. October 24, 1264, was the day that Chartres cathedral was consecrated. It's the pinnacle of Gothic architecture and what makes it even more impressive is that in 1194, most of the building was destroyed in a fire. It took 30 years to rebuild and the results have stood to this day. If they were doing reconstruction on this scale now, you'd never get the builders out, let alone after 30 years! The crypt in the cathedral is the largest in France and the cathedral itself has 172 stained glass windows. If you climb to the top of the north tower and steeple, over 100 metres high there are lovely views over the town and surrounding countryside.

It's well worth taking an express train from the station at Montparnasse in Paris; the journey covers 90km. We've done that trip and the magnificence of the cathedral repays many times over the effort of getting there. Chartres itself is a lovely town, much less spoiled than other places, like Versailles. The old town in Chartres covers about 60 hectares and you can wander around the many streets that date back to the Middle Ages. The town is also amply blessed with museums, so no shortage of things to do, and if the weather is fine, you can hire a pedalo or canoe on the River Eure, close to the cathedral and town centre.

Going on the river only in calm weather is the sensible thing to do. This week, among the many casualties of the great storm that ripped across southern Britain, northern France, through the Low Countries, into Germany and Scandinavia, was an unfortunate woman who was standing on the cliffs at Belle Ile in Britanny and was blown off those cliffs by the hurricane force winds.

There have been some near misses, too. The other day, a postal freight plane was taking off from Roissy, laden with thousands of parcels, when a propellor fell off. It tore a hole in the fuselage before falling to earth, but fortunately, the crew managed to make an emergency landing without any injuries.

Talking of transport, the latest addition to the TGV network has been announced. A high speed line is going to be built between Bordeaux and Toulouse and is due to open for service in 2024. At that stage, the journey time from Paris to Toulouse will be three hours and 10 minutes, an hour faster than at present. There's also talk of building a high speed line to connect south-western France and the north-west of Spain, with the first section going from Bordeaux to Dax, but at this earlier stage, there is so much opposition, the project seems a little less viable. Still, it's amazing that France has built such an impressive high speed rail network in not much more than a couple of decades, while the amount of ifs and buts that are plaguing the attempts to build England's first high speed rail links are astonishing. It's not just France, but other European countries, such as Belgium, Italy, the Netherlands, Spain and Germany, all of which have managed to create high speed rail networks.

I also noticed something else this week in which showed that mainland Europe is far ahead of GB. A referendum is coming up in Switzerland very shortly and if it's passed, it will set a minimum income for every Swiss citizen living in Switzerland equivalent to €2, 000 a month. It's all very commendable and all a far cry from the social divisive and imbecilic ' bedroom tax', that seems one of the main highlights of the current coalition government in London.

It's hardly surprising, having said all that, that Marks & Spencer is upping the ante in its return to the French market, despite France's economic doldrums. The group has just opened two more stores in Paris, one close to the Eiffel tower, the other in the Aéroville shopping centre near Roissy. M & S returned to France two years ago and now has four stores open. It's also linking up with Relay, a French chain of newsagents and convenience stores to present the M & S offerings at other outlets in the Paris area, such as stations and airports.

Meanwhile, the winter of discontent for Président Hollande just gets full of yet more dissatisfaction. A very recent opinion poll shows that more than 70 per cent of French people think there are too many taxes, while 80 per cent believe Hollande's economic policies are misguided. These days, more than a quarter of all French undergraduates have one ambition in mind, to emigrate, figures that are far higher for graduates with very marketable qualifications, as in IT. Just watch out for the rise and rise of the Front National—next year, it looks like delivering some serious shocks to the dysfunctional and archaic political establishment in France.

Still, we can't end without some funny stuff. A news website in Dublin, journal. ie, is great for publishing material many other media outlets won't touch, including all its funnies. This week, courtesy of the Redundant Proofreaders Society on Facebook, it published visuals of 10 signs in Ireland that could have been improved with a little proofreading. One fast food outlet in Dublin advertised ' the best cooked breastfast in Dublin', while a supermarket sign in its Cuisine de France bakery section read: "please use thongs or gloves provided". What a staggering thought!

November 6, 2013

Oops!

Everyone can have a senior moment, as the driver of the TGV from Paris to Nice proved on Monday.

The train was due to stop at Les Arcs in the Var départmente, but the driver completely forgot and the high speed express sailed right through, to the bemusement of many passengers who were getting ready to disembark from the train. The train stopped OK at the next scheduled stop, St Raphael, and they all had to be bussed back to Les Arcs, the slow way!

I was amused by another recent mistake in France. In Strasbourg recently, they put up street signs for the new esplanade François Mitterand, an outstanding former president, who lived from 1916 until 1966. The only problem was that on the street signs, his second name was spelled with just one 'r' when of course it should have had two. But what was even more amazing was that as soon as the spelling mistake went viral on the Internet, the authorities put up correct street signs within hours!

While we're on the subject of amusing stories, a parody of French president Hollande has been making waves on the Internet. He's singing about taxes to a Charles Trenet tune and it's all causing a lot of amusement.

But the opposition to the president is unprecedented. I was very surprised that at a couple to commemorate all those who fell in the first world war, groups of people actually started jeering the president. I certainly can't remember anything like that happening before at such a service in France. At least, tomorrow, Hollande is off to Monaco to meet up with Prince Albert II, so the two lads should have a bit of fun!

However, the French government has at least done something very positive within the past few days by announcing a €3 billion investment in the troubled city of Marseilles. It may be enjoying its current European cultural status, but behind all the glitzy new museums, art galleries and showcase events, there's a deeply troubled city, with 40 per cent youth unemployment in some areas and more than 20 per cent of the population living in poverty. The government plans to use this money to improve public housing, create jobs and help the poor, all very worthy aims, so lets hope that it all works out.

Marseilles is indeed a stunning city, especially around the port area, while the climb up to the hill to Nôtre-Dame-de-la-Garde cathedral will take your breath away. But the poor and the dispossessed can't be ignored any longer. At least they should be thankful they haven't got a British style government with David Cameron in charge—then, the only solution to the problems of Marseilles would be to impose a bedroom tax.

Another big scheme that's under way in France, this time in Bordeaux, should be even more interesting. A cultural centre for the Bordeaux wine industry is being created at a cost of €60 million. The design is said to resemble swirling wine in a glass! When it's completed in 2015, it should be a fantastic place for people to visit if they want to find out more about the wines of the region and indeed, do a little tasting.

While we're still in positive mode, I see that the latest tourist figures show that the south of France and indeed the rest of the country is holding its own. Last year saw upwards of 11 million people taking a holiday on the Côte d'Azur—this is about 10 per cent of the total number of holiday visitors to France in 2012. The Côte d'Azur now accounts for one per cent of global tourism.

In terms of the Côte d'Azur, 19 per cent of those visiting were Italian, while British and Irish visitors came to 18 per cent and Russians six per cent. A total of 27 per cent of visitors to the Côte d'Azur arrived by air, at Nice airport, which is now the second travel hub in France, after Roissy and Europe's third business aviation airport.

Still, behind the positive headlines, there's always a dark side. In Nice early last Saturday morning, a gang of about 20 very drunken teenagers broke into a bakery on the boulevard Carlone and created mayhem, smashing up the shop. Around 20 people were injured, ncluding the woman who is the manager of the bakery, and five policemen, one of whom had serious hand injuries. Then last weekend as well, a 24 year old woman fell out of the window of a fourth floor apartment in the north of Nice and was killed. Talking about this tragic incident on the avenue Montega, the police couldn't say whether the poor woman had lost her balance or had been pushed.

Apart from life on the dark side, sometimes, coverage of France can get so boring! I listened to a programme on Radio 4 the other night about the economic life of France, I n which it was stated that the public sector in France accounts for 57 per cent of GDP. It's the highest level in Europe, but most people would have guessed that anyway. Don't expect the French to suddenly reform and have an American approach to free enterprise!

Then just to make matters worse, this programme used the soundtrack of Je ne regrette rien by Edith Piaf. To my mind—and I love the music of Piaf and her near contemporary Jacques Brel- this is the ultimate musical cliché and I'm utterly sick of hearing it. This particular piece of music is one of the all-time favourites on Desert Island Discs—just shows how many boring people they have on that particular programme!

You could well say that the BBC often doesn't know its arse from its elbow! For Remembrance Sunday, they played a set of muffled cathedral bells, which were very impressive. When the announcer introduced them, he said they were recorded at Bristol

Cathedral, then when the segment was completed, he said that they were the bells of Worcester Cathedral!

There was another tragic event in recent days, this time in Paris, where a performance of a spectacle on 1789 was being prepared, Les Amants de la Bastille. It was being staged in the Palais des Sports in Paris. But some fireworks went off prematurely and 15 people were injured in the explosions, seven of them seriously. Then Marcus Toledano, the 41 year old technical director of the show, rushed to the scene to see what was happening. He then collapsed and died from a heart attack.

One Parisian anniversary caught my eye the other day. November 8, 1793 was the date on which the Louvre opened as an art gallery; previously, t had been a royal palace. It was a stunning transition and ever since, the Louvre has been a prime destination for millions upon millions of visitors to Paris.

Something else caught my ear in recent days, a superb documentary on Radio 4 about Telefon Hírmondó, launched in Budapest in 1893. It was billed as the world's first radio station, since it had the same kind of items that a good radio channel would have, news, current affairs, relays from the opera and theatre, in other words, a whole mix of features that wouldn't go amiss on Radios 3 and 4. But it operated by means of the telephone, rather than radio. People could listen in to the "station" at home or they could hear it in public places, where it was relayed through loudspeakers. All very avant garde and it worked well, until the second world war. The man who devised the whole system and got it up and running was Theodore Puskás. He died young, just before he was 50, but the service carried on after his death, a telling illustration of the inventive genius of Hungarians. After all, the humble biro was a Hungarian invention, in 1946!

I was also reading something about the world's first newspaper, which was launched in Strasbourg in 1605. The printer and publisher was German, Johann Carolus (1575-1634) and he started the paper with a really snappy title, Relation aller Furnemmen und gedenckwurdigen Historian. Try saying that in a hurry to your local newsagent! Naturally, the paper is normally just called "Relation". Carolus handset it, printed it and published between 100 and 200 copies once a week. Then at the end of each year, he bound all 52 copies of that year's paper into a book.

Talking about German style reminds me of a region of Austria we once visited that was an absolute delight. The jog to memory came from a Haydn concert performed at Esterházy in southeast Austria, near the Hungarian border. The great castle or schloss here at Eisenstadt was where Haydn was the composer in residence for many years. He worked for the Esterházy family for the best part of 40 years and today, the concert hall in the grounds of the estate is one of the most acoustically perfect in the world. After we had inspected the castle and listened to a performance of just a little sample of Haydn's music, we went to the nearby village of Rust, a most delightful place, with storks perched on the chimneys, as you find in Alsace. Beside the village is the Neusiedlersee, a great inland lake that seems to stretch for miles. This is also great wine country, so doubly interesting.

We completed this particular trip by going to the nearby border with Hungary, to look over the barbed wire into communist Hungary—this was a few years before the collapse of communism in central and eastern Europe.

Back home in Ireland, the news about yet more taxes and price hikes is as depressing and continuous as ever. A respected news commentator in Dublin, Declan Kiberd, who used to edit a Sunday business newspaper, said that Ireland is being battered by a whole new range of taxes, overt and covert. He pointed out what is happening in France, where Standard and Poors has just downgraded the country's credit rating. Kiberd said this shows what can happen to a once prosperous country when it succumbs to the thoughtless orthodoxies of the eurozone. He said that this former imperial power has been crucified by its ruinous acceptance of the common European currency and the austerity needed to sustain the foreign exchange regime.

Something else that's happening in present day Ireland and all under the radar, so no-one realises what's happening until it's too late—tax deadlines are being brought forward all the time, making life ever more difficult for householders and for small businesses. These small businesses are being crucified, according to Kiberd, to improve the government's cash flow, but at the same time, the large banks in Ireland, which are largely state owned, still aren't giving business enough credit!

People in Ireland seem to take it all lying down, in complete contrast to France. In Brittany, where companies have been badly hit by the new taxes on heavy lorries, protests are ongoing and since the beginning of November, over 30 roadside radar stations in Brittany that were being used to 'police' this new tax on lorries have been destroyed.

The government here is masterly imposing new taxes and new charges—hardly a day goes past without some new imposition. But it is singularly inept at deciphering social trends and reacting accordingly. Homelessness here in Ireland is at an all time high—it's a problem that doesn't even need a lot of money to solve, but plenty of organisation.

Yet the government's attitude to the problem is simply just to ignore it. It's the same with rental levels in the private sector, which are shooting up, so much so that lots of people can' now afford to pay current rent levels and are adding to the homeless totals. Yet the government is in blissful denial of the whole problem- it obviously hasn't the foggiest notion about what's happening, let alone figure out how to do anything about it.

But at least one recent survey portrayed the people of Ireland in a good light. It seems that around 75 per cent of the population has no objection to the proposed approval of gay marriage. A spirit of live and let live is very evident. In the old days, the Catholic church and its followers would have fulminated from on high at the very idea, but not now. It makes it all the harder to understand why there is such a venomous opposition to the same idea in France.

Having said all that, there has been much to recommend the weather in recent days here in Dublin, with daytime temperatures up to around 15 degrees Centigrade and some magnificent sunshine. Yesterday, I walked beside the Grand Canal in the city and the colours on the foliage were as striking as anything you'd see during the fall in the north-eastern US.

November 13, 2013

Anniversary week

T his week's blog means we've been doing this particular exercise since November, 2012, often good fun and always enlightening. It's so informative keeping up with the news as it's reported from within mainland Europe, since so often, the media in this part of the world, Ireland and Britain, shows little interest in what's happening in the rest of Europe. To find out what's happening on a day-by-day basis, especially in France, is always rewarding.

But this week is also time for anniversaries that are coming up, especially that on Friday, November 22, the 50th anniversary of the assassination of President Kennedy in Dallas on November 22,1963.It's quite true, everyone of a certain age remembers exactly where they were when they heard the news. As for myself, I was a third level student at university in the north of Ireland-I found the whole university business totally tedious and unproductive and couldn't wait to escape into the real world. Being at university created some of the most boring years of my life!Yuk. Anyway, to cut a long story short, that Friday night had seen the usual debate taking place in the main building of the university, a boring enough affair, but one way of passing the time. About eight o'clock, the debate finished and everyone wandered out into the main hall. All of a sudden, rumours began to fly that Kennedy had been shot and killed in Dallas. I had to wait until 10pm that night, when I got back to my digs and turned on the Radio 4 news to find out the whole story.

For my wife, Bernadette Quinn, it was even more dramatic and shocking, because she had met him during his visit to Ireland in June,1963.She was then working in the foreign ministry in Dublin and one night during his visit, the ministry staged an elaborate reception and dinner for the US president. It was there that she met Kennedy, who was so smitten with her that he wanted to take her back to |Washington with him. We all know what he had in mind!Her boss overheard the conversation;he had been enjoying the refreshments as had everyone else and he told the US president that no way was he going to take away the young woman working in his department. Not the short of thing you normally tell a US president!A short time later, an ominous sign happened, a portent of what was to come in Dallas. Bernadette was at a cocktail reception in the ministry she worked for when one of the diplomats, a little worse for wear, accidentally spilled a glass of red wine, which drenched her white cocktail dress. An ominous omen indeed.

On a more personal note, the present is also time for remembering a good friend in France, François Bonal, who died exactly 10 years ago, in November,2003,aged 89.He was a remarkable man, born in 1914,the year the great war started. His father had been a great military man, who was killed in that war. François himself went to the French military academy, St Cyr, from 1933 to 1935 then completed his training at the cavalry school in Saumur, from 1935 to 1936.His military career ended 30 years later, in 1967,when he retired from the French army. Then he found a new vocation, in Champagne, to where he moved when he left military service. He went on to become the head of public relations for the CIVC, the body based in Épernay that represents both the wine growers and the Champagne houses.

It was a role custom made for him;he travelled the world many times over, promoting the cause of Champagne and had friends of all ages, nationalities and religions on a global basis. My wife and I became great friends with him during our various trips to Champagne. He was fascinated with my wife's bottom and any time we met, he couldn't resist feeling its contours for himself!Everyone took this in good part, just part of the French way of life!If the same thing had happened today's politically correct world, he could have got himself into trouble!I always remember one of our trips to Champagne, when he organised for us to stay in the marvellous Royal Champagne hotel, which is six km outside Épernay. The rooms there are like self-contained apartments, looking out on the gardens and the vineyards.

François was extremely knowledgeable on every aspect of Champagne, so much so that he wrote 11 books on the subject, including his gold covered book of Champagne, which is an encyclopaedia on the subject. It's a vast book and has so much detail that since it was published, no-one has thought of trying to better it. François was such a wonderful host and he introduced us to the Champagne industry at all levels, from the poshest of the big Champagne houses to the small workaday firms that are so down-to-earth. It was a marvellous education in the history of this particular aspect of the French wine business and it's a sign of the respect in which François was held that after his death, one of the streets near the CIVC in Épernay was renamed in his honour. So if you ever see the rue François Bonal in that delightful town, the story behind it is well worth exploring!

On a more sombre note, I saw that last Friday, Libération, the left wing daily had decided to do an issue without photographs, to highlight the importance of photography in the media and to help promote the great photo exhibition that's currently on at the Grand Palais in Paris. That same day, last Friday, a gunman tried to shoot up a local TV station in Paris, then on Monday of this week, it became much more serious when the gunman stormed into the reception area of Libération in Paris and shot a 23 year old photographer, seriously injuring him. The poor guy had been working as a freelance and he was literally on the first morning of his new staff job at the paper. The gunman then escaped and went on to shoot up the headquarters of the Societé Génerale bank at La Défense. As of Wednesday morning, the gunman is still on the loose.

Meanwhile, in Nice, all kinds of awful things have been happening. Early last Friday morning, many parts of the Côte d'Azur were hit by winds of 100 kph as well as by a massive storm of hailstones. Then early last Friday morning, a gang of 20 very drunk male teenagers burst into a bakery in Nice and trashed the place, injuring a lot of people in the process, including the woman manager and five policemen, one of whom suffered serious hand injuries. Another frightful incident took place on Saturday in the north of Nice, when a 24 year old woman fell to her death from the window of a fourth floor apartment. After she died, the police were unable to say whether she fell out accidentally or had been pushed. It just shows, behind all the glitz and glamour of Nice and the Côte d'Azur, there's an awful lot of crime.

Dreadful weather events have been happening everywhere, not just in the Philippines and in Sardinia. Last week, an Air France flight took off from Rio de Janeiro bound for Paris, but it hadn't got far when it ran into a ferocious hail storm and had to return to Rio. Fortunately, no-one was hurt, but the amount of damage the hailstones did to the plane was unbelievable. Back in June,2009,an Air France plane on the same route wasn't so fortunate and came down in the south Atlantic during bad weather conditions.

Amid all these stories, the mood in France gets worse by the day. One secret report drawn up for the French Interior Ministry, but no longer secret, since it was leaked to Le Figaro, said that such was the level of anger and frustration in France that the country was now in an insurrectionary mood. One centre right leader, François Bayrou, said openly on radio the other day that France is on the verge of insurrection. At the same time, President Hollande's ratings have fallen to an all time low, with a mere 15 per cent approval rating. Will we see a rerun of 1968 or even 1789?We'll have to wait and see, but the present political situation in France and across much of mainland Europe is now so febrile that nothing can be ruled out, including insurrections, even political assassinations. No wonder that the Front Nationale in France has teamed up with its equivalent in the Netherlands, the Freedom Party, and that they seem set to make lots of hay in both countries in the European elections next May. It's hardly surprising-France has returned to recession and the tax burden is getting ever worse.

In one recent case, a woman in the small town of Peyrac in the Lot has seen her property tax increase from €411 last year to €6,050 this year. People in France have to pay two local taxes, one on their property and another to fund the municipality they live in, the taxe d'habitation. The mere fact that the government has suspended the very unpopular ecotax on heavy lorries will have little impact on the general bad mood. Meanwhile, lots of totally false stories are circulating on the Internet, all against the left. One false story is that the justice minister has a son who's doing time for murder, while another is that President Hollande has a secret daughter by the Socialist candidate for the mayor of Paris. These rumours are typical of the fractious spirit of unrest that's sweeping the country. But I was very amused by a photomontage in Le Monde's magazine the other day which showed Hollande and Angela Merkel apparently enjoying croissants, bretzels and orange juice while they were having breakfast together in bed!

One of the latest controversies in France could only happen there. The government is planning to bring in legislation that will penalise people who make use of sex workers. There's been an outcry against this and many celebrities have come out against this proposed new law, including Catherine Deneuve and Charles Aznavour. One of the petitions against what's planned is headed "Ne touche pas ma pute"-"don't touch my whore"!It could only happen in France!And talking of odd things, the other night in Toulouse, about midnight, a young man called Sébastien Bousquet was out having a look at the night sky when he saw three very strange bright objects. He concluded that they weren't aircraft, helicopters, Chinese fire lanterns or meteorological balloons, they had to be be OVNIs, the French word for ufos. So this has become the latest OVNI sighting in France.

At least, there was one piece of pleasant news from nearby Switzerland. The Belle Époque steamer that has long plied on Lac Léman (Lake Geneva) has been well restored after 18 months work that has brought the steamer back to its original state, although it now has some very modern navigational equipment. She makes a lovely sight sailing to and fro on the lake!

Meanwhile, back at the ranch here in Dublin, the other day I met someone I hadn't seen for a good while. He worked as one of the local street cleaners and binmen until nearly five years ago, when he reached retirement age with the city council. Since then, he was telling me, he has been driven demented because he has nothing to do all day. And he explained all this to me within earshot of his wife!It just shows, the old concept of retirement age is totally outdated, yet no-one is coming up with any solutions, so that people who thanks to modern medicine, have many years of productive life left in them, can continue making a useful contribution to society.

Also in Dublin, I see the latest example of indolence in the Obama administration in Washington. The last US ambassador to Ireland retired last December and hasn't been replaced. That means it could be well over a year before a new one is appointed. Since Irish-US diplomatic relations were initiated in 1927,there's never been such a gap between ambassadors, until now. Just shows. On his two visits to Ireland, Obama was full of enthusiasm for the country and its people;the reality is slightly different, as this ambassadorial delay shows what the US really thinks of Ireland.

I also saw for myself in Dublin this week the last incident of pavement pissing, which has become so prevalent here. I was walking past one of the top luxury hotels in the city centre when I saw someone behaving oddly. It was a young down and out, sprawled out on a bench, penis in hand, gaily pissing onto the pavement, creating his own equivalent of the fountain in the lake at Geneva. Really disgusting, but then, Dublin city centre is overrun with homeless down and outs and no-one in authority seems the slightest bit interested in helping them and in the process, solving the problem. Typical!It's just as bad in the UK, of course, where so many errors are being made in processing benefits to people who genuinely need them that if it weren't for all the food banks that have been set up, they would go hungry.

The JKF anniversary is taking up a lot of media time and space, but while we should honour the sudden end of a remarkable US President, we shouldn't forget the very pressing problems of the present!